INDUSTRIAL WAGE AND SALARY CONTROL

INDUSTRIAL WAGE AND SALARY CONTROL

ROBERT W. GILMOUR

Mercury Division
Ford Motor Company

NEW YORK · JOHN WILEY & SONS, INC.
LONDON · CHAPMAN & HALL, LIMITED

Library of Congress Catalog Card Number: 56–5637

Printed in the United States of America

To the Memory of My Father

Robert A. Gilmour

Preface

Industrial organizations have been devoting increased attention to the development and utilization of job analysis and evaluation techniques as a basis for controlling their wage and salary structures. Although several different systems with numerous variations are currently being used, point plans of evaluation have received the most widespread acceptance. In view of the general interest in this system, an attempt has been made to present practical suggestions concerning the development, installation, and administration of point evaluation plans as the basis for sound wage and salary controls.

The methods and procedures described have been primarily designed to meet the requirements of a large decentralized industrial organization. For those individuals who wish to install a similar system in a smaller company, the procedure outlined may be readily modified to meet their requirements. Although first consideration has been given to the establishment and control of hourly wage rates, persons interested in job analysis and evaluation as it pertains to salaried personnel will find that many of the ideas and methods may be used as a basis for their salary administration programs. Typical evaluation plans for both hourly and salaried personnel are presented in Chapter 3.

Since a large number of persons interested in job analysis and evaluation do not have a background in statistics, an explanation of the various statistical techniques which are used is provided in order to promote a greater understanding of the effectiveness of these measures in the field of wage and salary control. Detailed work sheets and examples have been included for those individuals who wish to apply the techniques to specific situations. Through the utilization of statistical methods, particularly in the development of a point evaluation plan, it is believed that new validity and logic are added to the system. Companies installing point evaluation systems have been too prone to accept plans which have not been specifically developed or adapted to fit their particular circumstances. When such plans have failed to produce logical results, skepticism has oftentimes developed concerning the reliability of point systems. This book places considerable emphasis upon the techniques which may be utilized to establish point weights for factors and degrees of factors. Research has indicated that the importance of this phase of job evaluation should not be underestimated. Despite the significance of point weight assignment, treatment of this aspect of point evaluation plans has been noticeably deficient.

It should not be implied that there is any system of job analysis and evaluation which will provide an automatic panacea for all the problems involved in the administration of wages and salaries. A carefully developed plan based upon factual information merely provides the basis for sound administration and improved cost control. The actual effectiveness of any such program is still largely dependent upon human judgment.

Many companies installing job analysis and evaluation plans have assumed that their wage and salary expense would be controlled automatically as a result of such a program. It is apparent that additional cost control techniques must also be utilized if maximum benefits are to be derived. Further research in the application of statistical and mathematical techniques to problems in labor cost control will undoubtedly result in the improved utilization of manpower and greater refinement in existing controls.

Unfortunately, it is impossible for me to acknowledge individually my indebtedness to the many contributors to this book. I can convey my expression of gratitude only by acknowledging this large group as a whole. I am especially grateful to those people who were connected with some of the studies outlined in this book, including Mr. S. R. Fontaine, Mr. D. E. Scriven, and Mr. L. T. Cox, and to the courtesy and cooperation of the many individuals, connected with some of the leading companies in the United States, who have consulted with me over a period of years. Whatever value this book may have is attributable in no small measure to their keen analytical abilities and helpful suggestions. The opinions and conclusions expressed here are solely mine, and any resemblance to policies or programs currently established within any company is purely coincidental.

ROBERT W. GILMOUR

January, 1956

Contents

ix

1

Introduction

In recent years, management personnel have become increasingly aware of the significant changes which are occurring within industry. Only a few years ago, "automatic" factories were unknown, advanced mathematical techniques were applied to industrial problems in only very limited areas, and electronic computers were restricted primarily to scientific calculations. Evidence is accumulating that these and similar products of human ingenuity are creating forces within industry which are certain to have a far-reaching influence upon all phases of business. It is becoming more and more apparent that the breaking down of boundaries between functions and techniques which at first appear to be totally dissimilar provides one of the richest areas for further cost reduction in industry. Exploration of these interrelationships and the benefits which can be derived is a long-range process limited only by individual imagination.

In management's quest for cost reduction and improved adminstrative controls, wages and salaries present one of the most lucrative areas for further research and development. A review of existing wage and salary controls in practically every company reveals problems such as the following:

1. Unexplained labor cost variances between similar units or operations.
2. Inconsistency of classification assignment within and between organizational units.
3. Employee dissatisfaction resulting from inequitable internal wage and salary relationships.
4. High labor turnover resulting from an inability to measure area rates accurately and establish competitive pay scales.
5. Inability to obtain accurate labor cost control reports on a current basis. These reports are needed within a matter of hours, not days or weeks.
6. Failure to measure or forecast periodically the relationship of actual manpower on the job to standard or budgeted manpower.

Although management is oftentimes aware of problems such as these, there has been a reluctance to act because ready solutions have not always been available.

If full advantage is taken of the changes occurring within industry, powerful new techniques will be added to those which now exist in the area of manpower control. Increased mechanization both in the plants and in the offices will contribute to defining and standardizing job requirements. There will continue to be, however, a very definite need for methods and systems analysis, the application of work simplification techniques, the development of effective organizational components, and the use of work measurement to aid in establishing a sound basis for cost controls. All too frequently management personnel apply controls without first investigating the foundation upon which the controls are being applied. Witness the number of incentive plans applied without first conducting a proper methods analysis, and the number of budgets approved for similar activities where little or no analysis is given to the wide variation in the classifications of persons assigned to perform the work.

The changes taking place within industry will not correct errors in management judgment but they will provide new situations and a new set of tools with which to work. Increased automation in our industrial plants will lead to standard manning tables for different levels of operation. In certain industries where labor requirements have been relatively small in relation to the capital investment for facilities, there has been greater progress toward standardizing manpower. In most companies, however, hourly workers have provided management with a substantial, yet oftentimes unpredictable, amount of variable expense. When production schedules fluctuated, it was possible for management to increase or decrease the number of hourly workers. Manning tables based upon normal operator performance and indicating specific classifications and numbers of persons required for different levels of operation have been either lacking or subjected to limited use. Oftentimes, changes in production schedules have occurred several days or even weeks prior to the time personnel adjustments were made. This lag, insofar as it has resulted in overstaffing, is expensive and is frequently accompanied by excessive manpower movement. When understaffing occurs, union grievances involving work standards may be filed or production objectives may not be met.

Although the introduction of automation in production operations will tend to result in labor's comprising a somewhat smaller portion of production costs, each employee will assume increased importance in the production process. Larger numbers of skilled personnel will be required. Their failure or inability to act will become more significant and their satisfaction or dissatisfaction more critical. Automation accompanied by other forces will also be instrumental in creating changes in the operation of production facilities and the assignment of personnel within the organization. Reduced working hours for each individual, increased utilization of facilities where large capital investments are involved, greater flexibility in production schedules to more nearly approximate sales, and more positive attempts to obtain greater overall stability in the work force are all within the foreseeable future. These factors will undoubtedly have a very pronounced influence upon even the day to day administrative controls over rates and classifications. For example, most companies have a standard practice of sending a job analyst into the plant to observe a new or recently reclassified employee in order to determine whether he has been assigned the proper classification. Thousands of man-hours are consumed each year by this costly practice. Standard manpower budgets listing the number of persons by classification for different production levels would substantially reduce the necessity for such on-the-job observations. Vastly improved internal communications, including rapid systems for manpower reporting and positive incentives to encourage greater stability in the work force, will also tend to improve manpower control.

There is evidence that management has been so engrossed in introducing automation in an attempt to reduce labor costs that it may have failed to explore other areas of labor cost control which could be of equal significance. Fortunately, however, executives who have experienced the economies to be derived from automation within production operations are usually willing to consider potential applications for other processes or techniques that appear promising.

Recently, increasing interest is being devoted to the application of mathematical and statistical techniques to industrial problems. In wage and salary control there are many fertile areas for the profitable use of these methods. Numerous situations exist where a refinement of existing practices appears to be in order. Such is the case with the development of job evaluation plans and the application of wage and salary controls in conjunction with such plans. A substantial amount of research remains to be done in connection with budget forecasting, the establishment of variable budgets, and the validating of new techniques used in the development of budgetary performance and manpower control reports.

Many of the changes which are now taking place within industry would be seriously delayed if it were not for the concurrent development and use of electronic data-processing machines. Again, in the field of wage and salary administration, these machines will help secure more reliable controls at speeds which only a few years ago sounded fantastic. In the development of job evaluation plans, in the conducting of area rate surveys, in the preparation of many statistical control reports, and in numerous other related applications, these electronic machines will provide more accurate and complete reports with sufficient rapidity for the data to be of maximum value from an administrative standpoint.

Internal forces such as automation and the application of new techniques are bringing about changes within industry, and at the same time certain external forces are also at work. Some of the most significant external forces include the day to day actions and periodic demands of labor unions. Numerous changes have occurred in practically every company as a result of union pressures to secure additional benefits. Management controls in the area of wages and salaries frequently represent one of the most controversial issues during discussions and negotiations with the union. It is an area where mutual understanding is oftentimes lacking, where decisions are sometimes reached on the spur of the moment without the aid of technicians, and where special groups gain concessions based upon their political strength. There has been a tendency in recent years for a leading company within an industry to establish the pattern, and other competitive companies oftentimes follow this pattern regardless of the long-range implications. Occasionally neither management nor union personnel are ready or willing to reach a decision for fear it may restrict future actions. There can be no question that union pressures relating to additional security during periods of layoff will result in management's devoting increased attention to manpower controls. Establishment of supplemental unemployment benefits similar to those negotiated in the automobile industry, or the adoption of other plans to serve a similar purpose, places a premium upon controls which will more adequately minimize layoffs. Other demands relating to a shorter work week will also influence management's desire for improved manpower controls.

Another external influence, especially during periods of national emergencies, is the Federal Government. Numerous companies have experienced difficulty in complying with federal wage and salary stabilization orders as a result of not having formalized pay structures and administrative regulations. Revisions or changes in the structure during a national emergency are sometimes difficult to accomplish, despite the fact that they may be designed to provide better control or eliminate inequities.

The constant influence of internal and external pressures on wages and salaries is apparent to every industrial executive. Failure on the part of management to establish well-defined labor cost controls, developed and effectively administered with the aid of the latest techniques, is almost certain to result in increased expense as well as employee dissatisfaction.

Many articles, short studies, and books have been written about the various phases of wage and salary control. In the chapters which follow, primary emphasis will be devoted to discussing certain aspects of the field of job evaluation and related cost controls which do not appear to have been treated adequately in the existing literature. The discussion takes into consideration the current internal situation in industry and the external forces which are certain to contribute to further changes. Obviously, company personnel will require a number of years to adjust to the new conditions under which they are beginning to operate. Careful advance study of existing wage and salary cost control practices will be required before certain revisions which appear desirable can be installed. In large companies, more precise controls oftentimes take several years to install and field-test. Where the end products might result in revisions to existing wage and salary structures, it is essential that caution be exercised and management motives be clearly understood by all personnel who are involved.

To the technicians in industrial engineering or industrial relations who are charged with the responsibility for developing procedures and salable job evaluation plans, it is hoped that the methods discussed in the chapters which follow will suggest a practical approach to the specific problems they have under consideration. To the analysts in fields such as manufacturing or finance who are conscientiously interested in cost reduction through improved administration, it is hoped that the demonstrated results of the techniques used here will act as a stimulus and provide a basis for further research in the area of wage and salary controls as related to their specific fields. To the executives, who perhaps have expressed doubts concerning the value of job analysis and evaluation, it is hoped that the fundamental need for effective programs of this nature will be clarified. Control of wages and salaries cannot be accomplished through the application of a single technique. Successful labor expense controls are necessarily the end product of a co-ordinated effort on the part of many persons within the company who treat different phases of the problem. Top-level recognition of job evaluation as an important administrative control is essential to its success. And finally, to students who expect within a few years to be associated with industry, it is hoped that the problems discussed and the techniques used to aid in their solution will be of assistance in providing a further understanding of the important area of labor cost control—an area where business concerns will be searching constantly for new and improved methods in the years ahead.

2

Planning a Job Analysis and Evaluation Program

Selection and Functions of a Nucleus Planning Group

The development and installation of a job analysis and evaluation program as a basis for labor cost control require careful planning in order to be certain that the program which is finally installed will adequately serve the needs of the organization. Before a final decision to proceed with the program is reached, a nucleus group of personnel should be appointed to conduct a thorough analysis of the existing situation. Such an analysis should include the basis upon which wages are now administered, the effectiveness of the program, the existing population distribution on wage rates and classifications, and a summary of administrative problems being experienced. Attention should also be devoted to progress in the field of wage administration and the relative success of programs introduced by other companies. Selected information and data developed at the time of this study should be prepared in the form of a written report. This report should be accompanied by suitable graphs and should include specific recommendations for consideration by top management. Regardless of the system being used by a company for wage control purposes, it is desirable to conduct periodic studies of this type. Individuals assigned to the nucleus group should not consist entirely of industrial engineering or industrial relations personnel currently working with the existing wage administration program; analytical personnel from other areas within the company, such as manufacturing, engineering, and finance, should also be included. On the basis of the preliminary information developed by the research group, top management may decide to initiate an analysis and evaluation program, or, if such a program is currently in existence, they may initiate a complete review of the existing system in order to determine where it may be improved.

At the time that a job analysis and evaluation program is first considered, management may be somewhat doubtful about the benefits to be derived from such a program. It is essential that any questions concerning the value of further analyses be answered to management's satisfaction at this stage. Insofar as programs of this nature have a direct influence upon operating costs and employee morale, the vital importance of top-level endorsement is evident. In some instances, efforts to accomplish job analysis and evaluation have been seriously delayed or even abandoned as a result of management's lack of interest or lack of knowledge concerning the full implications of such programs.

The decision to proceed with the installation or review of a job analysis and evaluation program raises numerous questions which require decisions. Emphasis is given here to the decisions which have to be reached at the time a program is being installed for the first time. In many instances, however, review of the existing program involves obtaining answers to the same or similar questions.

Scope of Program

One of the first decisions required involves the scope of the program. If the plan is to apply to hourly jobs, for example, decisions should be made as to whether job setters, utility men, relief personnel, and leaders should be covered. In many instances, it will be found that it may be desirable to develop the plan for hourly workers, excluding groups such as those just mentioned. These groups may be handled by means of negotiating separate agreements concerning rates to be paid. In most instances, these agreements will utilize the rate for a related classification as a basis for determining the amount to be paid the group under consideration. Thus, the rate for job setters may be established at a fixed differential of 10 cents above the rate paid the operators on the machines they service.

Releasing Information Concerning Program

As soon as the decision is reached to develop and install job analysis and evaluation, personnel whose jobs will be included should be informed of the program. Production supervision and other key supervisors should be acquainted with the nature of the program and the ultimate results expected by the company. It may be desirable, where the supervisory force is relatively large, to prepare a brief presentation treating such topics as the history of the company's wage structure and events leading up to job evaluation. An analysis of the existing wage structure may be presented, and where both single rates and rate ranges are in effect, the number and type of personnel subject to different pay practices may be outlined. In addition, current problems being experienced in the determination and administration of wage rates should be included in the presentation. Supervisors will also be interested in a broad outline of the job analysis and evaluation program, its influence upon the personnel under them, and the ultimate benefits of introducing the results secured. Throughout the presentation graphic illustrations should be developed to demonstrate the topics discussed. If the employees are represented by a union, it will be necessary to discuss the objectives of the program with their representatives. In some instances, the union may actually press management for some plan to eliminate wage rate inequities. If such is the case, the need for the program may be sufficiently apparent to make both parties eager to secure a workable solution.

Union Participation

Opinions differ as to whether it is wise to include union representatives in the meetings held during the developmental and testing phases of the program. It is probably true that a great deal of time can be wasted in extended discussions which may ultimately produce relatively few tangible benefits. Such negative results have to be considered in the light of counterbalancing factors, such as increased union understanding and acceptance of the plan, which can be valuable by-products of joint participation. It is practically impossible to give a definite decision concerning the advisability of complete union participation unless all the conditions are known. Such a decision usually rests with top management after consultations with personnel handling labor negotiations. If it is contemplated that the company will be discussing the program in detail with the union at a later date, union personnel should be thoroughly briefed concerning company objectives. This briefing becomes particularly important if the union is not to be brought into the developmental phases of the program. If at all possible, an agreement should be reached with union representatives whereby the results of the program will be reviewed periodically.

Personnel working with job analysis and evaluation have sometimes questioned the feasibility of discussing or attempting to negotiate an analysis and evaluation program with a union. They argue that the technique is primarily a management tool designed to assist in establishing rates. They point to the need for additional research in the field so as to resolve controversial issues. The fact remains, however, that wage rates have to be established and administered. Job analysis and evaluation programs, with the refinements which have been introduced in recent years, do provide a systematic method for accomplishing this task and thereby serve both management and the union.

If union personnel refuse to review the findings of the company or if after review they feel they cannot endorse the program, management should realize that numerous excellent reasons exist for maintaining the system and continuing to apply the results. Failure on the part of the union to accept the results will mean that the elimination of rate inequities within the company will be retarded. However, as jobs are eliminated and new jobs are created, a definite attempt can be made to negotiate evaluated rates. In the long range, such action will minimize or eliminate inequities remaining within the structure. From a management standpoint the advantages gained through improved control of manpower and labor costs as well as the numerous fringe benefits accruing from job evaluation are sufficient to justify continuation of the program.

Job Analysis and Evaluation Systems

The decision as to what type of job evaluation system to install is usually made near the beginning of the program. In general, the systems used may be classified into the following types:

1. The job-ranking system.
2. The grade description system.
3. The factor comparison system.
4. The point system.

Although variations exist within each of these systems, the important characteristics of each method may be described briefly as follows.

In the job-ranking system, judgment must be exercised to list jobs in their order of importance. The process makes no attempt to consider individual factors on a systematic basis. In actual practice, different raters list the jobs in what they consider the proper order from the most important to the least important. Information secured from written job analyses, organization charts indicating the relative importance of the work performed, and discussions with supervisors usually provide the basis for ranking jobs. Through further analyses and discussions, inconsistencies among raters are resolved. Upon completion of the ranking, jobs are grouped and standard wage rates are assigned each level.

The grade description system involves the defining of levels of work and the sorting of jobs into these various classes. The system differs from job ranking in that grades are usually defined in advance of the time when jobs are actually grouped or classified. Definitions of the grades usually deal primarily with the skills required to perform the work, the complexities of the duties, and the level of responsibility. After the classification of jobs on the various levels, standard wage rates are assigned each grade.

The factor comparison system involves the rating of jobs on a limited number of factors such as mental requirements, skill, physical requirements, responsibilities, and working conditions. A rating scale is developed by positioning key jobs on each level or degree of each factor. At the time the rating scale is constructed, the existing wage rate for each key job is prorated to the factors according to the estimated influence each particular factor exerts in relation to other factors. Where that portion of the rate of a key job distributed to a particular factor appears to be out of line, the job is usually eliminated as a benchmark. A job being rated on the scale is positioned on the degrees of a factor in relation to the key jobs on that factor, and the cents comparable to the degree are credited to the job. Addition of the cents applying to each factor results in the evaluated wage rate for the job.

Point evaluation plans involve the selection and definition of a group of factors which are believed to be influential in the determination of wage rates. Each factor is divided into several degrees or levels. To help the evaluator position jobs on the various degrees, benchmark statements and benchmark jobs are used to orient him to the various levels. Point weights are assigned to the factors and degrees of the factors. When the evaluation of a job has been completed, the points applying to each factor are totaled. A chart is constructed having total points on the horizontal scale and current hourly rates on the vertical scale. Each job is plotted on this chart, and a trend line is drawn through the plottings. Point totals are grouped to establish pay grades, and standard wage rates are determined for each grade.

The decision as to the type of job analysis and evaluation plan to be used for a particular situation will vary depending upon the nature and size of the organization as well as the characteristics and level of the jobs under consideration. A number of relatively small companies have adopted job-ranking or grade description systems and have effectively administered wages with these methods. Larger companies have used these methods successfully in connection with executive positions. The factor comparison method has been used by a variety of companies as a basis for administering wages. The majority of companies, however, have selected or developed a point evaluation plan. Since the predominant interest will probably be centered more and more in point plans, the major portion of this book is devoted to the development, installation, and administrative controls required for such a plan.

Among the point plans of job evaluation for hourly personnel, the National Metal Trades Association Plan and the National Electrical Manufacturers' Association Plan represent two systems which have been widely adopted by companies in the metal-working and electrical industries. As a result of the Directive Order of the National War Labor Board dated November 25, 1944, an evaluation plan was developed jointly by the steel industry and the United Steelworkers of America. This plan has general acceptance throughout the steel industry. Another plan, developed jointly by a company and a union, involves the Sperry Gyroscope Company and Local 450 of the United Electrical, Radio and Machine Workers, CIO, Brooklyn, New York. The American Institute of Bolt, Nut and Rivet Manufacturers have devised a system which may be adapted or modified to suit the needs of companies in that industry. The West Coast Aircraft Industry has also utilized an evaluation plan to assist in wage administration. Salaried job evaluation plans have been developed by major companies in practically all industries. Sample copies of these plans are frequently available for review in business libraries or may usually be secured by direct requests to the specific companies.

Analysis of the evaluation plans mentioned above will provide an excellent cross section of the various point systems. Personnel interested in developing a point evaluation plan should also review other types of evaluation systems, such as factor comparison or grade description plans. Ideas or policies expressed in other job evaluation systems may be of definite assistance in constructing a suitable point plan. All plans reviewed with the intent of applying them in another company should be studied critically, however, since certain plans have been more carefully developed than others.

Securing Outside Assistance

A decision will also have to be reached as to whether an outside consulting service should be used to assist in the development and installation of the program. Personnel employed by a progressive consulting organization using tested methods are often able to provide a number of short cuts in the installation of a job analysis program. Their experience is usually drawn from a sizable number of companies, and they have the advantage of observing the results of different ideas at the time they are field-tested. Any company hiring an outside consultant should be certain that every step proposed by individuals connected with such a service is understood. If a company is in a position to hire qualified personnel to develop and install the program, it may prove unnecessary to solicit the services of outside consultants except for certain phases of the program. It should be realized by companies hiring consultants that upon completion of the program, company personnel will be required to administer it. If the suggestions made by the consultant are impractical, the company may find their administration exceedingly difficult.

Organization to Install Program

Decisions will also have to be made as to what type of organization is required to develop and install a job analysis program. Regardless of the degree of decentralization within a company's production organization, it is usually desirable to establish a central staff wage analysis unit. In most instances, this unit is attached to the industrial relations or industrial engineering activity. Figure 1 presents a suggested organization designed to develop and install a wage administration program in a large company. The supervisor is primarily concerned with the recruiting, training, and direction of personnel and the overall administration of the program. The staff assistant for statistical and administrative controls is responsible for development of an evaluation plan, administrative procedures, manuals, and special presentations. It may be convenient to have clerical personnel assigned to this unit of the organization. The central editing group is concerned with editing job descriptions, checking jobs for consolidation, editing, coding, and titling job specifications, and maintaining central files. Supervising analysts are responsible for reviewing job analyses, conducting evaluation meet-

Suggested Organization Chart to Accomplish the Development and Installation of a Job Analysis and Evaluation Program

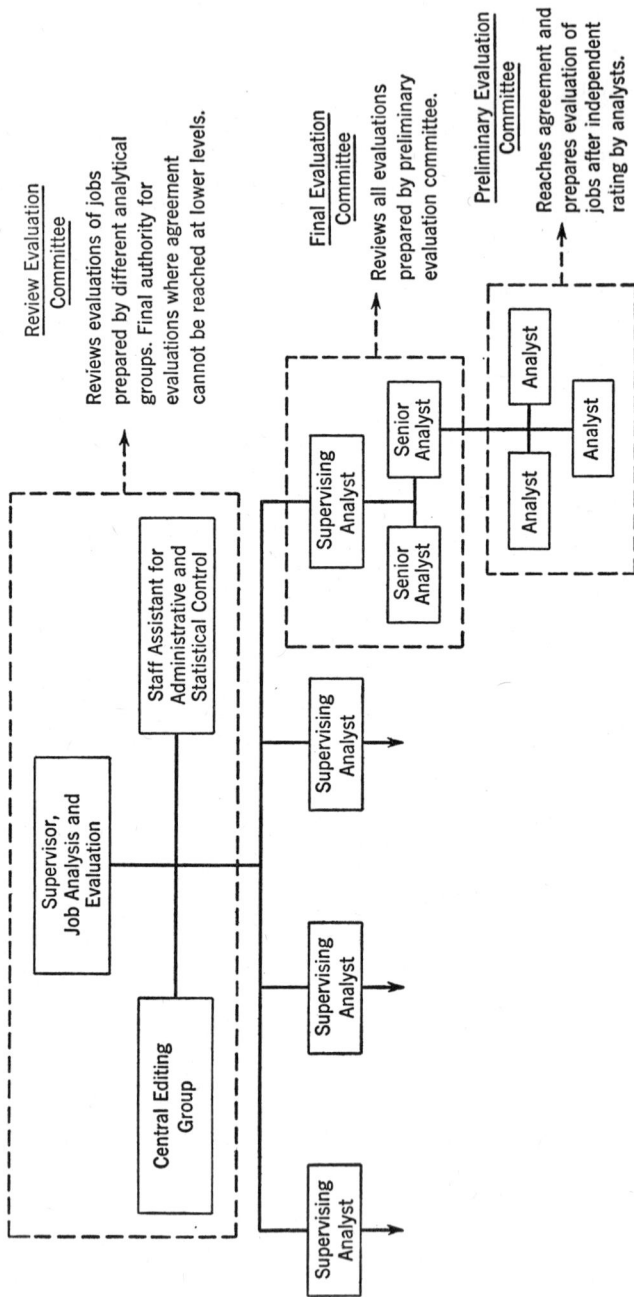

Review Evaluation
Committee

Reviews evaluations of jobs
prepared by different analytical
groups. Final authority for
evaluations where agreement
cannot be reached at lower levels.

Final Evaluation
Committee

Reviews all evaluations
prepared by preliminary
evaluation committee.

Preliminary Evaluation
Committee

Reaches agreement and
prepares evaluation of
jobs after independent
rating by analysts.

Supervisor,
Job Analysis and
Evaluation

Staff Assistant for
Administrative and
Statistical Control

Central Editing
Group

Supervising
Analyst

Supervising
Analyst

Supervising
Analyst

Supervising
Analyst

Senior
Analyst

Senior
Analyst

Analyst

Analyst

Analyst

Analyst

Figure 1

ings, and approving specifications for a particular area, plant, location, or organizational unit. Supervisors can be provided with assistance, as required, through the assignment of senior analysts and analysts. Figure 2 summarizes the responsibility for the major functions assigned the different units at the time a job analysis and evaluation program is undertaken. The chart also indicates the various committees required to evaluate jobs and review evaluations. In a smaller company, the central editing group could be merged with the staff assistant for administrative and statistical control. The classifications supervising analyst and senior analyst may also be unnecessary in a small organization.

Preliminary Training Program for Analysts

At the beginning of a job analysis and evaluation program, careful consideration should be given to the indoctrination and training of analysts. Oftentimes, this phase of the program is neglected, and within a short period of time inconsistencies in operating practices appear. The initial training material should present a broad outline of the program, including reasons for conducting the studies and the results desired. If personnel inexperienced in job analysis have been assigned to the program, it may be desirable to present a brief history of job analysis and the purpose it serves in controlling and administering rates. Thoroughness at this stage of the program will contribute materially to securing maximum effectiveness of the group within the shortest period of time.

Development of Procedure Manual and Periodic Progress Reports

As a guide for the installation of the job analysis and evaluation program and to aid in the training of analysts, it will be necessary to develop a written installation procedure. This procedure should be prepared in the form of a manual which will provide a step by step outline to be used by the supervisors and analysts connected with the program. It will usually be found as the program proceeds that some alterations will have to be made in the procedure. Although the tentative procedure for the entire program should be developed at the beginning of the study, individual steps should probably be issued just before they are actually required. In addition to outlining the steps involved in the analysis and evaluation, the procedure should also include various control reports which

Functional Flow Chart Summarizing Responsibility for a Job Analysis and Evaluation Program

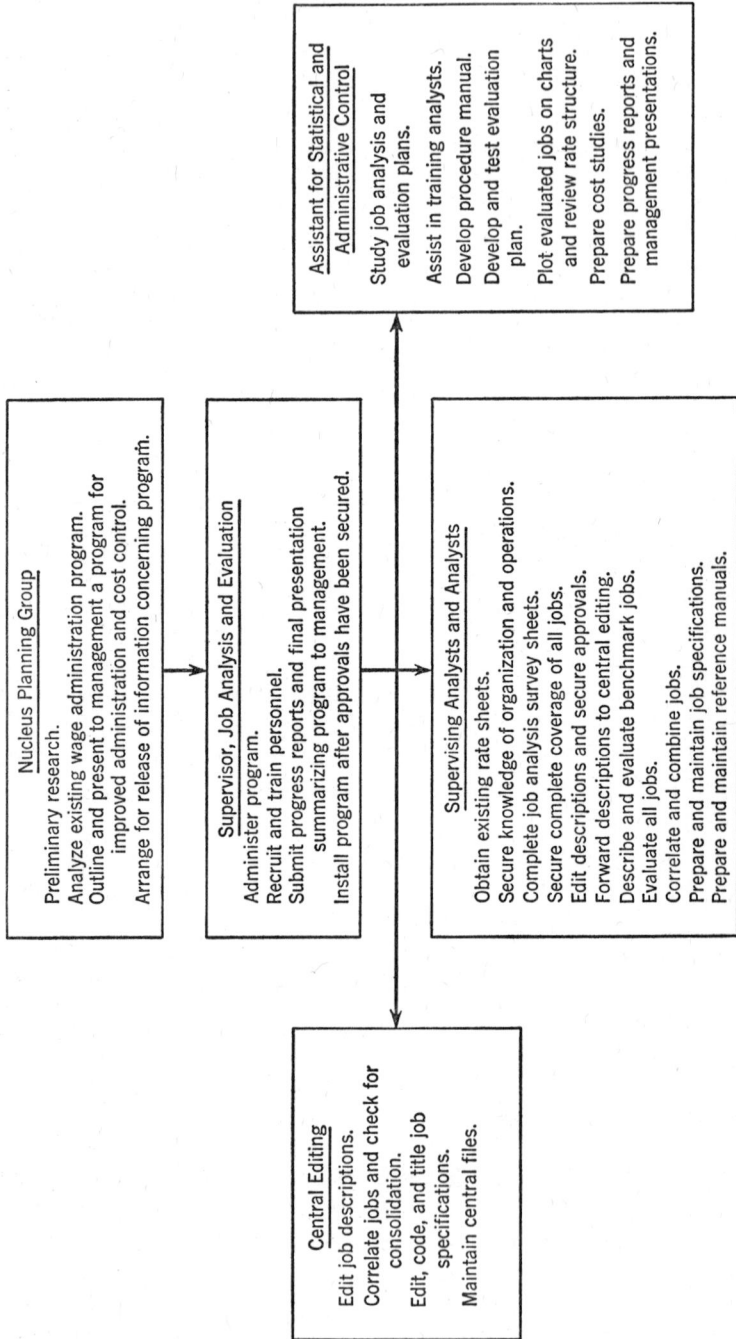

Nucleus Planning Group

Preliminary research.
Analyze existing wage administration program.
Outline and present to management a program for improved administration and cost control.
Arrange for release of information concerning program.

Supervisor, Job Analysis and Evaluation

Administer program.
Recruit and train personnel.
Submit progress reports and final presentation summarizing program to management.
Install program after approvals have been secured.

Supervising Analysts and Analysts

Obtain existing rate sheets.
Secure knowledge of organization and operations.
Complete job analysis survey sheets.
Secure complete coverage of all jobs.
Edit descriptions and secure approvals.
Forward descriptions to central editing.
Describe and evaluate benchmark jobs.
Evaluate all jobs.
Correlate and combine jobs.
Prepare and maintain job specifications.
Prepare and maintain reference manuals.

Central Editing

Edit job descriptions.
Correlate jobs and check for consolidation.
Edit, code, and title job specifications.
Maintain central files.

Assistant for Statistical and Administrative Control

Study job analysis and evaluation plans.
Assist in training analysts.
Develop procedure manual.
Develop and test evaluation plan.
Plot evaluated jobs on charts and review rate structure.
Prepare cost studies.
Prepare progress reports and management presentations.

Figure 2

will be submitted periodically and which will form the basis for reports to management concerning the progress of the program. In order that the program will be installed consistently throughout the organization, it is essential that all supervisors and analysts abide by the steps outlined. If a supervisor or analyst believes that the system can be installed more effectively by utilizing certain short cuts, these suggestions should be carefully analyzed. If it is decided that the suggested revisions will have advantages, the procedure should be changed. Until the actual changes are made, however, the procedure as outlined should be followed.

Major Steps in Program

A brief description of the major steps involved in analyzing and evaluating jobs is presented on the following pages. Key forms mentioned in the procedure are included in later chapters. Procedures similar to this have been tested and found suitable in a number of industrial companies of different sizes. Persons considering the utilization of this procedure in their particular company may find that certain modifications would be desirable to adapt it to their particular requirements. Steps in the procedure do not include the various functions performed by personnel responsible for developing the evaluation plan, establishing the wage structure, or installing the results of the program. These phases of the program are covered in greater detail in the chapters which follow.

Step 1.   Obtain and Analyze Existing Work Force Rate Schedules

The work force rate schedule should summarize the number of persons on each classification and rate within a specified organizational unit such as a department. This information will act as a guide in planning work loads and provide an indication of all job classifications and rates currently being used in each department. In addition, the report provides basic payroll data to be used by personnel responsible for development of the evaluation plan.

Step 2.   Obtain a Knowledge of the Organization Structure and the Operations Performed

Current organization charts should be reviewed in order to secure information concerning lines of authority and responsibility. Any other information such as instruction manuals, procedure manuals, training materials, or reports pertaining to organizational relationships should also be reviewed for the greatest possible familiarity with the existing situation.

Through discussion with supervisors, obtain a knowledge of all operations. Each analyst should be certain that he has a clear understanding of the activities involved before he starts analyzing jobs.

Step 3. Complete Job Survey Sheets

Information gathered in the preceding steps will provide background for the person analyzing the jobs. This step involves completion of a job analysis detail sheet designed to obtain data pertaining to the job elements, and a job description consisting of a brief summary statement followed by a paragraph outlining the detailed job content.

Step 4. Obtain Complete Coverage of All Jobs within a Particular Department

After completion of the job analysis detail sheets and the job descriptions, the information should be checked against the existing rate schedule and reviewed with production supervision in order to make certain that all jobs have been properly covered. A complete report should be prepared summarizing the conditions in the department.

Step 5. Prepare and Issue Progress Reports

In order that information as to the progress of the program may be obtained, weekly reports should be prepared. These reports should present information concerning the progress of individual analysts and of the program in different organizational units of the company.

Step 6. Edit Job Descriptions, Obtain Approval of Production Supervision, and Submit Job Folders to Supervising Analyst

When all jobs within a department have been investigated, analysts should edit their descriptions, being careful to insure that all phases of the jobs are adequately covered. After the approval of production supervision for all job classifications within a department has been obtained, job folders including the analysis forms and descriptions should be forwarded to the job analysis supervisor having jurisdiction over this phase of the installation.

Step 7.   Supervisors Will Approve the Contents of All Job Folders and Forward Them to Central Editing

After being approved by the supervisor, job folders for a department should be forwarded to the central editing office. This office will edit all job descriptions and titles, consolidate job descriptions so as to promote internal consistency, and be responsible for the maintenance of the central control files.

Step 8.   Expedite the Preparation of Job Descriptions and Evaluations for Benchmark Jobs

To assist in the evaluation of all jobs, benchmark jobs are positioned at the various degrees of the factors in the evaluation plan. It is necessary, therefore, to expedite the preparation of job descriptions and evaluations for these jobs. Benchmark jobs may also be used in the initial statistical studies to develop weights for the factors.

Step 9.   Establish Evaluation Committees and Tentatively Evaluate All Jobs

In general, there are two broad groups of jobs to evaluate:

1. Jobs individual to a particular plant.
2. Jobs common to several plants.

Committees responsible for jobs included in the first group should proceed by independently evaluating each job and then meeting as a group to resolve differences. Information pertaining to jobs in the second category should be brought together from all plants before these jobs are evaluated. The information should be reviewed carefully and the jobs slotted into groups according to their content. Throughout the evaluation process only the degree of each factor should be indicated, and no attempt should be made to compute total point values. Points may be added later just before the jobs are plotted. This regulation is emphasized since the evaluation of the job should not be influenced by the total points which result from the evaluation.

Step 10.   Correlate Jobs by Factors and Job Families.   Combine Jobs When Possible

Upon completion of the evaluation of all jobs within a plant or operation, each evaluation group should make comparisons between the jobs evaluated on the different degrees of each factor. In all cases, the evaluation should be consistent with the degree definitions and the benchmark jobs. Comparisons should also be made by job families (for example, all lathe operators), and any differences should be logical and justifiable.

When these studies are completed, the various jobs should be investigated from the standpoint of combining identical jobs in the plant or operation being studied. Job contents, as well as the evaluations on each of the factors, should be carefully compared. In no instance should jobs be consolidated where it is evident that a real difference exists on one or more factors. In addition, job contents must be practically identical before consolidation is recommended.

Step 11. Prepare Job Specifications after Clearance with Central Editing

The preparation of job specifications requires careful coordination in order to minimize duplications between the various evaluation committees. The central editing group should prepare and maintain control files of job specifications and records to indicate the plant or operation where each specification is active. Before specifications for jobs can be prepared, clearance must be obtained from the central editing group.

Step 12. Edit and Code Job Specifications and Maintain Specification Files

The editing group is responsible for editing the job descriptions and substantiating data covering the evaluations. They are also responsible for editing job titles and assigning a code number in accordance with a predetermined system. As the program nears completion, the central editing files will provide the basis for preparation of job specification manuals for each plant or operation. Specifications should be duplicated in order to provide the required copies. If a sufficient number of job specifications are being prepared, reproduction can be facilitated by typing the information on a preprinted stencil or duplimat.

Step 13. Prepare and Maintain Reference Manuals

In order that information developed during the job analysis program may be properly maintained, all supervisors should be responsible for the preparation of reference manuals for the plants and operations under their jurisdiction. These manuals should include information such as the following:

The names of all persons connected with the program who have worked in the particular plant recorded under the headings: analysis of jobs, evaluation of jobs and development of specifications, and administration and follow-up.

A list of the new classification titles, newly evaluated rates, and new classification code numbers for all departments.

Rate sheets currently being used to administer existing classifications.

An abbreviated organization chart, including production management for all three shifts and the areas over which they have jurisdiction.

A directory of key personnel (including industrial relations and industrial engineering) in the plant who may be contacted concerning job information.

Reports covering the results of meetings held with supervision concerning the development of job classifications.

Job evaluation sheets used for recording total points and plotting jobs.

A complete set of job specifications for the plant.

In this chapter, attention has been devoted to a discussion of some of the initial plans and decisions required at the time job analysis and job evaluation are undertaken. It is important that top management participate in most of these decisions and be familiar with the overall steps in introducing the program. For individuals interested in additional information concerning the historical background of job evaluation techniques and the systems which have evolved, and in a further discussion of the preliminary considerations relating to the introduction of these programs, reference may be made to several texts in the field, such as *Job Evaluation Methods*, by Charles Lytle, second edition, 1954, *Job Evaluation*, by Jay Otis and Richard Leukart, second edition, 1954, *Wage and Salary Administration*, by David Belcher, 1955, and other references listed in the bibliography at the end of this book.

In the chapters which follow, the results of research in the development of more adequate controls for wages and salaries are presented. Much of the success of any job evaluation program rests upon how thoroughly many of these techniques are applied in the development and administration of plans installed at individual companies.

3

Development of a Point Evaluation Plan:

Selection and
Definition of Factors

Basis for Selection and Definition of Factors

Most companies developing and installing a job evaluation program are primarily concerned with the elimination of internal rate inequities and the establishment of effective controls with a logical basis for administration of wages. With these objectives in mind, it is usually not the intention to create substantial changes in rates currently being paid. Actually, wage rates within a company are frequently in line with rates paid by other companies in the particular area, and radical changes in payment as a result of installing job evaluation would be undesirable.

It is essential that the basic objectives behind the development of a point evaluation plan be recognized at all times. Actually the process involves the establishment of wage rates by means of a selected group of factors having an influence upon rates. Although this approach has generally been recognized in the development of evaluation plans, sufficient attention has not been devoted to the process of defining factors and securing reliable weights on these factors so as to predict existing wage rate relationships with the greatest degree of reliability.

The installation of a job analysis and evaluation program should provide more than just a basis for establishment of rates, however. The plan should be designed to serve the needs of other groups or units within the organization, such as production management, personnel placement, safety, training, workmen's compensation, industrial engineering, and medical activities. Moreover, the plan which is finally installed should be capable of withstanding criticism from management as well as from the employees. It is essential, therefore, that factor definitions and degree definitions be determined on a logical basis substantiated by factual information.

Accomplishment of these objectives requires careful consideration of the types of jobs to be covered. Thus, if the plan is to cover jobs in assembly, foundry, and machining operations, the factors and degrees of the factors should be stated so as to cover adequately the various types of work performed. Benchmark statements will be of great assistance in positioning jobs with different characteristics on the levels of the various factors. Failure to define factors and degrees of the factors properly is certain to result in inconsistent evaluation. No matter how carefully the degrees of each factor are defined, it will usually be found that certain borderline jobs are exceedingly difficult to evaluate. As these jobs are encountered, it will be necessary to secure complete facts concerning the nature of the work performed in order that the jobs may be properly positioned on the factors.

In the discussion which follows, a number of statistical techniques are applied to the development of a point evaluation plan. As each of these techniques is mentioned, the method is described and actual cases are provided in order to clarify the process and demonstrate the results. It is evident from a review of a large number of point evaluation plans that lack of proper analyses of this type has been one of the major reasons for the failure of certain plans. For reference purposes, brief definitions of the various statistical techniques have been presented in Appendix A. Sample calculation forms which combine the calculation of several different statistical measures are presented in Appendix B.

One of the initial steps in the development of a point evaluation plan involves the selection of a group of factors which adequately describe the basic characteristics of the jobs being analyzed. An analysis of point evaluation plans currently in existence indicates that most factors are variations of four basic job characteristics:

1. Skill.
2. Effort.
3. Responsibility.
4. Working conditions.

These four characteristics are usually subdivided into several more specific factors, sometimes referred to as subfactors, which are defined and broken down into an appropriate number of degrees.

Number of Factors Required

Some of the early point evaluation plans had as many as fifty factors, whereas in recent years the tendency has been to reduce the number of factors. The determination of the exact number of factors to be used in any plan will vary somewhat with the jobs being covered. In general, plans designed to cover hourly workers should include not more than eight to ten factors. This number of factors, if carefully selected, will provide complete information concerning the various characteristics of the jobs performed. The addition of factors beyond this number usually results in some overlapping. This overlapping will tend to contribute to the cost of the program without providing compensating benefits. Moreover, statistical analyses have indicated that the results obtained have equivalent reliability. Several of these statistical studies have been conducted by Joseph Tiffin, Charles Lawshe, and others.* Most of these studies involve the use of the statistical technique of factor analysis to determine which characteristics or factors are playing an important part in rate determination. The process of factor analysis involves the selection of a reduced number of factors which will produce essentially the same result from a statistical standpoint as a larger number of factors would produce. Some of the factor analysis studies which have been conducted have indicated that plans having as many as eleven factors could be reduced to as few as three or four and secure approximately the same results. Although the relationship or correlation between total points for the longer system and total points for the shorter system is very significant, there is still some variance which remains to be explained. Failure of the short scale to account for practically all the variation will result in two somewhat different wage structures.

Little detail is given in Lawshe's studies concerning the definitions of the factors used in evaluating jobs. Most of the studies have indicated that the Skill factor can be used in the abbreviated scale. Using this factor, if it is broken down into a sufficient number of degrees, would have for all intent and purpose the same effect as job ranking. The process of making accurate defensible judgments on such a factor is usually difficult. For example, if the Job Training factor is broken down into a sizable number of degrees defined

---

* For studies of this type, see *Journal of Applied Psychology,* 1944, Volume 28, pages 189–198; 1945, Volume 29, pages 177–184; 1946, Volume 30, pages 177–184; 1946, Volume 30, pages 310–319; 1946, Volume 35, pages 426–434; 1950, Volume 34, pages 225–228.

almost entirely by variances in training times, it may be exceedingly difficult for different evaluators to position jobs consistently. A number of plans currently in existence use a breakdown on the Job Training factor such as the following: 3 months, 6 months, 9 months, 1 year, 1½ years, 2 years, 2½ years, 3 years, 3½ years, 4 years, 5 years, 6 years, 7 years, 8 years, 9 years, 10 years, and over 10 years. Obviously, such a fine breakdown makes it almost impossible for evaluators to judge whether a particular job requires 2, 2½, or 3 years of Job Training. Inconsistencies in evaluation are almost certain to develop, and where a union representing the employees is involved, it may be practically impossible to defend the evaluations adopted. Personnel responsible for developing an evaluation plan should recognize that they will not always be dealing with trained evaluators. The system which is developed should, after being explained, appear logical to persons with little or no experience in the field.

Although studies have indicated that it is possible to construct a job evaluation plan having relatively few factors, it is extremely doubtful whether such a plan should be installed by any company. Additional factors may not add substantially to the ability of the system to predict rates, but they do provide a means for recording information to be used elsewhere in the company. For example, factors such as Physical Effort or Work Surroundings may be of little assistance in predicting differences in rates between unskilled, semi-skilled, or skilled jobs, but the information developed may be of interest and use to placement, safety, training, and medical activities. It should be recognized at the time a job analysis and evaluation plan is developed that the program should be designed to serve as many purposes as possible within an organization in order that the initial cost of the program may be fully justified. As much data as possible concerning the various independent characteristics of each hourly job should be secured.

It should not be implied, however, that a large number of factors are essential to the proper operation of a job evaluation plan. In most instances, the addition of factors to a plan usually involves the division of each of the four basic factors into several subfactors. For example, the basic factor Responsibility may be divided into Responsibility for Material or Product and Responsibility for Tools and Equipment. Both of these factors represent slightly different job characteristics. In order to secure maximum consistency in evaluation, it is desirable to have factors which are independent of each other. The tendency to treat two different job characteristics as one results in confusion during evaluation. Thus, if Responsibility for Material or Product and Responsibility for Tools and Equipment are treated as one factor, jobs having one characteristic but not the other will be difficult to evaluate accurately on the factor.

Relationship between Factors and Rates

In practically every organization the way in which jobs are evaluated on these characteristics will have a relationship or correlation to rates paid. In other words, if a job evaluates high on a factor it will usually have a high rate. A relationship will also exist between the two factors. Thus, if a job tends to evaluate in a high degree on one factor, it will also tend to evaluate in a high degree on the other factor. Since the most reliable system of job evaluation from the standpoint of predicting rates involves the selection of as many independent factors as possible which correlate with rate, the tendency for factors to correlate with other factors in the plan serves to reduce the effectiveness of these factors in forecasting rates.

Correlation of Factors and Rates

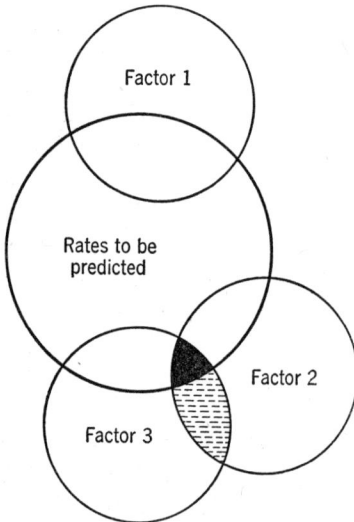

Figure 3

This tendency may be brought out more clearly through observation of Figure 3. If the center circle represents the rates to be predicted, the objective is to secure factors which overlap or correlate as high as possible with rates. In other words, as a job evaluates high on a factor, the existing rate will be high, and vice versa. For example, factor 1 correlates or overlaps rate and therefore might be considered a good predictor of rates. Factors 2 and 3 also correlate with rate and overlap rate but at the same time they overlap each other. This has a tendency to reduce the independent predictive value of factors 2 and 3. Obviously, a part of the variation in existing rates which factor 3 predicted (note area in solid black) had already been predicted by factor 2. If the correlation or relationship between two factors is sufficiently strong, it may be unwise to use both factors in the evaluation plan. For example, a factor such as Concentration would have a high correlation with Mental Effort, thus indicating that either one or the other factor should probably be eliminated. In this case, through proper definition, they might be combined.

The correlation between factors or between a factor and wage rates is measured by a statistical term called the correlation coefficient. The correlation coefficient usually designated by a small "r" indicates the similarity or relationship between factors or between

Perfect Negative Correlation

(Minus 1.00)

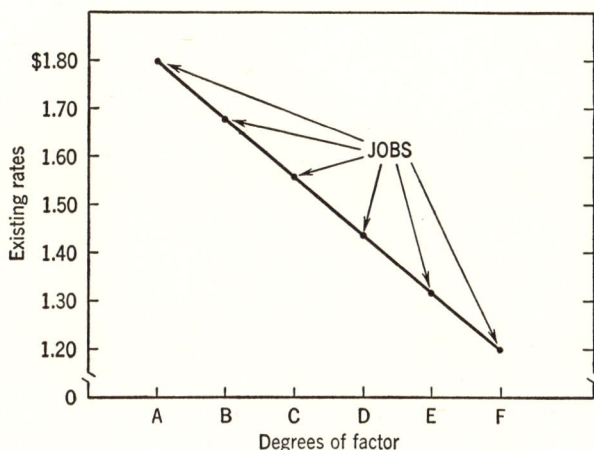

Figure 4

a factor and wage rates. It is a mathematical measure which is always stated in numbers ranging from a minus 1.00 to 0 and from 0 to a plus 1.00. A minus 1.00 correlation coefficient would mean that there is a perfect negative correlation existing between two groups of data. For example, if we were to evaluate a group of jobs on a particular factor and relate such an evaluation to existing rates, with the result that all jobs would fall exactly on a descending line (from left to right), it could be said that a perfect negative correlation existed between evaluation on the degrees of that factor and wage rates. Figure 4 indicates this relationship. If a group of jobs were evaluated on another factor and all jobs fell exactly on a line which had a tendency to rise, it could be said that a perfect positive correlation existed between the evaluation on the degrees of that particular factor and wage rates. Such a condition is shown in Figure 5.

In the analysis of wage data it is exceedingly unusual for jobs evaluated on the degrees of any single factor to have a perfect negative or perfect positive correlation with wage rates. Where any large number of jobs and rates is involved, such a condition would be practically an impossibility. Individual jobs would have a tendency to fall both above and below the trend line. In actual practice, the line would be calculated on the basis of the individual job

Perfect Positive Correlation

(Plus 1.00)

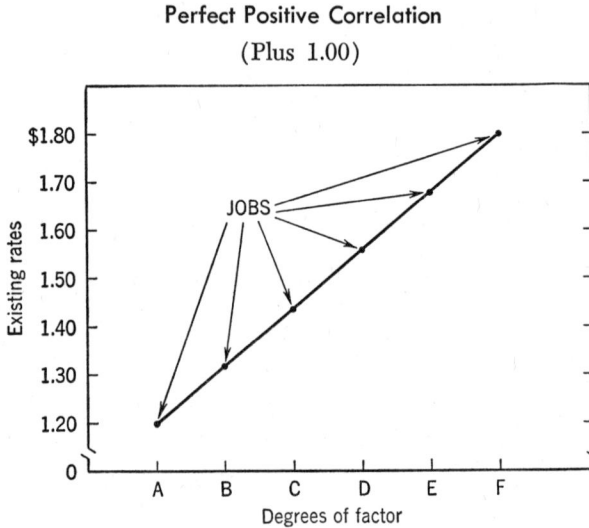

Figure 5

plottings and would be known as a least-squares trend line or line of best fit.

It becomes desirable when analyzing these job plottings to utilize a statistical measure which provides a summary of the deviations from the line of best fit passing through the data. The standard error of estimate provides this measure and indicates the range above and below the line within which approximately 68% of the jobs will fall if the scatter is normal. Within an area of two standard errors of estimate on each side of the line, about 95% of the cases would be included, and almost all cases (over 99%) would be found in an area within three standard errors. Figure 6 presents these relationships graphically.

In most instances, the factors selected in a job evaluation plan have a positive correlation with rate. This fact, as later studies will indicate, appears to be largely responsible for the apparent success of different point plans having a wide variety of weight distribution on similar factors.

In many instances, where a positive correlation exists between evaluation on the degrees of a factor and wage rates, the inter-correlations between the factor and other factors may also be fairly high. If the only intention of job analysis were to establish relative

Dispersion within a Wage Structure as Indicated by
Standard Errors of Estimate

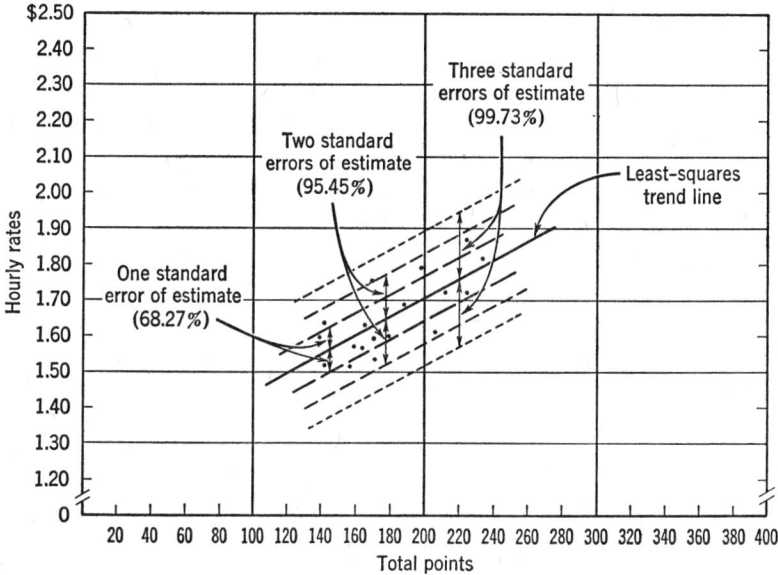

Figure 6

differences between rates, it would probably be possible to adopt some sort of an abbreviated scale where the factors all had a good correlation with rate and as low intercorrelations as possible.

Although studies have indicated that job characteristics such as Physical Effort and Work Surroundings have little correlation with rates, it is generally agreed that these factors should be included in any job evaluation system. Further analysis of the predictive value of these factors indicates that in the low rate production jobs as a group there is a tendency for Physical Effort and Work Sur-roundings to have a relationship to the rates paid. Thus, in the selection of factors for a job evaluation plan, it should be recognized that certain factors such as Job Training correlate with rates and exercise an influence throughout the entire structure, whereas other factors such as Physical Effort exert an influence within a restricted area of the structure.*

The determining element in the selection of job factors depends, to a large extent, upon the types of jobs being analyzed. If the plan is to be designed primarily for hourly non-supervisory workers and is not to include employees such as leaders, the factors should be selected to apply to the characteristics of the jobs to be covered by the plan. For example, if no leaders are to be included in the plan, it is doubtful whether a factor such as Responsibility for Work of Others should be included. On the other hand, such a factor would probably be desirable if an evaluation plan were being developed to cover supervisory personnel. Insofar as possible, factors should be independent of each other and generally considered as compensable.

Job Characteristics Determine Application of Evaluation Plans

The question is often raised whether the same evaluation plan can cover both hourly and salary jobs or both supervisory and non-supervisory jobs. The answer to these questions usually rests with an analysis of the job characteristics. A plan should be designed to cover a specific group and should reflect the job characteristics pertinent to that group. Evaluation of jobs on a plan not suited to the job characteristics will result in the creation of inequities as far as those jobs are concerned. Thus, under no circumstances should a plan designed for hourly personnel be used to evaluate jobs performed by salaried office personnel, foremen, or executives.

* A study of the Physical Effort factor was conducted on 1318 production jobs being paid three different rates. Data for the study were as follows. Average points are based upon the weights assigned the Physical Effort factor in the Hourly Plan presented at the end of this chapter.

Rates Paid	Number of Classifications Evaluating on Different Degrees of the Factor Physical Effort					Total No. Classifications	Average Points
	A	B	C	D	E		
$1.525	13(3.6%)	256(71.1%)	84(23.3%)	7(2.0%)	0	360	13.2
1.575	10(1.8%)	283(51.2%)	227(41.0%)	33(6.0%)	0	553	15.7
1.625	6(1.5%)	127(31.4%)	209(51.6%)	60(14.8%)	3(0.7%)	405	18.7

The Chi-Square test for a significant difference in point distribution between the $1.525, $1.575, and $1.625 levels was computed. Assuming that the $1.575 level represented a normal or expected distribution, differences in the $1.525 and $1.625 distributions proved to be highly significant. A similar study was conducted for the factor Work Surroundings with identical results.

Definition of Degrees of Factors

After the selection and definition of the factors, the next step in the development of a point evaluation plan is the careful definition of degrees of factors. Since each factor will provide the guide for classification of the various types of jobs, it is necessary that the degrees of factors be defined to include all of the various types of jobs to be evaluated on the plan. Analyses of characteristics of jobs at the extremes are helpful in preparing the degree definitions. Every attempt should be made at the time the degrees of factors are defined to provide a logical means of segregating jobs into groups. By so doing, evaluation on the plan will tend to be more consistent. Probably one of the best ways to secure information concerning degree definitions is to review a number of different job evaluation plans currently in use. Careful analysis of these plans will usually indicate the type of reasoning used to define the degrees of job factors. Every attempt should be made to clarify areas of controversy before they arise. Wherever possible, words and phrases should be selected which will be uniformly interpreted by persons evaluating jobs on the plan.

Number of Degrees Required

Some point plans have attempted to secure additional accuracy in evaluation by establishing a large number of degrees on each factor. In certain plans the number of degrees has reached 15 or more. It is probably desirable to establish between 3 and 8 degrees on each factor. A great many of the existing plans use 5 degrees on each factor. The number of degrees to be used depends upon the characteristics of the jobs being evaluated on the plan and the ability of evaluators to position jobs on the degrees after they have been established. For a certain type factor, only 3 degrees might be used, since the jobs in the organization would tend to slot themselves in 3 groups. For other factors it would probably be possible to have a larger number of degrees, since the jobs will group themselves satisfactorily into more levels. Whenever there is confusion about the evaluation of jobs on a particular factor, it may be because the factor is broken down into too many degrees and, through the process of human judgment, it is impossible to determine on any sort of a consistent basis just which degree should be used.

Attempts have been made to obtain greater accuracy in evaluation by using interpolation between degrees. Interpolation involves the assignment of a point weight to an area between two degrees in order that marginal cases may be positioned on one of these interpolated values. The contention is that by increasing the number of degrees by means of interpolation, increased accuracy in positioning of the jobs and consequently increased accuracy in the evaluation plan may be secured. In actual practice, however, the process involves additional work, and arguments frequently arise about the exact positioning of jobs. The statement has sometimes been made that interpolation may be used advantageously during union negotiations. If, for example, there is a controversy between two degrees, it may be possible to settle upon an interpolated value somewhere between the two extremes. However, it is somewhat obvious that the device may be used by union personnel or by management personnel as a means of trying to raise or lower a certain job by at least one pay grade. This is always a possibility, regardless of whether there are two separate degrees or whether there are interpolated values. Thus, in some instances, the interpolation may merely tend to complicate the plan. Since interpolation has a tendency to tax human judgment without providing compensating benefits from a mathematical standpoint, the use of this technique is not recommended.

For certain factors the definition of the degrees will have a pronounced influence upon the correlation which exists between the jobs evaluated on that factor and the total rates paid each of those jobs. For example, if only three degrees were placed on a factor such as Job Training, the correlation coefficient would probably be fairly high. As the number of degrees are increased, the correlation will tend to rise. Beyond a certain point (usually about eight degrees), however, the correlation begins to stabilize and addition of degrees beyond this point will have little effect upon the correlation. The creation of a large number of degrees (in excess of eight or nine) on this factor will usually lead to difficulty in evaluation, since the degree definitions themselves do not promote clear-cut evaluations.

Use of Objective Criteria in Degree Definitions

Every attempt should be made to define degrees of factors by objective criteria whenever possible. For example, the degrees of the factor Responsibility for Material or Product may be broken down into different gradations, depending upon the dollar amount of the loss. These dollar amounts tend to provide a tangible basis for evaluation. The selection of the dollar amounts should be made with considerable care, since lines of demarcation which are too fine will lead to inconsistent evaluation. It will be necessary also to consider the types of jobs which the plan is expected to cover. If, for example, the evaluation plan is to be designed for jobs where the dollar loss could never exceed $500.00, it would not be practical to use increments in excess of this amount. Objective criteria may also be developed in connection with factors such as Educational Background, Physical Effort, and Supervision of Others.

Sample Hourly and Salary Evaluation Plans

The evaluation plans for hourly and salaried employees presented on the following pages have been developed after careful review of a large number of existing plans. They have been used for evaluation of several thousand diversified jobs in numerous different types of industrial organizations. In each instance, point weights on factors and degrees of factors were developed after statistical studies similar to those outlined in this book. The Hourly Plan has been used as a basis for evaluation of jobs treated in the sample statistical studies discussed in this chapter and Chapter 4. It is believed that these plans may provide some suggestions to personnel interested in developing job evaluation plans suitable for their particular organizations. During the developmental stages and after the factors and degrees of the factors have been defined and the plan has been tested for a trial period, it will probably be found that certain modifications and changes will have to be made to clarify some of the original definitions. Any difficulties experienced by evaluators using the plan should be carefully analyzed so as to provide the basis for making changes which will eliminate confusion and bring about more consistent evaluations.

Modifying Plans for Small Companies

A review of the job evaluation plans presented on the following pages indicates that they have been designed for large industrial organizations having a variety of different types of classifications. Modification of these plans to permit their use in smaller companies would not be difficult. Persons faced with such a responsibility should remember that the characteristics of the jobs to be evaluated should form the basis for whatever changes are made. A group of typical jobs should be selected and related to each factor and the degrees of the factors. In the Hourly Plan, for example, an analysis of jobs within the company might reveal that no jobs would evaluate in the highest degree of Educational Background. Such might be the case when a small company is subcontracting work which requires highly skilled personnel. When such a condition exists, personnel developing the plan might consider the possibility of not including the highest level of Educational Background. Later, if the company should expand or decide to acquire employees with high-level skills, the degree could be added. Since jobs differ between companies, benchmark statements and benchmark jobs will differ, and these differences should be incorporated into the plan. It is important during this stage to develop a plan where the job classifications fall into logical groups. In certain instances, this objective may result in the addition of a degree to a factor. Factors such as Physical Effort, Work Surroundings, and Hazards should be carefully reviewed, since there is usually a significant variance in these factors between different companies. The factors Responsibility for Material or Product and Responsibility for Tools and Equipment may be restated to incorporate an increasing dollar amount of damage into each degree, thereby eliminating the multiple choice which currently exists under the degrees of these factors. For example, the second degree of the factor Responsibility for Material or Product could be worded "Property loss due to damage, scrapping of materials, or loss of production is seldom over $50.00." Where a large number of diversified jobs does not exist, the development of a simplified plan will have a tendency to increase the speed of the evaluation phase of the program. It is also possible that local practices within a company may result in the addition of a factor. For example, Responsibility for Work of Others might be included if certain hourly employees are responsible for instructing and overseeing employees such as apprentices.

In a similar manner, factors and degrees in the salary plan may be reviewed in relation to the jobs being evaluated on it. If it becomes apparent that further changes are required in the plan as the evaluation progresses, it is far better to revise the wording than to continue experiencing difficulty in positioning jobs on the degrees of the factors.

Conversion Chart—Points to Dollars

Pay Grade	Hourly Plan			Salary Plan			
	Point Range (inclusive)	Rate	20-Cent Range	Point Ranges (inclusive)	Mid-point	35% Ranges Rounded to Outside $5.00 Min.	Max.
1	Up to including 35	1.32		Up to including 36	170.25	140	205
2	36–52	1.37		37–59	193.92	155	230
3	53–69	1.42		60–82	217.59	175	260
4	70–86	1.47		83–105	241.26	195	285
5	87–103	1.52		106–128	264.93	215	315
6	104–120	1.57		129–151	288.61	235	340
7	121–137	1.62		152–174	312.28	255	370
8	138–154	1.67		175–197	335.95	275	395
9	155–171	1.72	1.62–1.82	198–220	359.62	295	425
10	172–188	1.77	1.67–1.87	221–243	383.29	315	455
11	189–205	1.82	1.72–1.92	244–266	406.96	335	480
12	206–222	1.87	1.77–1.97	267–289	430.63	355	510
13	223–239	1.92	1.82–2.02	290–312	454.30	370	535
14	240–256	1.97	1.87–2.07	313–335	477.97	390	565
15	257–273	2.02	1.92–2.12	336–358	501.64	410	590
16	274–290	2.07	1.97–2.17	359–381	525.32	430	620
17	291–307	2.12	2.02–2.22	382–404	548.99	450	650
18	308–324	2.17	2.07–2.27	405–427	572.66	470	675
19	325–341	2.22	2.12–2.32	428–450	596.33	490	705
20	342–358	2.27	2.17–2.37	451–473	620.00	510	730
21	359–375	2.32	2.22–2.42				
22	376–392	2.37	2.27–2.47				

Evaluation Plan for Hourly Employees

I. EDUCATIONAL BACKGROUND

Educational Background consists of the intelligence, practical knowledge, or schooling required as a basis for satisfactory performance of the work involved. Formalized education or schooling is oftentimes not essential for the fulfillment of occupational requirements and is offered in the degree definitions, therefore, as an additional guide to assist in the positioning of job classifications. In all instances, specific job requirements should be carefully analyzed to determine the knowledge or mental level required.

Degree	Degree Definitions and Benchmark Statements	Benchmark Jobs	Code No.	Points
A	*Requires the ability to carry out simple specific verbal instructions and/or read and comprehend simple statements. Equivalent to fourth-grade education.* Perform rough work not requiring close supervision. Operate machines or equipment with push button or simple controls. Make simple tool changes requiring little or no adjustment. May use simple fixed gauges to check work. Perform routine repetitive assembly operations where the possibility of making errors is slight and where practically no decisions are required. Tolerances may be liberal. Possibility of errors minimized since practically no judgment is required.	Body bolter Shakeout man Masker Reamer, hand Cleaner, general— Group I	4210 0541 4192 7295 1111	2
B	*Requires the ability to read and write and to perform simple arithmetic calculations, such as adding, subtracting, multiplying, and dividing of decimals and fractions. Equivalent to eighth-grade education.* Perform assembly operations where adjustments or selection may be necessary to obtain proper fit. Make routine setups or adjustments to machinery or tools. Perform simple repetitive machining operations where the tolerances are not completely controlled by the machine. Read and comprehend simple information shown on charts, blueprints, and drawings. Do reading of sketches or blueprints which consists only of taking direct information from the prints, such as dimensions, material, and finish specifications.	Grinder, crankshaft- pin bearing Industrial lift truck operator Stoveman Crib attendant Glass polisher	8943 3260 3897 3201 0030	8

- Use measuring instruments such as rule, caliper, micrometer, square, and other simple measuring gauges and meters.
- Do routine checking involving the completion of standard forms not of a complex nature.
- Operate motor-driven truck or overhead crane.
- Perform simple numerical or alphabetical filing.

C   *Requires the ability to read and write, use and perform mathematical calculations involving a knowledge of the fundamentals of shop mathematics, algebra, or geometry. Equivalent to two years high school and approximately six months of specialized training.*

- Make difficult setups on machines.
- Perform machining operations requiring the use of the fundamentals of shop mathematics and a knowledge of feeds and speeds.
- Follow established routine which requires variations of procedure from cycle to cycle.
- Use variety of precision measuring instruments requiring some trade knowledge in a specialized field or process.
- Make minor repairs to machinery involving practical knowledge of mathematical or electrical principles.
- Perform diversified clerical work which may involve the completion of various reports and/or the use of different methods or routines (such as touch typing) to perform different phases of the job.

D   *Requires the ability to make applications acquired through study of such subjects as shop mathematics, algebra, physics, chemistry, shop practice, and mechanical drawing. Equivalent to two-year high school program plus two years of specialized training.*

- May have to interpret complicated drawings and specifications and use wide variety of precision measuring instruments and broad shop trade knowledge.
- May have to interpret large detailed assembly drawings or complex part drawings involving a large number of dimensions where it is difficult to locate and visualize finished surfaces.

Job	Code	
Melter, cast steel	0525	15
First helper, open hearth	3650	
Painter	0985	
Clerk-typist	6394	
Slotter operator	1397	24
Roller, hot strip	3573	

Evaluation Plan for Hourly Employees—Continued

I. Educational Background—Continued

Degree	Degree Definitions and Benchmark Statements	Benchmark Jobs	Code No.	Points
	Plan diversified work of a complex nature.			
	Make repairs involving a knowledge of mathematical or electrical principles.			
	Independently interpret a wide variety of reports and determine appropriate action.			
E	*Requires a basic technical knowledge sufficient to deal with complicated and involved mathematical, electrical, or other engineering problems. Equivalent to four years high school and four or more years of specialized training.*	Electrician	1001	35
	Perform difficult analytical or developmental work.	Die sinker	1373	
	Interpret and/or write comprehensive technical reports.	Die maker	1402	
	Perform highly skilled work requiring a four-year apprenticeship.	Patternmaker, wood	1387	

II. Job Training

Job Training measures the period of time required to attain mental and manual skills in order to perform the job satisfactorily. Consider the complexity of the work, the variety of situations which occur, and the total amount of actual experience required in order to be *thoroughly familiar with all phases of the job*. Manual dexterity and muscular coordination required for successful manipulation of materials, parts, tools, machines, or equipment to accomplish the job should also be taken into consideration. Review carefully the frequency and speed of movements, the coordination which must be developed between sensory cues and physical responses, the accuracy or precision of movements, the repetitiveness of movements, and the independence of finger, hand, foot, and/or leg movements.

Fundamental knowledge ordinarily obtained through formalized schooling or apprenticeship training should be included under Educational Background, not Job Training. The measure of time should include only the actual job training required on the work to be performed *plus necessary experience on directly related work*. In all instances, the total time should be based upon continuous progress. Where advancement to a higher classification is retarded because of slow turnover on the job ahead, such time will not be considered a part of the normal training period.

		Code	Points
A	Up to and including 2 weeks		6
	Block handler	0535	
	Assembler, hood	4199	
	Cleaner, general—Group I	1111	
	Drill press operator	9681	
B	3 weeks through 2 months		17
	Clerk-typist	6394	
	Body and motor decker	4208	
	Core assembler	0534	
	Industrial lift truck operator	3260	
	Lathe operator, crankshaft	9963	
C	3 months through 6 months		28
	Grinder, crankshaft-pin bearing	8943	
	Balancer, flywheel	9846	
	Clerk, department	6407	
	Checker, receiving	6380	
D	7 months through 12 months		39
	Stoveman	3897	
	Plumber-pipe fitter	0997	
	Gas furnace patrolman	3808	
	Repairman, trim	8026	
	Checker, material control	6379	
	Discrepancy adjuster, receiving	6396	
E	13 months through 24 months		50
	Electrician	1001	
	Glass roller, master	0059	
	Chemist, artificial leather	3298	
	Cutter grinder A	1405	
F	25 months through 36 months		64
	Melter, cast steel	0525	
	Speed operator A	3577	
	Fixture repairman, general	1386	
G	37 months through 60 months		82
	First helper, open hearth	3650	
	Patternmaker, wood	1387	
	Die maker	1402	
	Gear man, all-round	1388	
H	Over 60 months		110
	Die sinker, layout	1417	

Evaluation Plan for Hourly Employees—Continued

III. Mental and Visual Effort

Mental and Visual Effort measures the degree of *concentration or attention* required throughout the shift in order to perform the work involved satisfactorily. Analyze the job to determine the degree of initiative, judgment, and resourcefulness required to accomplish the work. Consider the intricate or exacting nature of the job, the reasoning powers which must be exercised in order to reach decisions, and the necessity for carrying out assignments not covered by usual standards or precedents. Determine the frequency, intensity, and continuity of visual effort to assemble parts, manipulate tools, set up machines, inspect materials, record information, check data, and perform service operations.

Degree	Degree Definitions and Benchmark Statements	Benchmark Jobs	Code No.	Points
A	*Minimum mental application required for performance of simple routine tasks.* Walk, clean up, use simple tools for rough work, handle crude materials. Operate simple controls not requiring adjustment and where cycle of operations is not rapid. Few relatively simple decisions required where proper course of action is apparent. Operation practically automatic and/or duties require attention only at long intervals. Job duties definitely and clearly established. No choice of procedure and practically no resourcefulness required. Coordination of hand and eye not important in accomplishing task.	Cleaner, general— Group I	1111	4
B	*Light mental and/or visual attention where the flow of work is intermittent or the operation involves waiting for a machine or process to complete a cycle with little attention or checking.* Coordination of hand and eye required at intervals in order to accomplish task. Occasional close visual attention required to perform the work. Decisions limited to few possibilities. Limited selection among well-defined procedures. Work may require some discretion in applying variations of standard procedures.	Crane hooker Mud mixer Monkeyman Oiler	3252 0520 3894 1004	18

		33

Body bolter	4210	
Bullard operator	9625	
Clerk-typist	6394	
Glass polisher	0030	

C *Continuous mental and/or visual attention for sustained period where the flow of work is repetitive or the operation requires constant alertness.*

Perform repetitive short-cycle assembly or machining operations involving continuous visual attention.

Perform duties involving close tolerances.

Set up machines and make adjustments which require frequent decisions to detect variations from proper operations.

Maintain continuous observation of pressure gauges or electrical instruments.

Perform repetitive inspection or checking work where continuous mental and visual attention are required to prevent defective workmanship.

Perform clerical work requiring constant visual attention to prevent errors.

Job may require some original thinking and planning since standard procedures do not always apply to all phases of the work.

| | | 51 |

Die maker	1402	
Patternmaker, wood	1387	
Hydraulic journeyman	1003	
Molder, jobbing A	0532	
First helper, open hearth	3650	
Checker, material control	6379	

D *Concentrated mental and visual attention involving planning and laying out of complex work.*

Careful judgment required to select proper methods.

Decisions required to properly organize and lay out intricate work.

Job requires resourcefulness and ingenuity to perform work.

Concentrated mental attention required to analyze and interpret a variety of reports.

| | | 75 |

| Gear man, all-round | 1388 | |
| Roller, blooming mill | 3557 | |

E *Concentrated and exacting mental and visual attention involving planning and laying out of very involved and complex jobs.*

High concentration required involving unusual coordination of mind, eye, and physical responses.

Decisions required after extensive investigation, careful analysis, and weighing of complex factors.

Superior reasoning, initiative, and judgment required.

Perform work requiring extreme accuracy and precision.

Evaluation Plan for Hourly Employees—Continued

IV. PHYSICAL EFFORT

The factor Physical Effort measures the physical exertion required by the job and the frequency with which such physical exertion occurs. Where material handling devices such as hoists, cranes, or other mechanical aids are available, such conditions should be taken into account. In all instances the weight lifted or equivalent exertion in pushing or pulling should be considered. Where the job involves rapid short-cycle operations (i.e., where the machining time is less than the handling time), sufficient consideration should be given to the effort expended as a result of the rapidity of movement as well as the weight of the materials handled when positioning jobs on the various degrees of this factor.

Degree	Degree Definitions and Benchmark Statements	Benchmark Jobs	Code No.	Points
A	*Minimum physical exertion.* Perform light work where the major portion of the job is accomplished in a sitting position with occasional standing or walking. Operate push-button controls where the major portion of the work is in a sitting position.	Clerk-typist Gas dispatcher Checker, glass assembly	6394 3802 2805	2
B	*Light physical exertion.* Use light hand tools, sweep, clean up. Pick up, position, or assemble small parts or materials. Perform most duties in a standing position. Operate light controls or valves.	Masker Industrial lift truck operator Sprayer, paint Die maker Checker, receiving	4192 3260 1630 1402 6380	11
C	*Moderate physical exertion.* Handle medium-weight materials using a variety of medium-sized hand tools. Operate heavy controls and valves or medium-weight hand power tools. Work in awkward positions for a major portion of the time. Work from ladders. Use moderate effort to push or pull heavy materials where occasional lifting is involved.	Millwright Assembler, headlining Strander, merchant mill	1023 4146 3541	20

D *Heavy physical exertion.*
Manually lift heavy tools and materials.
Operate heavy pneumatic tools.
Continually move heavy materials in wheelbarrows.

Block handler	0535	31
Sand slinger	0516	
Iron worker, structural	1020	
Third helper, open hearth	3652	

E *Extreme physical exertion working with heavy-weight materials.*
Move or drag extremely heavy materials with tongs or bars.
Lift or manually move materials such as exceedingly heavy parts or castings.
Perform work requiring lifting of extremely heavy materials and involving continued strain because of exceedingly difficult working positions.

Balancer, crankshaft finish	9851	45

V. RESPONSIBILITY FOR MATERIAL OR PRODUCT

Responsibility for Material or Product measures the probability and extent of damage to or loss of materials or products as a result of the actions of a worker. The worker's responsibility extends only to what he can control. The material or product is what is actually being worked upon and in some instances may include parts, raw materials, inventory, fuels, acids, oils, gas, and any other material with which the worker is involved in controlling the processing and which directly or indirectly becomes a part of the manufactured or merchandized product. Materials may not always be product since the equipment worked on by maintenance workers is considered materials for those jobs. For clerical jobs, consider the care required to prevent errors resulting in shortages, loss of materials, or rechecking. Where work involves the controlling of fluids or gases, only the material handled or supplied is to be considered material for the job. Both the care required by the worker and the probable monetary loss are to be considered. In determining the loss, consider the nature of the material being worked upon, the probability that it can be damaged, the length of time before the damage is detected, the quantity of material spoiled, the cost of repair or replacement, and the salvage value. In all instances, the dollar amount should be based upon the estimated expenditure resulting from a single loss.

Degree	Degree Definitions and Benchmark Statements	Benchmark Jobs	Code No.	Estimated Cost	Points
A	*Possibility of damage is unlikely.* Because of the nature of the materials being worked upon and the process performed, damage is unlikely. Products worked with difficult to damage (rough castings).	Shakeout man	0541	Under $25	6
		Block handler	0535		
		Cleaner, general— Group I	1111		

Evaluation Plan for Hourly Employees—Continued

V. RESPONSIBILITY FOR MATERIAL OR PRODUCT—Continued

Degree	Degree Definitions and Benchmark Statements	Benchmark Jobs	Code No.	Estimated Cost	Points
B	*Damage is possible but exercise of ordinary care and attention will prevent loss.*			$ 25	15
	Perform repetitive task with liberal tolerances and specifications where material can be damaged through improper handling or processing.	Bullard operator	9625	100	20
	Mechanically handle or transport material occasionally subject to damage or material which is adequately protected.	Sander, wet	1596	500	26
	Perform clerical work requiring ordinary attention and checking to prevent loss or damage to material.	Cutter, rough glass	0094	Over 500	34
	Handle materials subject to damage on and off production units.				
	Use ordinary care in making simple setups or adjustments to prevent damage to materials.				
C	*Damage is possible but can be prevented by considerable care and attention.*	Industrial lift truck operator	3260	$ 25	21
	Set up and operate processing unit where specifications are partially obtained by mechanical control.	Plumber-pipe fitter	0997	100	29
	Perform repetitive work where close attention is required only during checking of product for tolerances.	Charging car operator	3898	500	38
	Mechanically handle and transport material subject to damage from handling devices.	Glass roller master	0059	Over 500	49
	Perform diversified clerical work relating to the production program and requiring careful checking.	Cycle checker	6395		
	Inspect or check products where close attention is required to prevent further processing or use of defective material.				

			$100	33
D	*Damage is probable but can be prevented by sustained high degree of care and attention.*			
	Set up and operate units having a variety of detail requiring frequent checking and adjustment to determine size, shape, finish, or physical properties.	Patternmaker, wood	$100	33
		First helper, open hearth	500	43
	Perform skilled work requiring frequent checking and close tolerances.	Speed operator A	1000	55
			1500	69
	Perform skilled inspection work involving close tolerances and a great variety of details and dimensions.	Welder, high-pressure pipe	Over 1500	85
		1387		
		3650		
		3577		
		1010		
E	*Damage is probable and can be prevented only by extreme care and attention.*	Roller, hot strip	$100	43
	Perform highly skilled work involving a great degree of precision or variety of detail.	Die sinker	500	58
	Have responsibility for product on complex units requiring constant checking.		1000	75
			1500	94
	Constant concentrated attention required.		Over 1500	115
		3573		
		1373		

VI. RESPONSIBILITY FOR TOOLS AND EQUIPMENT

Responsibility for Tools and Equipment covers the obligation imposed upon the worker to prevent or minimize damage to tools and production equipment. Responsibility of this nature is judged according to the probable cost or loss which might result from an error in using or handling tools or machines improperly where everything possible has been done through automatic equipment to prevent damage. The mere fact that the machine operated is large or expensive does not merit placing a high rating on this factor. Consider the care required to avoid damage and the estimated cost of the damage when it occurs. Tools and equipment may be defined as those items in which the company has made a capital investment. In all instances the dollar amount should be based upon the estimated expenditure resulting from a single loss. Equipment repaired or installed by maintenance personnel is considered as material and is credited under the factor Responsibility for Material or Product. Definitions of degrees of probable damage are:

Minor damage	Up to $25.00
Intermediate damage	$26.00 through $500.00
Major damage	Over $500.00

Evaluation Plan for Hourly Employees—Continued

VI. RESPONSIBILITY FOR TOOLS AND EQUIPMENT—Continued

Degree	Degree Definitions and Benchmark Statements	Benchmark Jobs	Code No.	Estimated Cost	Points
A	*Possibility of damage is unlikely.* Use no tools or equipment. Use simple hand tools of such a nature that damage is unlikely (shovel, pick, sledge). Use no precision tools or equipment which would be damaged as a result of being dropped.	Masker	4192		2
		Oiler	1004		
		Stock chaser	3230		
		Assembler, sandwich	0034		
		Assembler, radiator tube	4169		
B	*Damage is possible but exercise of ordinary care and attention will prevent loss.* Exercise reasonable care to recognize obvious trouble and shut down hand power tools and routine machines to prevent or minimize damage. Use or handle tools or equipment subject to damage, such as micrometers, calipers, gauges, and office machinery.	Hoist operator	3137	Minor	7
		Body bolter	4210	Intermediate	10
		Bricklayer	0993	Major	14
		Hobbing machine operator	9281		
		Sand slinger	0516		
C	*Damage is possible but can be prevented by considerable care and attention.* Prevent damage to dies, power-driven cutting tools, rolls, and other processing equipment. Prevent damage to highly complex machines or moderate-sized production lines while performing operations. Exercise close attention to prevent damage to mobile equipment such as trucks and cranes.	Industrial lift truck operator	3260	Minor	11
		Stoveman	3897	Intermediate	14
		Manipulator	3607	Major	19
		Cutter grinder A	1405		
		Glass roller master	0059		
D	*Damage is probable but can be prevented by sustained high degree of care and attention.* Prevent damage to major equipment, responsibility for which is placed directly on the operator.	First helper, open hearth	3650	Minor	17
		Powerhouse and substation operator	4669	Intermediate	21
				Major	30

Control rapidly changing conditions which require immediate action to avoid damage to complex high-speed machines and production lines.

Sustained high degree of care and attention required in observing rapidly changing instrument readings to prevent damage to equipment.

E *Damage is probable and can be prevented only by extreme care and attention.* Prevent damage to equipment where responsibility exists for acts of others as well as own acts on large and complex operating units. Expert judgment and fast and accurate reactions required to prevent damage.

Roller, hot strip	3573	Minor 27
		Intermediate 32
		Major 45

VII. Responsibility for Safety of Others

The factor Responsibility for Safety of Others appraises the care required to avoid or prevent injury to other workers, considering the nature of the job performed. Only direct acts of the workers performing the job should be considered when positioning jobs on this factor. It is assumed that all employees are complying with safety regulations and that safety devices for which workers are not directly responsible are in order. Consider the probability of injury and the seriousness of the injury.

Degree	Degree Definitions and Benchmark Statements	Benchmark Jobs	Code No.	Points
A	*Little care required to prevent injury to others.* Work done in an isolated area or on machines where others are seldom exposed to hazards of the job. Material handled is usually light and injuries resulting therefrom are unusual. Work done in enclosed areas or with equipment where the possibility of injury to others is remote.	Clerk-typist Crib attendant Stapling machine operator Checker, gears	6394 3201 4329 2783	1
B	*Ordinary care and attention required to prevent injury to others.* Operate equipment where others are exposed to minor cuts, bruises, or burns.	Cleaner, general — Group I	1111	4

Evaluation Plan for Hourly Employees—Continued

VII. Responsibility for Safety of Others—Continued

Degree	Degree Definitions and Benchmark Statements	Benchmark Jobs	Code No.	Points
	Coordinate work where individual accident may injure others. Handle materials manually where other employees are exposed to injury. Work with power-driven machine tools, power-driven hand tools. Perform work exposing one other person, such as helper, where likelihood and probable seriousness of accidents are small. Use simple burning or welding equipment.	Bullard operator Patternmaker, metal Plasterer	9625 1414 1008	7
C	*Considerable care and attention required to prevent injury to others.* Operate large presses where several other employees are exposed to accidents despite operation of safety devices. Normally work in position above others. Operate power-driven mobile equipment where others are exposed but probability of accident is low. Handle inflammable liquids or gases where safeguards minimize the probability of fire or explosion.	Shakeout man Sinter plant operator Industrial lift truck operator Roofer	0541 3906 3260 0994	
D	*Sustained high degree of care and attention required to prevent injury to others.* Be responsible for flow of electric power, molten metal, or steam. Operate high-pressure vessels where others are exposed to accidents. Perform general electrical work.	Electrician First helper, open hearth Monkeyman	1001 3650 3894	10
E	*Extreme care and attention required to prevent injury to others.* Handle, control, or transport highly inflammable explosives or molten materials where others are constantly exposed to serious injury. Control high-voltage equipment and transmission lines. Inherent hazard on job cannot be safeguarded. Safety of others depends entirely upon course of action of employee on job being rated, and carelessness may result in total disability or fatal accidents to others.	Metal pourer, bull ladle Gas holder attendant Crane operator, bridge type, molten metal	0537 3809 3216	15

VIII. WORK SURROUNDINGS

The factor Work Surroundings pertains to the environment or physical conditions under which the work must be performed and over which the employee has no control. These conditions cannot be eliminated or minimized and tend to influence the employee's mental or physical well being. Physical discomfort frequently involves such factors as heat (hot metal operation), noise (motor testing), dirt (foundry), smoke (heat treating), vibration (air hammer), and glare (arc welding).

Degree	Degree Definitions and Benchmark Statements	Benchmark Jobs	Code No.	Points
A	*Disturbing influences, such as dirt, oil, grease, or noise, are present to a negligible extent.* Inside, well heated, lighted, and ventilated. Work in enclosed areas for a major portion of the time. Clean work and working conditions.	Clerk-typist Elevator operator Checker, glass assembly	6394 5194 2805	2
B	*Some dirt, oil, grease, or noise are present to a moderate degree.* Inside machine shop or average factory type of building. Machining or assembly operations where the parts handled are greasy or oily. Inside and outside weather conditions, but worker not required to remain out in extreme weather.	Wire brush operator Bullard operator Die maker Body bolter Stock checker	0031 9625 1402 4210 6430	8
C	*Some element or elements of disagreeableness continuously present to a substantial degree.* Continuous exposure to exceedingly noisy operations. Exposure to all weather conditions. Continuous exposure to heat, dirt, dust, smoke, fumes, and/or oil to a considerable degree.	Plumber-pipe fitter Hardener Die setter Press operator	0997 1407 6904 6761	15
D	*Some disagreeable element or elements continuously present to an intense degree.* Continuous exposure to extreme dust, smoke, and fumes. Exposure to extreme heat for a major portion of the time.	Melter, cast steel Strander, merchant mill	0525 3541	24
E	*Continuous exposure to extremely disagreeable surroundings.* Exceedingly disagreeable conditions, such as extreme heat approaching the point of endurance for the worker and requiring the scheduling of periodic rest periods.	Shakeout man	0541	35

Evaluation Plan for Hourly Employees—Continued

IX. Unavoidable Hazards

The factor Unavoidable Hazards takes into consideration the frequency of exposure to accidents and the probability and severity of resulting injuries to which an employee is subjected on any particular job. Consider the material being handled, the machines or tools used, and the work location. Assume that the worker is exercising reasonable care and observing safety regulations.

Degree	Degree Definitions and Benchmark Statements	Benchmark Jobs	Code No.	Points
A	*Accident hazard unlikely.* Perform assembly work involving light-weight parts where possibility of injury is unlikely. Perform clerical work. Perform work having practically no accident hazards. Accident hazard consists only of occasional minor cuts, bruises, and burns.	Clerk-typist Masker Gas dispatcher	6394 4192 3802	1
B	*Accident hazard moderate and probable injury consists of cuts, bruises or burns.* Manually operate machines, machine tools, burning and welding equipment, and material handling equipment, or control movement of material when exposed to moving machinery. Handle medium-weight material or parts for a major portion of the shift. Perform manual tasks such as feeding or piling light- or medium-weight materials. Exposure to flying objects, such as chips and scales. Occasional exposure to hot objects which may cause moderate burns. Occasional exposure to falls such as might occur while working on low ladders and scaffolds.	Diemaker Wire brush operator Assembler, radiator tube Drill press operator Industrial tow tractor operator	1402 0031 4169 9681 3172	6
C	*Frequent exposure to severe injuries.* Manually handle heavy materials for a major portion of the shift. Perform heavy maintenance work to repair, set up, or tear down equipment. Regularly adjust moving machinery.	Varnish cooker Furnace operator, cyanide	1601 5803	11

Work on low-voltage electrical equipment.
Frequently climb on moving rolling stock.
Frequent exposure to second-degree burns, severe cuts, or bruises.
Exposure to inflammable or volatile liquids or gases.

D *Frequent exposure to injuries resulting in total disability or death.*
Exposure to high-voltage electricity at frequent intervals.
Exposure to severe burns from handling, transporting, or controlling flow of molten metal.
Exposure to falls as a result of normally performing duties on high structures and roofs.

E *Continual exposure to injuries resulting in total disability or death.*
Frequent exposure to volatile gases, liquids, or other hazards where failure to exercise extreme care and judgment at all times might cause an accident which would result in total disability or death.
Continuous work on high-voltage equipment where climbing is involved.

Title	Code	
Die setter	6904	
Block handler	0535	17
Electrician	1001	
Monkeyman	3894	
Iron worker, structural	1020	
Metal pourer, bull ladle	0587	
Gas holder attendant	3809	25
Gas furnace patrolman	3808	

Evaluation Plan for Salaried Employees

I. KNOWLEDGE REQUIRED

The factor Knowledge Required consists of the general knowledge, such as grammar and arithmetic, or specialized knowledge, such as chemistry, engineering, accounting, or merchandising, required by the position. Consider the inherent ability and acquired knowledge necessary to perform the duties effectively. To help evaluate position classifications, degree definitions are stated in terms of formalized education or schooling. In all instances, specific position requirements should be carefully analyzed to determine the mental level involved.

Degree	Degree Definitions and Benchmark Statements	Benchmark Jobs	Points
A	*Requires the ability to read and write and to perform simple arithmetic calculations. Equivalent to a high school education.* Follow simple written or verbal instructions. Do simple routine tasks where practically no decisions are required. Make only judgments well established by precedents. Do simple operations on office machines, such as adding or subtracting, which require only normal reaction time. File folders or forms alphabetically or numerically.	Messenger File clerk B Duplicating equipment operator B	3
B	*Requires the ability to use fractions, decimals, and commercial arithmetic. Basic knowledge of English grammar required. Equivalent to a four-year high school education and six months of specialized training.* Develop simple procedures according to general instructions. Operate various types of office machinery such as a typewriter or comptometer which require fast reaction times. Perform clerical duties involving the securing, recording, and arranging of various types of information. Follow established routines which require occasional modifications in procedures.	Typist A, B Stenographer A, B Tabulating equipment operator B Comptometer operator A, B Test driver	12
C	*Requires the ability to perform moderately complex mathematical calculations. Must organize diversified information and apply fundamental principles of a science. Equivalent to a four-year high school education and two years of specialized training.*	Industrial relations clerk A Mechanic, senior Reporter, publications Secretary A	22

34

50

Safety inspector

Accountant A, B
Purchase analyst, A
Industrial relations representative A
Buyer B
Staff assistant B
Project engineer, senior

Labor relations umpire representative
Tax specialist A
Cost analyst, senior
Financial analyst A

D

Perform bookkeeping and simple accounting procedures.
Organize a variety of statistical figures.
Understand basic office practices, techniques, and methods.
Apply knowledge of basic procedures or methods pertaining to manufacturing processes or design engineering.
Develop procedures of moderate difficulty and complexity according to general instructions.
Perform diversified clerical duties where considerable planning and judgment are required.
Requires the ability to understand complex mathematical formulas, charts, and engineering drawings. Equivalent to a four-year college education leading to a degree, or four years of specialized training.
Apply the principles of a science or a complex technical subject in such fields as design engineering, production engineering, industrial engineering, or accounting.
Understand cost distribution and accounting procedures.
Develop complex procedures where numerous variables must be taken into account.
Edit technical business correspondence or procedure manuals.
Plan diversified work of a complex nature.

E

Requires the ability to apply exceedingly complex procedures and methods involving a technical knowledge in a specialized field. Equivalent to a four-year college education and one or more years of graduate work or specialized training leading to advanced degrees.
Formulate policies requiring original thinking and the application of exceedingly complex technical or professional information.
Perform original technical research in a specialized field.
Analyze and develop solutions for unusual or highly complex problems pertaining to manufacturing, accounting, industrial relations, sales, or purchasing.
Do creative thinking involving product designs where advanced technical knowledge is essential.

Evaluation Plan for Salaried Employees—Continued

II. EXPERIENCE

The factor Experience measures the period of time required to absorb mental and manual skills in order to perform the work required satisfactorily. Consider the time normally required for an individual with the proper educational background or intelligence to acquire necessary practical experience to be able to assume full responsibility for the work and perform it effectively. Fundamental knowledge ordinarily obtained through formal education should be considered under education rather than under experience. The measurement of experience should include only that period when the work is actually being performed, plus necessary experience on directly related work. In all instances, the total time should be based upon continuous progress. Where advancement to a higher classification is retarded because of slow turnover on the position ahead, such time will not be considered a part of the normal training period.

Degree	Degree Definitions and Benchmark Statements	Benchmark Jobs	Points
A	Up to and including 2 weeks.	File clerk B Messenger Comptometer operator B Typist B Stenographer B	7
B	3 weeks through 2 months.	Typist A File clerk A Teletype operator B	17
C	3 months through 6 months	Stenographer A Tabulating equipment operator B Mechanic B	29
D	7 months through 12 months.	Personnel representative B Hourly employment inter- viewer A Job analyst B	43

		57	74	95	120
E	13 months through 24 months.	Industrial relations clerk A Secretary B Test driver Accountant B			
F	25 months through 60 months.		Budget analyst B Layout draftsman B Secretary A Industrial relations research analyst B Tabulating equipment operator, senior Safety inspector Buyer B Accountant A Purchase analyst A Shop instructor A Designer A		
G	61 months through 96 months.			Cost accountant A Financial analyst A Labor relations representative A Draftsman, senior Project engineer A	
H	Over 96 months.				Tax specialist A Product cost analyst Project cost appraiser Project engineer, senior Supervisor, drafting

Evaluation Plan for Salaried Employees—Continued

III. MENTAL EFFORT

This factor appraises the frequency, intensity, and continuity of mental attention required to perform the work involved. Consider the extent to which duties are standardized, the degree of independent action, the judgment and planning required, the type of decisions made, and the creative effort or resourcefulness required in devising efficient methods for accomplishing work assignments.

Degree	Degree Definitions and Benchmark Statements	Benchmark Jobs	Points
A	*Minimum mental effort.* Work performed under immediate supervision or involves relatively few choices or decisions. Decisions required follow well-established precedents.	Messenger File clerk B Duplicating equipment operator B Typist B	4
B	*Light mental effort.* Intermittent thinking required to carry out predetermined procedure or sequence of operations of limited variability. Work may be sufficiently repetitive for a habit pattern to be formed. Repetitive work for which the decisions required are limited to few possibilities. Occasional mental effort required to select correct method from several standard procedures which are available.	File clerk A Typist A Stenographer A, B	16
C	*Moderate mental effort.* Work requires some original thinking and planning, since standard procedures do not always apply to all phases of the job. Considerable judgment required to reach decisions involving the use of various methods or routines to solve moderately complex problems. Perform successive operations, selecting and combining steps included in one or more standard procedures.	Accountant B Safety inspector Industrial relations clerk A Job analyst B Layout draftsman B	29

D   *Concentrated mental effort.*

Close mental attention required for planning operations involving considerable detail, a high degree of coordination, and a variety of decisions. Resourcefulness and ingenuity must be applied to perform work. Work requires very careful planning and judgment while making decisions for which only general procedures or policies are available for guidance.

44

Industrial relations research analyst B
Machine tool operator
Layout draftsman A
Purchase follow-up man, senior
Buyer B

E   *Concentrated and exacting mental effort.*

High degree of concentration required where the volume and character of work involve unusual coordination of mind and eye. Sustained periods of analytical thinking required in order to develop solutions to complex problems. Work may deal with technical or specialized problems involving keen analysis.

Superior reasoning, initiative, and judgment required. Highly diversified complex work requiring a high level of sustained mental effort and consistent careful advance planning. Originality and judgment required to devise new methods or procedures for carrying out complex work assignments.

65

Financial analyst A
Area supervisor, labor relations
Supervisor, drafting
Cost analyst, senior
Project engineer, senior

IV. PHYSICAL EFFORT

This factor considers the nature and frequency of physical exertion required to perform the duties involved. The working position, weights normally lifted, and continuity of effort should be carefully analyzed.

Degree	Degree Definitions and Benchmark Statements	Benchmark Jobs	Points
A	*Minimum physical effort.* Majority of work performed in sitting position with intermittent standing and walking. Handle light materials in a sitting position.	Keypunch operator A, B Typist A, B Secretary A, B Financial analyst A File clerk A, B	1

Evaluation Plan for Salaried Employees—Continued

IV. PHYSICAL EFFORT—Continued

Degree	Degree Definitions and Benchmark Statements	Benchmark Jobs	Points
B	*Light physical effort.* Perform most work in a standing position. Occasionally lift and carry light-weight materials. Occasionally work in difficult positions. Handle light materials in a standing position. Walk for considerable periods of time.	Messenger Draftsman, senior Tabulating equipment operator B Wage analyst Job analyst B	11
C	*Moderate physical exertion.* Work in awkward positions for sustained periods of time. Occasionally handle heavy-weight materials, equipment, or supplies. Walk continuously or for prolonged periods.	Guide Motion picture cameraman Shipping and receiving clerk	25

V. RESPONSIBILITY FOR COMPANY PROPERTY, MATERIALS, AND EQUIPMENT
(Financial Responsibility)

Responsibility for Company Property, Materials, and Equipment measures first, the degree of care and attention which must be exercised to prevent errors leading to increased costs or capital losses, and second, the estimated normal amount of a single loss. Financial losses to the Company may involve raw materials, work in process, inventory, tools, machines, or the unnecessary expenditure of funds or utilization of manpower as a result of reaching incorrect decisions. Analyze the nature of the decisions which are required, the length of time before damage is detected, the extent of the damage, and the normal cost of correcting the error. The employee's responsibility extends only to those decisions for preventing financial losses and protecting Company investments which are under his direct control.

Degree	Degree Definitions and Benchmark Statements	Benchmark Jobs	Estimated Cost	Points
A	*Possibility of damage or loss is unlikely.* Responsibility for property, materials, and equipment may be negligible. Materials worked with difficult to damage. Errors easily detected or when not detected can only result in minor loss of time or money.	Messenger	Under $25.00	6

	Definition	Jobs	Responsibility	Points
B	*Damage or loss is possible but exercise of ordinary care and attention will prevent loss.* Perform duties where property or materials may be damaged through improper handling or processing. Work is subject to checks and controls. Work may be verified by others in subsequent operations.	File clerk A, B; Typist A, B; Duplicating equipment operator B; Teletype operator A, B	Up to and Including $100	16
			Over 100	26
C	*Damage or loss is possible but can be prevented by considerable care and attention.* Careful checking required to prevent damage or loss of Company property or materials. No specific controls exist to expose errors. Control the operation of complicated office machinery such as IBM printers or multipliers where damage to the machines may result in delays.	Industrial relations clerk A; Tabulating equipment operator B; Medical stock man, senior; Mechanic A, B; Test driver; Safety inspector	Up to and Including $250	37
			Over 250	48
D	*Damage or loss is probable but can be prevented by sustained high degree of care and attention.* Responsibility for the care of large amounts of Company money. Supervisory responsibility involving the care of Company funds or property. High degree of care required to prevent errors during the purchasing of materials or equipment.	Buyer B; Purchase expediter; Accountant A; Designer A; Staff assistant B	Up to and Including $500	61
			Over 500	76
E	*Damage or loss is probable and can be prevented only by extreme care and attention.* Responsibility for the care or purchasing of extremely large amounts of materials. Constant concentrated attention required in order to prevent costly mistakes. Little possibility of shifting responsibility to others through checks or controls where an exceedingly important course of action is taken.	Financial analyst A; Area supervisor, labor relations; Research engineer A; Project engineer A; Cost analyst, senior	Up to and Including $1000	92
			Over 1000	110

Evaluation Plan for Salaried Employees—Continued

VI. RESPONSIBILITY FOR PERSONAL CONTACTS

This factor measures the extent to which the position requires an individual to contact or work with other personnel within or outside the Company. The relative frequency and significance of the transactions handled and the potential effects of such contacts on Company good will and policies should be considered.

Degree	Degree Definitions and Benchmark Statements	Benchmark Jobs	Points
A	*Position involves relatively few contacts with personnel outside the immediate work unit. Information handled is routine.* Work performed requires little self-expression. Little contact with others except to provide information or ideas gained while performing required duties.	Typist A, B File clerk B Comptometer operator A, B	3
B	*Position involves contact with personnel inside and/or outside the Company where the nature of the information provided usually follows an established pattern.* Receive service orders or complaints. Contact individuals in other sections of the Company to secure routine statistical data. Contact outside personnel where the type of data handled or information provided is routine. Discuss a variety of information with other personnel in the work unit.	Messenger Librarian Mechanic A, B Manufacturing clerk A Accountant B Layout draftsman B	13
C	*Position involves frequent contact with persons inside or outside the Company where the matters discussed require some resourcefulness, tact, and a working knowledge of Company policies and procedures.* Job requires close contact with the public through letters or personal interviews. Some judgment required in securing or providing information to outsiders where the data are not entirely routine.	Unit supervisor, guest relations Secretary A Hourly employment interviewer Insurance reviewer Job analyst B Plant protection shift supervisor	24

Degree		Benchmark Jobs	Points
D	Important discussions with personnel both outside and inside the Company which materially affect Company policies and procedures. Ability to convey ideas through speaking, writing, or graphic presentations required. Considerable tact required while securing or releasing information. Must take direct responsibility for public relations and the building and maintaining of good will.	Buyer B Tax specialist A Research engineer A Cost analyst, senior Supervisor, drafting	37
E	Constant and almost continuous contact of a highly significant nature with executives or key personnel both outside and inside the Company. Handle matters of major importance to the welfare of the Company. Secure information concerning grievances and other controversial issues. High degree of discretion required at all times in the securing or releasing of information.	Seniority representative, senior Area supervisor, labor relations Purchase expediter	55

VII. RESPONSIBILITY FOR SUPERVISION OF OTHERS

This factor considers the amount of direct responsibility inherent in the position or placed there by supervisory authority for the planning, direction, instruction, and coordination of other people in order to promote effective use of their time and abilities. Although the number of persons normally supervised has been provided as an aid in evaluating jobs on this factor, it is not to be considered as the only criteria for reaching decisions. The nature of the group supervised and the complexity of the supervision provided should be carefully evaluated.

Degree	Degree Definitions and Benchmark Statements	Benchmark Jobs	Points
A	Responsible for own work and normally not required to direct or supervise other personnel. Perform routine duties not involving the training or indoctrination of personnel. Occasionally explain certain routine phases of the work to other employees.	Messenger Typist A, B Secretary A, B Machine tool operator Test driver	3

Evaluation Plan for Salaried Employees—Continued

VII. RESPONSIBILITY FOR SUPERVISION OF OTHERS—Continued

Degree	Degree Definitions and Benchmark Statements	Benchmark Jobs	Points
B	*Work involving the immediate supervision of from one to three individuals performing routine work.* Supervise a small group performing routine tasks where few decisions are required. Plan and allocate routine work for one or two assistants.	Cost accountant C Industrial relations clerk B Buyer B	14
C	*Work involving the supervision of a small group of individuals, normally about four to eight people.* Supervise a group of employees working on a non-routine job. Supervise a small group of employees where some knowledge of manufacturing processes or operations is required. Plan and allocate specialized work for one or two assistants.	Supervisor, teletype Accountant A Industrial relations research analyst B Industrial relations clerk A Project engineer, senior Labor relations representative A	26
D	*Work involving the supervision of a medium-sized group, normally about nine to twenty people.* Be responsible for the effective utilization of personnel in a medium-sized group performing various operations requiring judgment. Be responsible for a small group performing analytical or highly specialized work.	Accountant, senior Financial analyst A Cost analyst, senior	41
E	*Work involving the supervision of a large group of personnel, normally over twenty persons.* Be responsible for a medium-sized group performing analytical or highly specialized work.	Area supervisor, labor relations Plant protection, shift supervisor	60

VIII. WORK SURROUNDINGS

This factor pertains to those physical conditions surrounding the work which are disagreeable, uncomfortable, or otherwise adverse in nature. Environmental influences, such as illumination, ventilation, atmosphere, and noise, should be analyzed. In addition to these elements, the hazards inherent in the work, including the possibility, severity, and frequency of exposure to injury, should be included under this factor. These conditions cannot be eliminated or minimized and tend to influence the employee's mental or physical well-being.

Degree	Degree Definitions and Benchmark Statements	Benchmark Jobs	Points
A	*Disturbing influences present to only a minor extent.* Inside, well heated, lighted and ventilated. Occasional disagreeable conditions, such as moderate heat, dust, or noise. Most of work performed inside office. Occasional exposure to outside weather conditions. Perform work having little or no accident hazard. Injuries sustained would be minor.	Librarian A Secretary A, B Accountant A, B	1
B	*Disagreeable elements present to a moderate degree.* Some elements of disagreeableness continuously present. Work in areas where moderate degrees of noise from machines or assembly operations are evident. Outside weather conditions, but worker protected part of time. Work performed both inside and outside. May be exposed to moderate accident hazards and probable injuries consisting of cuts, bruises, or burns.	Labor relations representative A Mechanic A, B Manufacturing clerk A	7
C	*Several disagreeable elements present for a major portion of the time.* Exposure to dust, smoke, fumes, and considerable noise. Occasional exposure to considerable heat from manufacturing operations. Outside most of the time. Exposure to all weather conditions. May be frequently exposed to severe injuries resulting in lost time.	Wage analysts, senior and A	15

4

Development of a Point Evaluation Plan:
Weighting of Factors
and Degrees of Factors

Value of Statistical Techniques in Developing Factor Weights

As additional research has been done in the field of job evaluation, the concept has grown that weighting applied to factors should be designed to reflect the general wage structure or overall job to job relationships as closely as possible. In other words, the weighting system should be devised to maximize the combined predictive force of the factors in determining wage rates. At the same time, the purely arbitrary effect which weighting of the factors and degrees of the factors has upon final evaluated rates should be minimized.

Personnel designing point plans have often assumed that the factors used have certain intrinsic values in determining rates. The decisions they have reached concerning the amount of these inherent weights or values have varied or were subsequently altered as a result of producing wage structures which were unsalable. Variations which were made usually followed no consistent pattern and a review of numerous different point plans reveals considerable inconsistency in weight assignments. The process of assigning weight to factors and degrees of factors without resort to the type of information derived from statistical studies has actually resulted in the creation of some distortion in wage structures. Changes in job rates resulting from evaluation on plans of this type have sometimes been illogical and exceedingly difficult to defend.

In most instances, after a point evaluation plan has been developed and jobs have been evaluated on the plan, an attempt has been made to describe the resulting wage structure by means of a straight line. This straight line describes the relationship between total points and current wage rates on each job. Sometimes little thought has been given to the fact that the data may not be adequately represented by a straight line. In other words, degrees of the factors may be weighted in such a manner that the relationship within the overall wage structure could more adequately be described by means of a curve. In such instances, the forcing of a straight line through the data has a tendency to create inequities within the wage structure. Some personnel working in the field of job analysis and evaluation have recognized this apparent difficulty, and various systems of progression on the factors have been adopted so as to produce a structure which could best be described by a straight line. It appears evident that, from the standpoint of simplicity, use of a straight line to describe the resulting structure should be one of the basic objectives in the development of a point plan.

It should be realized by persons developing a job evaluation plan that it is possible, through improper weighting of the factors or degrees of the factors, to create actual distortions in the wage structure. Thus, by applying too much weight to certain factors such as Physical Effort and Work Surroundings, jobs having these characteristics to a high degree will usually be increased in rate. The application of sizable amounts of weight to such factors will result in increased dispersion from the trend line. This will have the effect of creating changes in job rates which are not justifiable.

In order to eliminate the arbitrary effect which weighting of the factors has upon job rates, the statistical technique of multiple correlation may be used. This technique provides information concerning the relative importance of the various factors in the plan as far as predicting rates is concerned. The results of the multiple correlation analysis provide the basis for reweighting factors so as to produce a more reliable estimate of wage rates. The technique also results in reducing to a minimum the number of rates changed as a result of weights applied to factors and degrees of factors. It is believed that this process is essential to the development of a mathematically sound point evaluation plan. It provides a sound basis for weight distribution and at the same time produces a logical wage structure.

In the development of weights for factors and degrees of factors, questions frequently arise concerning the total points to be used. Where statistical calculations are contemplated, it is important to use numbers sufficiently large to eliminate the necessity for using fractions. Point systems where the values are too high tend to complicate the calculations. Each of the plans presented in Chapter 3 has a possible maximum of 500 points. The numerical values used in these plans have been found suitable for statistical calculations.

Despite the stress placed upon creation of factor weights and degree weights which are mathematically sound, it is evident that the evaluation plan finally developed will be judged upon its ability to classify or segregate jobs into logical groups, thereby providing a sound basis for establishing standard wage rates for each group. The type of mathematical analysis which may be used in the development of an evaluation plan should be directed toward securing answers which appear to be logical and can be substantiated. Thus, the use of statistical methods is merely an aid in the development of the plan and is no substitute for sound judgment. In his book entitled *Methods of Correlation Analysis*, Mordecai Ezekiel points out that:

The place of statistical analysis in scientific research is no different from the place of any other technical aid the investigator may employ. It furnishes a means of measuring the elements that are involved and of examining the way in which they are related; but it does not of itself furnish an explanation of phenomena. Except insofar as the effort to reduce the variables to specific numerical statement, definitely related, forces the investigator to think more clearly and definitely about his problem, statistical analysis is not a substitute for logical analysis, clear-cut thinking, and full knowledge of a problem. . . . Instead, it is an aid which may make that thought and skill even more productive of worth-while results.*

Selection of Typical Jobs as Basis for Developing Plan

To provide the basis for development of a point evaluation plan, a representative cross section of the various types of jobs which will be subject to the evaluation plan should be selected. This sample should be chosen with extreme care since it will provide the basis not only for checking definitions of factors and degrees of factors but also for statistical calculations. The size of the sample will be directly dependent upon the number of classifications in the organization and the population distribution on these classifications.

If only a few hundred classifications are involved, it may be possible to select a sample of about 100 jobs. If this number will not represent all the various characteristics of the jobs in the organization, the number should be increased to the point where it will

* *Methods of Correlation Analysis*, Mordecai Ezekiel, John Wiley & Sons, 2nd edition, 1941, p. 453.

be truly representative of all classifications. If only a few hundred classifications are involved, it will usually be found that the population is concentrated on a relatively few jobs, and these jobs should in most instances, be included in the sample. If several thousand classifications are included in the wage structure, it may be necessary to include 250 or more jobs in order to obtain a representative sample.

The jobs chosen should provide not only an adequate basis for the development of the definitions of the factors and the degrees of the factors but also the basis for statistical studies involving the assignment of point weights. Careful thought should be given to the exact type of information to be secured about each hourly job used in the sample. The information collected will then provide sufficient data so that these jobs will not have to be re-analyzed at a later date. Thus, the initial expenditure of time devoted to gathering of information concerning jobs used in the sample will not be lost. Information obtained for this sample group should be complete in all respects, since it will provide the basis for development of factor definitions, degrees definitions, and point weights.

Some of the considerations which should be taken into account during the time this sample is being selected are as follows:

1. Jobs which are selected should be representative of all of the various types of operations performed within the organization. For example, if the company has a foundry, machine shop, and assembly operations, all three of these activities should be represented.

2. Jobs with different characteristics in the various operations should be chosen. For example, foundry jobs should be selected from the core room as well as from the hot metal operations.

3. Jobs should be chosen which appear to have both a high or low rate in relation to other similar jobs. The selection of these jobs will be based, to a large extent, upon a knowledge of the existing rates and classification system.

4. The number of job classifications chosen in each rate area should have a strong relationship to the population distribution within the organization. In other words, if a large population exists on a certain rate or rates, a larger number of classifications should be selected in this area. To make certain that a strong relationship does exist between population distribution and the number of classifications chosen, the correlation coefficient may be computed. The correlation coefficient which is obtained will be high, usually falling somewhere above .90 if the sample has been carefully selected. By selection of the proper types of jobs in different areas of the wage structure, it will be possible to secure a correlation which is practically perfect.

5. An attempt should be made to select classifications on which there is a large population distribution.

6. Since the job sample will be used for statistical calculations, it is

important that jobs with rates which are known to be out of line be excluded from the sample. Permitting such jobs to become a part of the sample will have a tendency to distort the results. For example, job content for a particular classification may undergo a period of gradual change. This may result in the job's being substantially undervalued or overvalued in relation to other jobs. If this distortion reaches 15 or 20 cents, the job should be reviewed from the standpoint of dropping it from the sample.

During the selection of the job sample, it may be found that an unusual group of jobs exists within the company. These jobs may have been subject to a different rate history. For example, a company which has been negotiating with two unions may find that one union has succeeded in securing a rate schedule considerably higher or lower than that received by the other union. A similar situation results when there is an area differential in rates. An area differential exists when rates paid for similar jobs vary between different geographical locations. Either of these situations will produce within the company a group of jobs which have a different rate relationship as compared to other jobs in the company.

It will be necessary at the time the sample is selected to determine whether jobs with these unusual characteristics should be included as part of the job sample. Where area differentials of a substantial nature exist, such jobs should probably not be included in the job sample. This is particularly true if there are area differentials in only a few operations of the company. If a representative group of jobs can be secured from one operation, the statistical studies can be developed on the basis of these jobs. Jobs in locations where the rates differ will plot out either higher or lower than the jobs in the sample. It will then be necessary for management to determine the rate schedule or schedules to be adopted at the various locations. The prime objective in selecting the job sample is to secure a good representative cross section of all of the various types of jobs performed within the company. Since the statistical computations will take into consideration rates currently being paid for these jobs, it will also be necessary to select jobs which have been subject to the same rate pattern.

Evaluation of Typical Jobs

Upon completion of the definition of the factors and degrees of the factors, the typical jobs selected should be evaluated on the various factors of the plan. This evaluation will reveal some of the difficulties which will probably be experienced on factors and degrees of factors in view of the way they are presently stated. As many alterations as possible should be made at this time in order to clarify the existing definitions. The evaluation on the plan should probably be made by a group of trained evaluators acting independently. If groups of three evaluators are used, it will be possible for each person to evaluate the jobs independently and then for all to meet to discuss their thinking and reconcile any differences. Since no point weights are available at this stage, evaluators will merely be able to position each job on the degrees of the factors. It will be impossible to convert evaluations into rates and the evaluators will not, therefore, be influenced by the current rate on the job as compared with the new rate.

It should be recognized that there are certain limitations in applying all job evaluation systems. No matter how carefully factors and degrees of factors are defined, there will always be borderline jobs. In such instances it is essential that every possible fact be gathered concerning the job in order that the evaluation may be as accurate as human judgment will allow. The final wage rate of the job will depend not only upon the facts but also upon a certain degree of bias which is present among evaluators. Proper construction of the job evaluation system will tend to eliminate a substantial amount of this bias. If point weights or any means of converting the evaluation to current rates are not available to evaluators, the influence that these forces would have upon their evaluation is reduced.

When the evaluation of the typical jobs is complete, an analysis should be made of the number of jobs evaluating on the degrees of each factor. Such an analysis will indicate whether the degrees of a particular factor have been so stated to exclude practically all jobs within the company. For example, a plant where employees are handling materials up to thirty pounds in weight and where heavy physical effort does not exist will find that no jobs would evaluate on a degree designated as extreme physical exertion, involving the lifting of materials weighing over sixty pounds.

Degree definitions and factors should be modified to cover the jobs for which the plan is designed. Degrees which are not used should be eliminated. It may also be found during the course of this analysis that a factor has been described in such a way that practically all jobs in the plant are evaluated on a single degree. This has the effect of adding a constant weight to all evaluations. Such a factor adds little to the evaluation plan and should, therefore, be redefined or eliminated.

Considerable time should be spent in checking the evaluations of all the jobs on the plan which has been tentatively developed in order to be certain that changes in evaluations will not have to be made at a later date. During the course of the study it will be advisable to check with production supervision concerning the period of time required to learn particular types of jobs. Although some research has been done in this field, it is evident that considerable more work could be done in determining learning periods for different types of work. Individual judgments will vary as to the learning time required. There is a tendency for individuals who are familiar with a certain type of work to underrate the learning time involved. On the other hand, when an evaluator is unfamiliar with the job performed, there is a tendency to overrate learning time. This bias should be taken into account at the time jobs are evaluated. Before statistical studies are undertaken, all differences of opinion between evaluators about the rating of a job should be reconciled. In most instances, personnel charged with the responsibility of developing a plan are anxious to secure point weights as rapidly as possible. Actually, it is far better to concentrate upon the development of definitions for factors and degrees of factors and the consistent evaluation of jobs rather than to try and secure point weights immediately. It will probably be impossible to make all of the necessary changes to the factors and degrees of the factors on the basis of the sample group of typical jobs. Further clarification of the plan will have to be made during the development and testing period.

It is desirable, at this stage, to determine the exact factors to be used in the evaluation plan. Information will have to be secured concerning the job content of the group of typical jobs. This process is described more fully in the next chapter. If decisions cannot be made as to what factors should be used in the plan at the time the jobs are analyzed, it may be necessary to obtain information on all factors which might be used in the plan. It is essential that as much information as possible be secured concerning the work performed by persons on typical jobs.

Use of Tabulating Machines to Perform Calculations

If a point evaluation plan is being designed to cover a large number of jobs, it will probably be desirable to use tabulating machines to perform the necessary computations. The mechanical devices described briefly on the following pages may be leased from the International Business Machines Corporation, 590 Madison Avenue, New York City. Similar machines are available from Remington Rand Division, Sperry Rand Corporation, 315 Fourth Avenue, New York City. For those individuals who are not familiar with the capabilities of these machines, detailed information may be secured from the various sales offices. A brief description of some of the basic principles follows.

The process of mechanical tabulation involves reducing all data to a numerical or alphabetical code. These code numbers are then punched into designated areas on tabulating cards. It is of vital importance that all data placed on tabulating cards be carefully verified and checked before computations are made. Constant alertness is required to prevent computational errors from entering the data and making the results meaningless or actually misleading. Tabulating cards may be punched with a numerical or alphabetical key punch machine or with a reproducer or summary punch. Certain areas on the card may then be multiplied by other areas or divided by other areas and the results punched in another designated location on the card. The cards may then be sorted by means of a mechanical sorter. The information is listed by numerical or alphabetical listing machines, which may be controlled to print only the information desired and secure totals of columns as required.

The cards designed by International Business Machines have eighty columns with twelve positions for punching in each column. At the time the card passes through a sorting machine, an electrical contact is made through the hole and the card is routed to a particular compartment corresponding to the punched number on which the sort is being made. In a tabulating machine, the electrical impulse is transferred by means of wires to a plug board which in turn indicates the disposition of the card. When a hole is punched in a specific position it can:

1. Add itself to another number.
2. Subtract itself from another number.
3. Post itself.
4. Eliminate itself.
5. Select itself.
6. Produce an automatic balance forward.
7. Cause a form to feed to a predetermined position or to be ejected automatically or to space from one position to another.
8. Cause a total to be printed.

The three basic types of machines found in practically all installations include:

1. Key punch machines.
2. Card-sorting machines.
3. Listing machines.

In addition to the ability of tabulating cards to handle numerical data, alphabetical data may also be recorded on the cards. It is essential for those individuals who intend to use the facilities offered by tabulating machines to understand the capabilities and limitations of the equipment. One prerequisite is that whatever calculations are desired, it is necessary that they be stated in simplified form. For example, if computations for a least-squares line are required, it will be necessary to break down every step of the computations and list exactly what operations are required to obtain the proper answers. It is beneficial where lengthy computations are involved to establish internal checks or to process two independent studies. The results can then be checked, and if they are inconsistent, the errors can more readily be located.

Sample Instructions for Tabulating Unit

There are numerous short cuts in the use of tabulating machines, and it is strongly suggested that persons not familiar with their operation discuss their plans with individuals responsible for operating the machines. For a better understanding of the methods of presenting data to persons in charge of tabulating equipment, sample instructions appear on the following pages. The manner in which this information is presented provides an example of the type of request which may be turned over to a supervisor in charge of tabulating equipment.

This sample study provides information concerning the punching of a master deck of cards (one card for each job classification), the reproducing of the deck and addition of certain areas, and the reproducing of the deck and multiplication of certain areas. In each instance, tabulating machine wiring will be facilitated if the instructions include the maximum number of digits which will result from the action desired.

1. *Punch and Verify Basic Data on Tabulating Cards.* One card is to be punched for each classification. Space on the card has been allocated to meet the requirements of a plan somewhat similar to the hourly job evaluation plan in Chapter 3.

Areas	Card Columns	Description
1	1–5	Abbreviated job title
2	6–8	Job code (no more than 3 digits)
3	9–10	Point weight on factor Educational Background (no more than 2 digits)
4	11–13	Point weight on factor Job Training (no more than 3 digits)
5	14–15	Point weight on factor Mental and Visual Effort (no more than 2 digits)
6	16–17	Point weight on factor Physical Effort (no more than 2 digits)
7	18–19	Point weight on factor Responsibility for Material (no more than 2 digits)
8	20	Code assigned to level (dollars) within degree
		0—First degree (under $25.00)
		1—$25.00
		2—$100.00
		3—$500.00
		4—Over $500.00
		5—$1000.00
		6—Over $1000.00
9	21–22	Point weight on factor Responsibility for Tools and Equipment (no more than 2 digits)
10	23	Code assigned to level within degree
		1—Low
		2—Intermediate
		3—High
11	24–25	Point weight on factor Responsibility for Safety of Others (no more than 2 digits)
12	26–27	Point weight on factor Work Surroundings (no more than 2 digits)
13	28–29	Point weight on factor Unavoidable Hazards (no more than 2 digits)
14	30–32	Total points assigned classification (no more than 3 digits)
15	33–36	Average rates (no more than 4 digits)
16	37–40	Estimated population on classification (no more than 4 digits)

2. *Addition.* Reproduce deck of cards and list, printing totals for the following areas:

3	9–10	Maximum of 4-digit number
4	11–13	Maximum of 5-digit number
5	14–15	Maximum of 4-digit number
6	16–17	Maximum of 4-digit number
7	18–19	Maximum of 4-digit number
9	21–22	Maximum of 4-digit number
11	24–25	Maximum of 4-digit number
12	26–27	Maximum of 4-digit number

13   28–29   Maximum of 4-digit number
15   33–36   Maximum of 5-digit number

3. *Multiplication.* Reproduce on new deck columns 1–5 (Area 1), 6–8 (Area 2), 30–32 (Area 14), 33–36 (Area 15), and 37–40 (Area 16), in first 19 columns as follows:

1–5   Alphabetic code of job title (for fast identification)
6–8   Job code (numerical)
9–11   Total evaluation points
12–15   Average rate for classification
16–19   Estimated population

Multiply as follows:

1. Columns 9–11 by columns 9–11 and punch in columns 20–25 (maximum of 6-digit number).
2. Columns 20–25 by columns 16–19 and punch in columns 26–35 (maximum of 9-digit number).
3. Columns 12–15 by columns 12–15 and punch in columns 36–42 (maximum of 7-digit number).
4. Columns 36–42 by columns 16–19 and punch in columns 43–53 (maximum of 11-digit number).
5. Columns 9–11 by columns 12–15 and punch in columns 54–60 (maximum of 7-digit number).
6. Columns 54–60 by columns 16–19 and punch in columns 61–70 (maximum of 10-digit number).
7. Columns 20–25 by columns 12–15 and punch in columns 71–78 (maximum of 8-digit number).

In the future, computing machines of much higher speeds will aid in the solution of problems where sizable numbers of computations are involved. This electronic equipment, operating with magnetic tapes, magnetic drums, magnetic cores and other high-speed storage and calculating devices, will greatly facilitate the use of mathematical techniques in industry.

Demonstration of Statistical Methods to Derive Point Weights — 25-Job Sample

In order to demonstrate the various statistical techniques used in the weighting of factors and degrees of factors, a sample group of 25 jobs has been selected and evaluated on the plan for hourly workers presented in Chapter 3. As was pointed out earlier in this chapter, a sample of this size would not ordinarily be sufficiently large to produce statistically significant results. The primary purpose of this study is to demonstrate the various methods used to weight factors and degrees of factors. Failure to develop proper weights on factors and degrees of factors has probably been one of the greatest shortcomings in point evaluation plans. Many persons connected with the introduction of point plans have failed to recognize that these weights have a pronounced influence on the frequency and magnitude of rate changes occurring at the time a plan is installed. Improper weighting frequently results in excessive installation costs and greater disturbance to existing job rates than would otherwise be required. A review of the results of this study also indicates the value of statistical techniques in analyzing wage structures and developing administrative controls. The following steps are involved in the study, and the objectives of the steps are indicated.

Step 1. Selection of 25 typical jobs as a basis for statistical analysis. *Objective:* 25 jobs were selected for purposes of demonstrating the statistical techniques involved in developing an evaluation plan and analyzing a wage structure. A relatively small sample was selected in order to reduce computations to a minimum while still demonstrating the principles involved.

Step 2. Plotting of 25 jobs with equal weights on all factors and arithmetic progression on degrees of factors. *Objective:* No other basis being available for allocating weight to factors and degrees of factors, equal weight was assigned each factor and arithmetic progression was applied to the degrees of the factors. The intention of this portion of the study was to observe the results of these weight assignments and compare them with results obtained in the following steps.

Step 3. Experimentation with arithmetic and geometric progression on degrees of factors. *Objective:* Since the nature of the progression used on the factors has a very definite bearing on the results of the study, experimentation was conducted using arithmetic and geometric progression on the degrees of the factors. The results obtained were tested by means of various statistical measures. The intention was to develop a wage structure which could be adequately described by a straight line.

Step 4. Utilization of multiple linear correlation to assist in the weighting of factors. *Objective:* Realizing that a logical evaluation plan would not involve the weighting of each factor equally, personnel developing the plan decided to obtain a system of weights which would provide the most reliable prediction of wage rates for the jobs in the sample. The technique of multiple linear correlation was utilized in order to secure these results.

Step 5. Analysis of results of Step 4 and computation of a second multiple correlation. *Objective:* Although the first multiple correlation gave an indication of which factors should receive more weight in order that rates could be predicted with increased reliability, it was realized that a second multiple correlation using the results secured at the time of the first study would provide additional facts upon which to base decisions concerning reweighting of the factors.

Step 6. Analysis of results of Step 5 and computation of a third multiple correlation. *Objective:* The results of the multiple correlation computed under Step 5 were analyzed with the further reweighting of factors in mind.

A complete description of the processes used in each step and a summary of the results obtained are presented. Charts and graphs have been prepared in order to illustrate and explain the information developed.

Step 1. Selection of 25 Typical Jobs

Description of Step 1. As a basis for the statistical study demonstrating the methods used in the assignment of weights to factors and degrees of factors, 25 different jobs have been selected representing several different types of work content. Although some attempt should be made to select jobs with rates corresponding to the population distribution within a company, the size of this sample has limited the selection from such a standpoint. Where a large sample is being selected for purposes of developing weights on factors and degrees of factors, it is important that the number of job classifications selected has a strong correlation with the population distribution in the organization. Such a relationship may be checked by means of computing the correlation coefficient between the number of jobs selected on each rate and the number of persons in the company receiving these rates. In order to obtain information concerning the characteristics of the sample, the jobs were plotted using the same weights on factors and degrees of factors as those indicated for the evaluation plan for hourly employees in Chapter 3. Various statistical measures, including the following, were computed:

1. Least-squares trend line.
2. Correlation coefficient.
3. Standard error of estimate.
4. Second-degree curve.

The data in this step are presented as follows:

1. List of job specifications covering the 25 jobs which have been selected for use in this study. A sample job specification appears in Chapter 6.
2. Table presenting the points assigned each degree of each factor for the Hourly Plan presented in Chapter 3.
3. Summary of evaluation for the 25 jobs which have been selected. (In order to conserve space, job point evaluations for all steps have been included here.)
4. A tabulation of the number of jobs on each degree of each factor.
5. Presentation of graphic information, Figure 7.
6. Summary of results obtained in Step 1.

List of Job Classifications for 25-Job Study

Job Title	Code No.	Job Title	Code No.
Plumber-pipe fitter	2	Paint sprayer, production	120
Painter	10	Cut off and threading ma-	
Material control checker	28	chine	121
Picker and packer, parts	38	Hanger, door	139
First roller, 44-in. mill	75	Metal finisher	142
Scarfer	78	Core maker, jobbing A	170
Subassembly water pump	85	Metal pourer, bull ladle	180
Balancer, crankshaft finish	93	Body decker	196
Engine tester, dynamometer	96	Body bolter	200
Reamer, hand	104	Welder, spot and gun	204
Drill press operator	106	Die maker	218
Punch press operator	109	Keller operator	220
Lathe operator, crankshaft	113	Cleaners, general plant	246

Weight Assigned Each Degree of Each Factor
Hourly Plan, Chapter 3

Factors	Degrees of Factors and Points							
	A	B	C	D	E	F	G	H
1. Educational Back-ground	2	8	15	24	35			
2. Job Training	6	17	28	39	50	64	82	110
3. Mental and Visual Effort	4	18	33	51	75			
4. Physical Effort	2	11	20	31	45			
5. Responsibility for Material or Product	6	$25–15 100–20 500–26 0–500–34	$25–21 100–29 500–38 0–500–49	$100–33 500–43 1000–55 1500–69 0–1500–85	$100–43 500–58 1000–75 1500–94 0–1500–115			
6. Responsibility for Tools and Equipment	2	M– 7 I–10 M–14	M–11 I–14 M–19	M–17 I–21 M–30	M–27 I–32 M–45			
7. Responsibility for Safety of Others	1	4	7	10	15			
8. Work Surroundings	2	8	15	24	35			
9. Unavoidable Hazards	1	6	11	17	25			

Summary of Evaluation for 25 Jobs and Points Used in Statistical Analyses

Code No.	Classi-fication	Rate or Rate Range	Avg. Rate	1	2	3	4	5	6	7	8	9	Total Points
2	Plumber, pipe fitter	1.62–1.87	1.85	E	D	C	C	C	B	C	C	D	
								$100 Minor					
	Points used for Step No. 1			35	39	33	20	29	7	7	15	17	202
			2	56	25	29	29	24	10	29	29	42	273
			4	56	20	24	24	14	9	24	24	38	233
			5	35	50	39	23	49	8	8	19	19	250
			6	35	39	33	20	29	7	4	11	27	205
10	Painter	1.57–1.82	1.80	C	D	C	C	C	B	C	C	D	
								$100 Minor					
	Points used for Step No. 1			15	39	33	20	29	7	7	15	17	182
			2	29	25	29	29	24	10	29	29	42	246
			4	24	20	24	24	14	9	24	24	38	201
			5	19	50	39	23	49	8	8	19	19	234
			6	15	39	33	20	29	7	4	11	27	185
28	Material con-trol checker	1.62–1.72	1.72	C	D	C	B	C	A	A	B	A	
								$500					
	Points used for Step No. 1			15	39	33	11	38	2	1	8	1	148
			2	29	25	29	16	28	3	3	16	3	152
			4	24	20	24	13	18	2	3	13	3	120
			5	19	50	39	12	57	2	1	11	1	192
			6	15	39	33	11	38	2	1	6	2	147
38	Picker and packer, parts	1.52–1.62	1.61	B	C	C	C	C	A	B	B	B	
								$25					
	Points used for Step No. 1			8	28	33	20	21	2	4	8	6	130
			2	16	18	29	29	20	3	16	16	16	163
			4	13	14	24	24	10	2	13	13	13	126
			5	11	35	39	23	41	2	4	11	7	173
			6	8	28	33	20	21	2	2	6	10	130
75	First roller 44 in. mill	2.33	2.33	D	G	E	B	E	E	C	B	B	
							Over $1500 Major						
	Points used for Step No. 1			24	82	75	11	115	45	7	8	6	373
			2	42	48	56	16	56	56	29	16	16	335
			4	38	43	56	13	56	56	24	13	13	312
			5	27	95	75	12	115	45	8	11	7	395
			6	24	82	75	11	115	45	4	6	10	372
78	Scarfer	1.58	1.58	B	B	C	C	B	B	B	C	B	
								$25 Minor					
	Points used for Step No. 1			8	17	33	20	15	7	4	15	6	125
			2	16	10	29	29	8	10	16	29	16	163
			4	13	9	24	24	7	9	13	24	13	136
			5	11	20	39	23	16	8	4	19	7	147
			6	8	17	33	20	15	7	2	11	10	123

Summary of Evaluation for 25 Jobs and Points Used in Statistical Analyses—Continued

Code No.	Classi- fication	Rate or Rate Range	Avg. Rate	Evaluation Factors, Degrees and Points									Total Points
				1	2	3	4	5	6	7	8	9	
85	Subassembly water pump	1.53	1.53	A	B	C	B	B	B	B	B	B	
								$25 Intermediate					
	Points used for Step No. 1			2	17	33	11	15	10	4	8	6	106
			2	3	10	29	16	8	15	16	16	16	129
			4	3	9	24	13	7	12	13	13	13	107
			5	2	20	39	12	16	12	4	11	7	123
			6	2	17	33	11	15	10	2	6	10	106
93	Balancer, crankshaft finish	1.71	1.71	B	C	C	E	C	B	B	B	C	
								$25 Minor					
	Points used for Step No. 1			8	28	33	45	21	7	4	8	11	165
			2	16	18	29	56	20	10	16	16	29	210
			4	13	14	24	56	10	9	13	13	24	176
			5	11	35	39	45	41	8	4	11	13	207
			6	8	28	33	45	21	7	2	6	18	168
96	Engine tester, dynamometer	1.73	1.73	C	D	C	B	C	B	B	C	B	
								$100 Intermediate					
	Points used for Step No. 1			15	39	33	11	29	10	4	15	6	162
			2	29	25	29	16	24	15	16	29	16	199
			4	24	20	24	13	14	12	13	24	13	147
			5	19	50	39	12	49	12	4	19	7	211
			6	15	39	33	11	29	10	2	11	10	160
104	Reamer, hand	1.53	1.53	A	A	C	B	B	A	B	B	B	
								$25					
	Points used for Step No. 1			2	6	33	11	15	2	4	8	6	87
			2	3	3	29	16	8	3	16	16	16	110
			4	3	3	24	13	7	2	13	13	13	91
			5	2	6	39	12	16	2	4	11	7	99
			6	2	6	33	11	15	2	2	6	10	87
106	Drill press operator	1.53	1.53	A	A	C	B	B	B	B	B	B	
								$25 Intermediate					
	Points used for Step No. 1			2	6	33	11	15	10	4	8	6	95
			2	3	3	29	16	8	15	16	16	16	122
			4	3	3	24	13	7	12	13	13	13	101
			5	2	6	39	12	16	12	4	11	7	109
			6	2	6	33	11	15	10	2	6	10	95
109	Punch press operator	1.57	1.57	A	A	C	B	B	B	B	B	B	
								$25 Intermediate					
	Points used for Step No. 1			2	6	33	11	15	10	4	8	6	95
			2	3	3	29	16	8	15	16	16	16	122
			4	3	3	24	13	7	12	13	13	13	101
			5	2	6	39	12	16	12	4	11	7	109
			6	2	6	33	11	15	10	2	6	10	95

Summary of Evaluation for 25 Jobs and Points Used in Statistical Analyses—Continued

Code No.	Classi-fication	Rate or Rate Range	Avg. Rate	Evaluation Factors, Degrees and Points									Total Points
				1	2	3	4	5	6	7	8	9	
113	Lathe opera-tor, crankshaft	1.68	1.68	B	B	C	D	B $25 Intermediate	B	B	B	C	
	Points used for Step No. 1			8	17	33	31	15	10	4	8	11	137
			2	16	10	29	42	8	15	16	16	29	181
			4	13	9	24	38	7	12	13	13	24	153
			5	11	20	39	34	16	12	4	11	13	160
			6	8	17	33	31	15	10	2	6	18	140
120	Paint sprayer, production	1.58	1.58	A	B	C	B	B $25 Minor	B	B	C	B	
	Points used for Step No. 1			2	17	33	11	15	7	4	15	6	110
			2	3	10	29	16	8	10	16	29	16	137
			4	3	9	24	13	7	9	13	24	13	115
			5	2	20	39	12	16	8	4	19	7	127
			6	2	17	33	11	15	7	2	11	10	108
121	Cut off and threading machine	1.63	1.63	B	B	C	C	B $25 Intermediate	B	B	B	B	
	Points used for Step No. 1			8	17	33	20	15	10	4	8	6	121
			2	16	10	29	29	8	15	16	16	16	155
			4	13	9	24	24	7	12	13	13	13	128
			5	11	20	39	23	16	12	4	11	7	143
			6	8	17	33	20	15	10	2	6	10	121
139	Hanger, door	1.53	1.53	A	A	C	C	B $25 Minor	B	B	C	B	
	Points used for Step No. 1			2	6	33	20	15	7	4	15	6	108
			2	3	3	29	29	8	10	16	29	16	143
			4	3	3	24	24	7	9	13	24	13	120
			5	2	6	39	23	16	8	4	19	7	124
			6	2	6	33	20	15	7	2	11	10	106
142	Metal finisher	1.67	1.67	B	C	C	C	C $25 Minor	B	B	C	B	
	Points used for Step No. 1			8	28	33	20	21	7	4	15	6	142
			2	16	18	29	29	20	10	16	29	16	173
			4	13	14	24	24	10	9	13	24	13	144
			5	11	35	39	23	41	8	4	19	7	187
			6	8	28	33	20	21	7	2	11	10	140
170	Core maker, jobbing A	1.88	1.88	E	D	D	C	D $100 Minor	B	B	D	B	
	Points used for Step No. 1			35	39	51	20	33	7	4	24	6	219
			2	56	25	42	29	29	10	16	42	16	265
			4	56	20	38	24	16	9	13	38	13	227
			5	35	50	57	23	60	8	4	27	7	271
			6	35	39	51	20	33	7	2	17	10	214

Summary of Evaluation for 25 Jobs and Points Used in Statistical Analyses—Continued

Code No.	Classi- fication	Rate or Rate Range	Avg. Rate	Evaluation Factors, Degrees and Points									Total Points
				1	2	3	4	5	6	7	8	9	
180	Metal pourer, bull ladle	1.68	1.68	B	B	C	C	B	B	E	D	D	
								$25 Minor					
	Points used for Step No. 1			8	17	33	20	15	7	15	24	17	156
			2	16	10	29	29	8	10	56	42	42	242
			4	13	9	24	24	7	9	56	38	38	218
			5	11	20	39	23	16	8	15	27	19	178
			6	8	17	33	20	15	7	10	17	27	154
196	Body decker	1.62	1.62	B	B	C	C	C	B	C	B	B	
								$100 Minor					
	Points used for Step No. 1			8	17	33	20	29	7	7	8	6	135
			2	16	10	29	29	24	10	29	16	16	179
			4	13	9	24	24	14	9	24	13	13	143
			5	11	20	39	23	49	8	8	11	7	176
			6	8	17	33	20	29	7	4	6	10	134
200	Body bolter	1.58	1.58	A	A	C	D	A	B	B	B	B	
								Minor					
	Points used for Step No. 1			2	6	33	31	6	7	4	8	6	103
			2	3	3	29	42	3	10	16	16	16	138
			4	3	3	24	38	3	9	13	13	13	119
			5	2	6	39	34	6	8	4	11	7	117
			6	2	6	33	31	6	7	2	6	10	103
204	Welder, spot and gun	1.58	1.58	A	A	C	C	B	B	B	C	B	
								$25 Minor					
	Points used for Step No. 1			2	6	33	20	15	7	4	15	6	108
			2	3	3	29	29	8	10	16	29	16	143
			4	3	3	24	24	7	9	13	24	13	120
			5	2	6	39	23	16	8	4	19	7	124
			6	2	6	33	20	15	7	2	11	10	106
218	Die maker	1.82– 2.02	1.94	E	G	D	B	D	C	B	B	B	
								$500 Intermediate					
	Points used for Step No. 1			35	82	51	11	43	14	4	8	6	254
			2	56	48	42	16	33	27	16	16	16	270
			4	56	43	38	13	21	17	13	13	13	227
			5	35	95	57	12	68	22	4	11	7	311
			6	35	82	51	11	43	14	2	6	10	254
220	Keller operator	1.87– 2.07	2.06	E	G	D	C	D	C	B	B	B	
								$500 Intermediate					
	Points used for Step No. 1			35	82	51	20	43	14	4	8	6	263
			2	56	48	42	29	33	27	16	16	16	283
			4	56	43	38	24	21	17	13	13	13	238
			5	35	95	57	23	68	22	4	11	7	322
			6	35	82	51	20	43	14	2	6	10	263

Summary of Evaluation for 25 Jobs and Points Used in
Statistical Analyses—Continued

Code No.	Classi- fication	Rate or Rate Range	Avg. Rate	Evaluation Factors, Degrees and Points									Total Points
				1	2	3	4	5	6	7	8	9	
246	Cleaners, general plant	1.28– 1.38	1.38	A	A	A	B	A	A	B	B	A	
	Points used for Step No. 1			2	6	4	11	6	2	4	8	1	44
			2	3	3	3	16	3	3	16	16	3	66
			4	3	3	3	13	3	2	13	13	3	56
			5	2	6	4	12	6	2	4	11	1	48
			6	2	6	4	11	6	2	2	6	2	41

Evaluation of 25-Job Sample

A Tabulation of the Number of Jobs on Each Degree of Each Factor

Factors	Degrees								
	A	B	C	D	E	F	G	H	Totals
1. Educational Background	9	8	3	1	4				25
2. Job Training	7	7	3	5			3		25
3. Mental and Visual Effort	1		20	3	1				25
4. Physical Effort		10	12	2	1				25
5. Responsibility for Material or Product	2	11	8	3	1				25
6. Responsibility for Tools and Equipment	4	18	2		1				25
7. Responsibility for Safety of Others	1	19	4		1				25
8. Work Surroundings		15	8	2					25
9. Unavoidable Hazards	2	18	2	3					25

Summary of Results Obtained in Step 1. Since it is important that the jobs selected for purposes of developing weights on factors and degrees of factors be representative of all of the various types of work performed, a check should be made of the tabulation indicating the number of jobs on each degree of each factor. This tabulation provides information concerning those degrees not used. It appears obvious that if a plan is to be developed to cover jobs in a particular organization, each degree in the plan should be utilized. A review of the statistical measures* computed along with the plotting of jobs indicates that the least-squares trend line and the second-degree curve are practically identical. The correlation coefficient was .9912, indicating a very strong relationship between total points and current rates. The standard error of esti-

---

* A condensed computing form designed for rapid calculation of statistical measures such as those mentioned in this step is presented in Appendix B.

mate was $.0260, indicating very little dispersion in the data. It may be concluded that for this sample the weights assigned to factors and degrees of factors produced a linear wage structure and a strong correlation between total points and wage rates.

Plotting of 25 Jobs Using Hourly Plan in Chapter 3
with Existing Geometric Progression

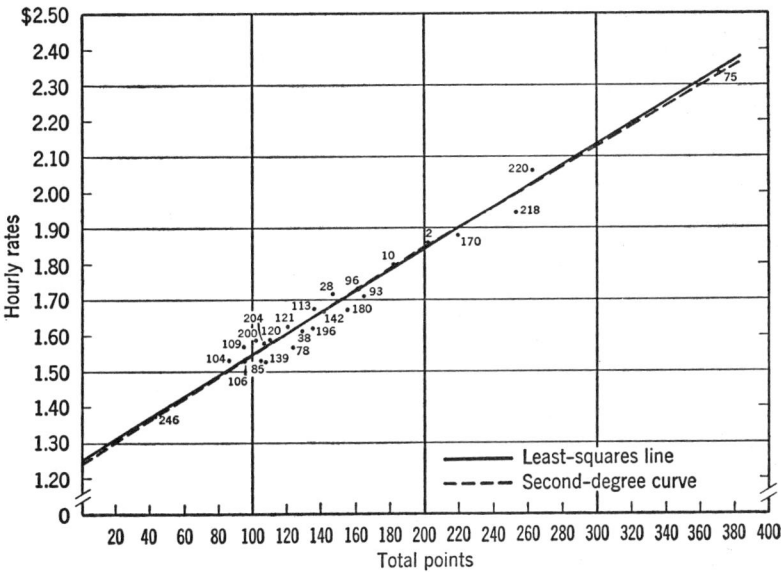

Figure 7

This step indicates that the 25-job sample which was selected produced a straight-line wage structure with the jobs grouped closely around the trend line, provided the point weights were used as indicated for the Hourly Plan in Chapter 3. The next several steps proceed to utilize variations in point weights in order to determine the influence on the wage structure.

Step 2. Plotting of 25 Jobs with Equal Weights on All Factors and Arithmetic Progression on Degrees of the Factors

Description of Step 2. In order to determine the effects of equal weight on all factors and the arithmetic progression on the degrees of the factors, the 25 jobs were evaluated on a plan having these characteristics. Using this system, the evaluators assigned 56 points to each factor, and the total points available amounted to 504. Five percent of the total weight was given to the lowest degree on each factor, and arithmetic progression was established between the degrees of the factors. Various statistical measures were computed as follows:

1. Least-squares trend line.
2. Correlation coefficient.
3. Standard error of estimate.
4. Second-degree curve.

The data included in this step are presented on the following pages:

1. Table presenting the points assigned each degree of each factor.
2. Plotting of 25 jobs having equal weight on the factors and arithmetic progression on the degrees of the factors, Figure 8.
3. Summary of results obtained in Step 2.

Equal Weights on Each Factor
with Arithmetic Progression

(Constant Base Value of 5% of Maximum Points on Each Factor)

Factors	Degrees of Factors and Points							
	A	B	C	D	E	F	G	H
1. Educational Background	3	16	29	42	56			
2. Job Training	3	10	18	25	33	40	48	56
3. Mental and Visual Effort	3	16	29	42	56			
4. Physical Effort	3	16	29	42	56			
5. Responsibility for Material or Product	3	$25– 8	$25–20	$100–29	$100–40			
		100–12	100–24	500–33	500–44			
		500–16	500–28	1000–37	1000–48			
		0–500–20	0–500–32	1500–41	1500–52			
				0–1500–45	0–1500–56			
6. Responsibility for Tools and Equipment	3	M–10	M–22	M–34	M–46			
		I–15	I–27	I–39	I–51			
		M–20	M–32	M–44	M–56			
7. Responsibility for Safety of Others	3	16	29	42	56			
8. Work Surroundings	3	16	29	42	56			
9. Unavoidable Hazards	3	16	29	42	56			

Summary of Results Obtained in Step 2. An analysis of the relationship existing between the least-squares trend line and the second-degree curve appearing on the plotting indicates that the data would probably be best described by a curve. It appears evident that if a straight line were used as a basis for establishing pay grades, considerable distortion would result in present rates. The correlation coefficient is lower (.9293 compared to .9912) and the standard error

Plotting of 25 Jobs Using Plan Having Equal Weights (56 Points on Highest
Degree) on All Factors and Arithmetic Progression on Degrees of Factors

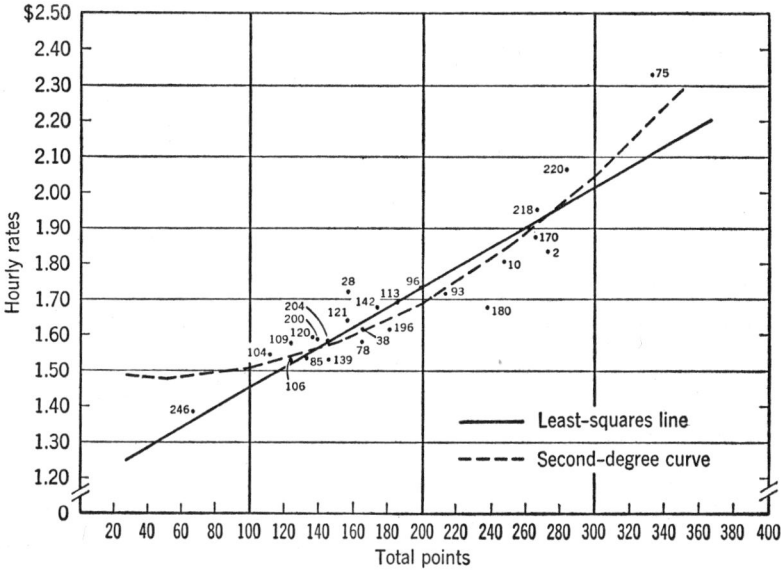

Figure 8

of estimate is higher ($.0725 compared to $.0260) than comparable
figures secured in the study conducted under Step 1.

It is noted, however, that a fairly strong relationship exists between
total points and present rates despite the fact that equal weight was
applied to each factor. The relationship which exists between points
and dollars, in spite of the application of equal weight on each factor,
is apparently one reason why point evaluation plans have succeeded
reasonably well, even though the weighting applied to factors varies
substantially from one plan to another.

It is apparent from these studies that the type of progression
applied to degrees of factors has a very definite effect upon the final
wage structure. The use of arithmetic progression tends to create a
curve in the wage structure. When data which are basically curvilinear are described by means of a straight line, sound statistical
principles are violated and the results secured cannot be logically
substantiated. Since one of the objectives of installing a job evaluation plan is to create a minimum disturbance traceable to point
weights, it is important that further statistical studies be conducted
in order to eliminate the arbitrary effect which the assignment of
points will have upon the wage structure finally developed.

Step 3. Experimentation with Arithmetic and Geometric Progression on Degrees of Factors

Description of Step 3. In Step 2 it was indicated that the type of progression assigned to the degrees of each factor appeared to have a definite effect upon the type of wage structure finally developed. The forcing of a straight line through data which lend themselves to description by a curve violates sound statistical principles. In order to investigate the relationships between total points and dollars, different types of progression were used. The following progressions were adopted and investigated:

1. Arithmetic progression.
2. Geometric progression which produces a straight line when plotted on semi-logarithmic paper.
3. The variation of geometric progression which produces a straight-line relationship between the degrees of the factor and present rates (based upon large sample).
4. The variation of geometric progression which produces a straight-line relationship between the degrees of the factor and present rates (based upon 25-job sample).

The factor Job Training, which has a strong correlation with rate, was selected for experimental purposes. The 25 jobs were plotted on three separate charts, with points on the factor on the horizontal scale and current rates on the vertical scale. The points varied with the type of progression used. Least-squares trend lines and second-degree curves were computed in order to indicate whether a linear relationship existed when the various types of progression were used. A token weight was established on the first degree in each instance. Although such a value would not necessarily have to be granted on the first degree of a factor, the adoption of a small weight appears to be psychologically sound.

If an evaluation plan is being developed to cover a large number of jobs, it is essential that the relationship between each factor having a correlation with rate and total rate be analyzed. The type of analysis made should be similar to that made on the factor selected for this study. Analyses of this nature should only be made on the basis of a large number of jobs distributed on all degrees of the factors under consideration. After the results of the progression studies had been considered, the 25 jobs were then evaluated on a plan having equal weight on all factors with geometric progression on the degrees of the factors. The results of this study are presented in Step 4.

The data covered in this step are presented as follows:

1. Table presenting arithmetic progression and variations of geometric progression applying to the factor Job Training.

2. Arithmetic progression on the factor Job Training. Graphic presentation, Figure 9.

3. Geometric progression (straight line on semi-log paper) on the factor Job Training. Graphic presentation, Figure 10.

4. Variation of geometric progression resulting in a linear relationship between the degrees of the factor Job Training and present rates (based upon large job sample). Graphic presentation, Figure 11.

5. Variation of geometric progression which produces a straight-line relationship between the degrees of the factor Job Training and present rates (based on the 25-job sample). Graphic presentation, Figure 12.

6. Summary of results obtained in Step 3.

Job Training Factor No. 2

Study of Arithmetic Progression and Geometric Progression
(5% Weight on Base)

	Degrees of Factors and Points							
	A	B	C	D	E	F	G	H
Arithmetic progression	6	21	36	51	65	80	95	110
Geometric progression, straight line on semi-log paper	6	8	13	20	30	47	72	110
Variation of geometric progression (Hourly Plan, Chapter 3)	6	17	28	39	50	64	82	110
Weights giving best linear relationship (25-job sample)	6	17	24	42	51	66	85	110

Summary of Results Obtained in Step 3. Observation of the results secured on the factor Job Training indicated that utilization of arithmetic progression on the degrees of the factors produced a curved relationship. As points increased, rates increased more rapidly, resulting in a curve which had a tendency to swing upward. An analysis of the results of using geometric progression (straight line on semi-log paper) on the factor indicated that as points increased present rates failed to increase as rapidly. The result was a curve which had a tendency to flatten out as point values increased. An analysis of the variation of geometric progression used in the Hourly Plan presented in Chapter 3 indicated that the progression was sufficient to compensate for practically all of the curve in the wage structure (for this sample) and produce a linear relationship between points and dollars.

In order to improve the straight-line relationship for the factor Job Training, minor alterations were made in the smooth progression. Computation of a least-squares trend line, correlation coefficient, standard error of estimate, and second-degree curve revealed that these alterations resulted in a minor increase in the correlation coefficient. The second-degree curve was practically identical with the least-squares trend line. The alterations made in the progression may be attributed primarily to the size and characteristics of the

Plotting of 25 Jobs Using Arithmetic Progression Factor Job Training

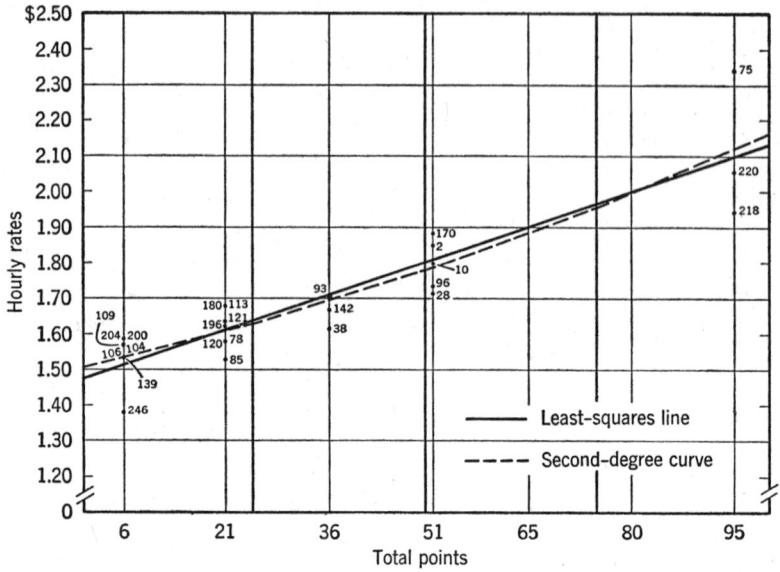

Figure 9

Plotting of 25 Jobs Using Geometric Progression Straight Line on Semi-log Paper Factor Job Training

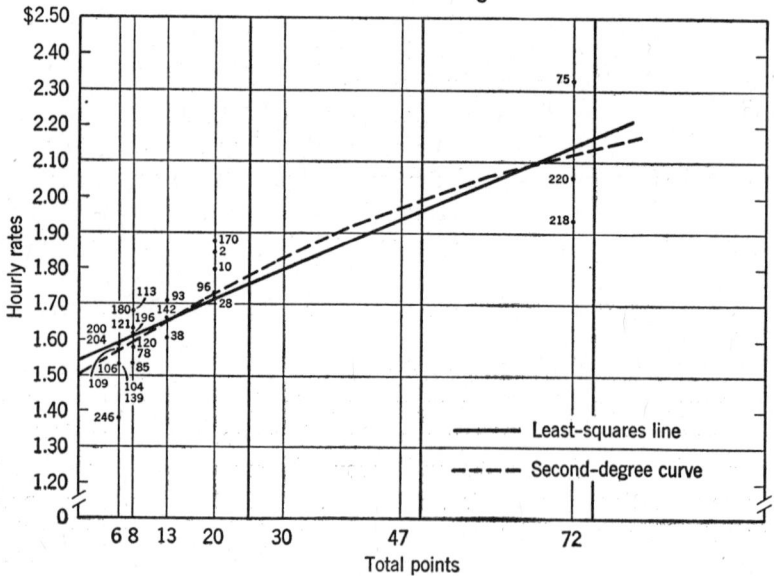

Figure 10

Plotting of 25 Jobs Using Hourly Plan in Chapter 3 with Existing Geometric
Progression
Factor Job Training

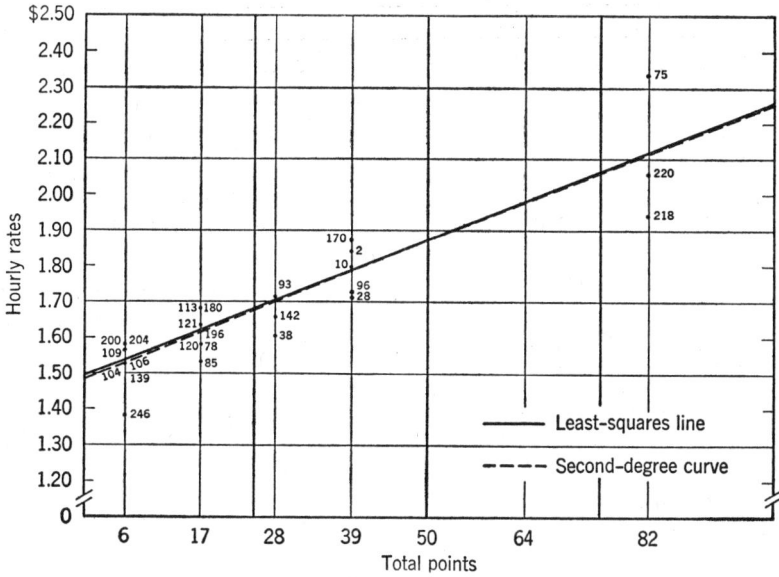

Figure 11

Plotting of 25 Jobs Using Weights Giving Best Linear Relationship
Factor Job Training

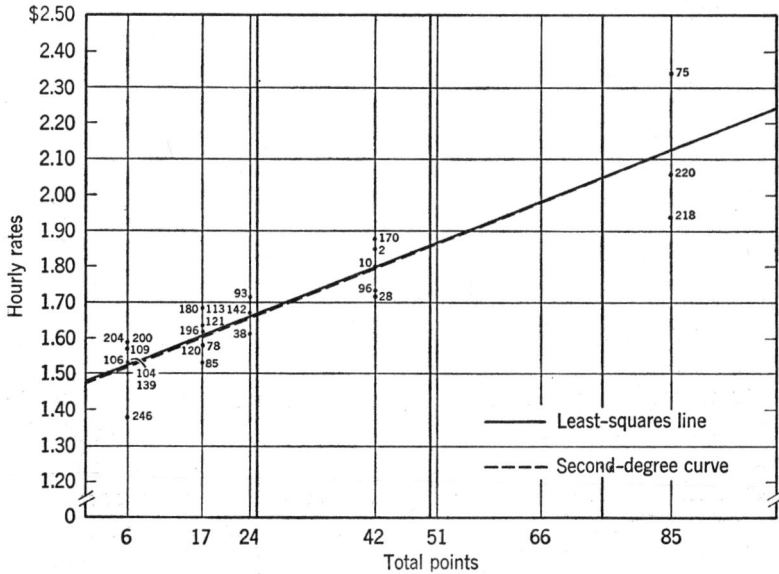

Figure 12

25-job sample. For larger samples, variations in the data which are attributable to individual jobs tend to disappear and a smoother progression can be adopted. It should be noted that as the relationship between points and dollars approaches a straight line, the correlation coefficient tends to increase and the standard error of estimate tends to decrease. Correlation coefficients and standard errors of estimate for the progressions indicated above are as follows:

	Correlation Coefficient	Standard Error of Estimate
Arithmetic progression	.9122	$.0804
Geometric progression straight line on semi-log paper	.8768	.0943
Variation of geometric progression. Hourly Plan Chapter 3	.9149	.0792
Weights giving best linear relationship	.9173	.0781

Although this study has undertaken the analysis of only one factor, a further analysis may be made of all factors having a correlation with rates. The curvilinear relationship will be particularly noticeable where the factor has a high correlation with rates. It is necessary to analyze the type of curve which actually exists within the particular wage structure. Since the objective is to define the final wage structure by means of a straight line, it is necessary to determine the exact nature of the curve existing within the structure and compensate for the curve by adopting a progression which will yield a straight-line relationship on those factors having a strong correlation with rate. Probably one of the best methods for investigating the relationship between a particular factor and total rate is to plot the data, then proceed to compute a least-squares trend line, standard error of estimate, correlation coefficient, and second-degree curve. Through alteration of the progression, a straight-line relationship may be obtained. The progression which is finally adopted should be smoothed in order that the weights will increase by an increasing amount. The primary objective in developing weights for the degrees of a factor is to establish a progression which will result in a linear relationship between the factor and the total rates being predicted.

As the analysis proceeds to those factors which have an exceedingly low correlation with rate, there will be considerable dispersion in the plottings, and it will be apparent that no basic curve exists within the data such as there was for those factors having a strong correlation with rate. These plottings result since factors such as Physical Effort or Work Surroundings do not have the ability to predict variations in rates throughout the entire wage structure. In other words, the fact that a job evaluates high on a factor such as Work Surroundings does not necessarily mean that the job will be paid a high rate in relation to other jobs. Thus, these factors account for little of the variance in rates throughout the wage structure. They do, however, account for variances between jobs which are similar. For example, if all factors for two jobs evaluate the same, except Physical Effort, the classification requiring the greater physical effort should be compensated accordingly (see pages 29 and 30). It is believed that from a logical standpoint weight should be assigned to those factors which have little or no correlation with rates on the same geometric basis that weight assignments are made to those factors having a strong correlation with rates. A further discussion of weight assignment to degrees of factors is presented under Step 4.

Adoption of geometric progression may be explained from a logical standpoint, since the degrees of the factors are so stated that as a job evaluates higher on a factor the conditions or requirements are progressively greater. It appears logical therefore that points should be allocated to the higher degrees in progressively increasing amounts.

Step 4.   Utilization of Multiple Correlation To Assist in the Reweighting of Factors

Description of Step 4. After degrees of the factors have been weighted to secure a linear relationship between total points and present rates, the next problem involves weighting of the factors to produce a more reliable prediction of rates. The statistical technique of multiple correlation is of assistance in assigning these weights. Utilization of this technique is based upon the assumption that job analysis and evaluation involve the selection of a group of factors which influence rates and which, in most instances, have a tendency to predict rates. Average rates for the 25 jobs were used as the basis for statistical calculations.

By using multiple correlation, it is possible to develop a system of weights where the variation in the evaluation on the combined factors will adequately predict the variation which now exists in wage rates. Thus, it is usually true that those factors which have a high correlation with rates will usually have more weight in the plan than those factors having a low correlation with rates. The process of multiple correlation indicates those factors which should be weighted more heavily in order to obtain a more reliable prediction of rates. The technique involves correlating each factor with rates and each factor with every other factor in a manner which will indicate where more weight should be applied, or where weight should be subtracted, to increase the predictive value of the factors used.

It may be desirable to weight all factors equally at the time the first multiple correlation is computed. It would be possible, however, to apply weight which is similar to the weight applied in other plans. The results secured will be in the form of a regression equation indicating the amount each factor contributes to the prediction of rates.

The application of multiple correlation in the development of a point evaluation plan assumes that the relationship between each factor and total rates is linear. In this step, the factor progression for the Hourly Plan in Chapter 3, which was developed on the basis of a large sample to produce a straight-line wage structure, was adopted and equal weight was applied to each factor. The following statistical measures were computed:

1. Least-squares trend line.
2. Second-degree curve.
3. Correlation coefficient.
4. Standard error of estimate.
5. Multiple correlation.

The data covered in this step are presented in the following order:

1. Table presenting the points assigned each degree of each factor.
2. Presentation of graphic information, Figure 13.
3. Summary of results in Step 4.

Present Progression with a Maximum of 56 Points on Each Factor

Factors	Degrees of Factors and Points							
	A	B	C	D	E	F	G	H
1. Educational Background	3	13	24	38	56			
2. Job Training	3	9	14	20	25	32	43	56
3. Mental and Visual Effort	3	13	24	38	56			
4. Physical Effort	3	13	24	38	56			
5. Responsibility for Material or Product	3	$25– 7	$25–10	$100–16	$100–21			
		100–10	100–14	500–21	500–28			
		500–13	500–18	1000–27	1000–37			
		0–500–17	0–500–24	1500–34	1500–46			
				0–1500–41	0–1500–56			
6. Responsibility for Tools and Equipment	2	M –9	M–14	M–21	M–34			
		I–12	I–17	I–26	I–40			
		M–17	M–24	M–37	M–56			
7. Responsibility for Safety of Others	3	13	24	38	56			
8. Work Surroundings	3	13	24	38	56			
9. Unavoidable Hazards	3	13	24	38	56			

Plotting of 25 Jobs Using Plan Having Equal Weights
(56 Points on Highest Degree) on All Factors and
Geometric Progression on Degrees of Factors

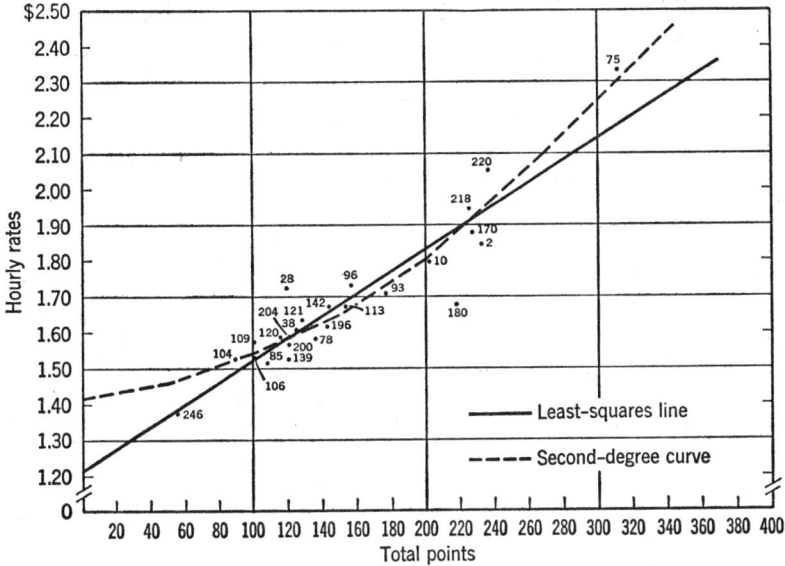

Figure 13

Summary of Results Obtained in Step 4.   A review of the plotting resulting from the weights applied to factors and degrees of factors indicated that the relationship between total points and present rates was more linear than the plotting presented in Step 2 (equal weights on factors with arithmetic progression). The correlation was higher (.9333 and .9293), and the standard error of estimate was lower ($.0705 and $.0725). This is true since the correlation coefficient and standard error of estimate are statistical measures which assume linearity of the data. Although the plotting revealed a more linear relationship as compared with the plotting presented in Step 2, the data appeared to be more accurately described by means of a curve rather than a straight line. This result is attributed to the particular characteristics of the small sample. As will be shown in the steps which follow, reweighting of the factors with the aid of multiple correlation results in the development of a straight-line structure for this sample.

Based upon the assignment of equal weight of 56 points on each factor and a linear progression on each factor, the following contributions for the factors were secured as a result of computing a multiple correlation: *

Factors	Contributions
Educational Background	.00210
Job Training	.00436
Mental and Visual Effort	.00344
Physical Effort	.00174
Responsibility for Material or Product	.00727
Responsibility for Tools and Equipment	.00182
Responsibility for Safety of Others	− .00064
Work Surroundings	.00090
Unavoidable Hazards	.00273

The multiple correlation coefficient was computed and found to be .9914.

A review of the contributions of each factor indicates that the following factors should receive more weight:

1. Job Training.
2. Mental and Visual Effort.
3. Responsibility for Material or Product.

On the factor Unavoidable Hazards weight should remain approximately the same.

Weights should be reduced on the following factors:

1. Educational Background.
2. Physical Effort.
3. Responsibility for Tools and Equipment.
4. Responsibility for Safety of Others.
5. Work Surroundings.

At the time these results are reviewed, the factor correlations with rate and the correlations between factors should also be considered. It is noted that in many instances where a factor has a strong correlation with rate it also has strong correlations with other factors which correlate well with rate. Thus, the independent predictive force of these factors is somewhat reduced. Despite the fact that Educational Background has a strong correlation with rate, the multiple regression equation indicated that less weight should be applied to this factor. It will be noted that a strong correlation exists between Educational Background and Job Training. Job Training appears to be a better independent predictor of rate, with the result that the regression equation indicates that more weight should be applied to this factor.

* A condensed computing form designed for calculation of a multiple correlation appears in Appendix B.

An analysis of factor correlations with rate will usually reveal that a factor such as Job Training has one of the highest correlations with rate. The correlation of this factor with rate will usually be dependent upon the number of degrees established on the factor. It will frequently approach or even exceed .90. As the number of degrees on such a factor is increased, the correlation is also increased. It should be recognized, however, that benefits derived from an increase in correlation may not be compensated for by the increased difficulty in evaluating accurately on the factor. If evaluation on the factors begins to become inconsistent, it may be necessary to reduce the number of degrees in order that judgments will become more accurate and consistent. Any loss in correlation on an individual factor as a result of this process will usually have only a slight influence on the overall correlation. The overall correlation may be increased through reweighting of factors using the regression equation as a basis.

It will be found, during the course of these studies, that certain factors, such as Physical Effort, Work Surroundings, Responsibility for Safety of Others, and Unavoidable Hazards, usually have a very low correlation with rate, and if it were merely a problem of establishing proper job-to-job relationships throughout the wage structure, these factors could probably be dropped. However, it is generally agreed that some of these factors do contribute to rate determination and should, therefore, be retained.

It will usually be found, at the time the multiple correlation is computed, that results will consistently indicate application of greater weight to a factor such as Job Training. Although consistent application of increased weight to this factor will usually result in a slight improvement in correlation within the overall data, it will, at the same time, involve sizable steps or differences in point values between degrees of the factors. Such steps will mean that if a job is positioned on the next degree higher than it presently is, there will probably be a change in more than one pay grade. Rather than continue to apply weight to this factor, it will probably be desirable to select another factor having a good correlation with rates and apply weight to that factor. It will be observed that the intercorrelation between these two factors is usually strong, indicating that weight can be shifted from one to the other without any appreciable effect on the end result. It should always be borne in mind that the objective is to obtain a high correlation with rates through the combined factors used in the plan, not just through application of increased weight to a single factor.

In view of the fact that the multiple regression equation computed for 25 jobs indicated that weights should be shifted to make them somewhat similar to the weights in the Hourly Plan in Chapter 3, it was decided that the next multiple correlation should utilize these weights. It is expected that use of these revised weights will increase the correlation coefficient and reduce the standard error of estimate. Computation of additional multiple correlations for the 25-job sample should result in further improvements in the factor weights being used.

Step 5.   Analysis of Results of Step 4 and Computation of a Second Multiple Correlation

Description of Step 5.   In order to secure weights for factors which would more adequately predict wage rates, the results of Step 4 were analyzed with the reweighting of factors in mind. It was decided that weights currently being used in the Hourly Plan in Chapter 3 should be adopted. The least-squares trend line, standard error of estimate, and correlation coefficient for these weights were computed under Step 1. Since a straight-line relationship adequately described this structure, it was evident that the curved relationship which developed in Step 4 was attributable to the characteristics of jobs within the small sample. In order further to verify this conclusion, it was decided to adopt a system of weights having the same maximum values as those currently being used in the Hourly Plan in Chapter 3 and to assign arithmetic progression to the degrees of the factors. By using these weights, the following statistical measures were computed:

1. Least-squares trend line.
2. Second-degree curve.
3. Correlation coefficient.
4. Standard error of estimate.

After completing these calculations, weights presently being used in the Hourly Plan in Chapter 3 were used to compute a second multiple correlation.

The data prepared in this step are presented in the following order:

1. Table presenting points assigned the degrees of each factor (arithmetic progression on degrees of factors and weights on factors the same as those being used in the Hourly Plan, Chapter 3).
2. Presentation of graphic information, Figure 14.
3. Summary of results obtained in Step 5.

Present Maximum Weights in Hourly Plan, Chapter 3,
with Arithmetic Progression on Degrees

Factors	Degrees of Factors and Points							
	A	B	C	D	E	F	G	H
1. Educational Back-ground	2	11	19	27	35			
2. Job Training	6	20	35	50	65	80	95	110
3. Mental and Visual Effort	4	21	39	57	75			
4. Physical Effort	2	12	23	34	45			
5. Responsibility for Material or Product	6	$25–16 100–25 500–33 0–500–41	$25–41 100–49 500–57 0–500–66	$100–60 500–68 1000–76 1500–84 0–1500–92	$100–82 500–90 1000–99 1500–107 0–1500–115			
6. Responsibility for Tools and Equipment	2	M– 8 I–12 M–16	M–18 I–22 M–26	M–27 I–31 M–35	M–37 I–41 M–45			
7. Responsibility for Safety of Others	1	4	8	11	15			
8. Work Surroundings	2	11	19	27	35			
Unavoidable Hazards	1	7	13	19	25			

Plotting of 25 Jobs Using Hourly Plan in Chapter 3
Present Maximum Weights and Arithmetic Progression on Degrees of Factors

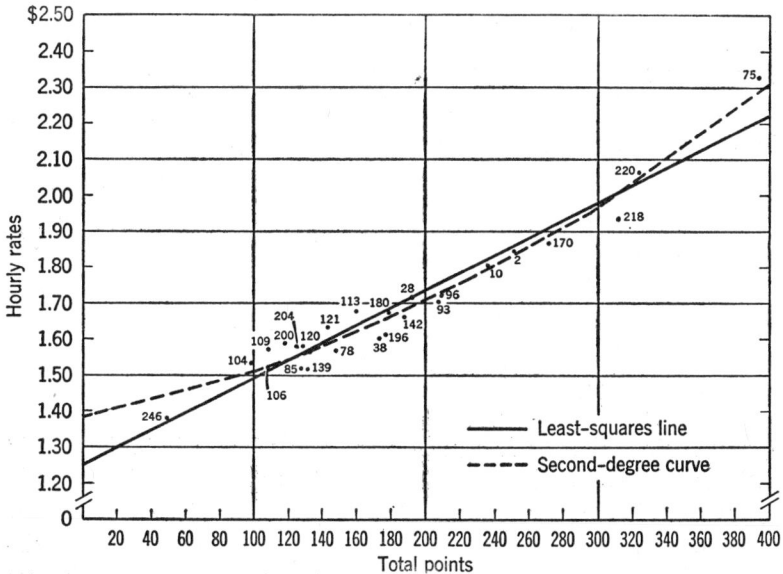

Figure 14

Summary of Results Obtained in Step 5. As a result of using the same weights on the factors as those used in the Hourly Plan in Chapter 3 and arithmetic progression on the degrees of the factors, the wage structure, as indicated by the plotting, is best described by a curve. The curve is attributed to the assignment of arithmetic progression to the degrees of the factors.

As a result of the multiple correlation study, using the factor and degree weights as indicated in the Hourly Plan in Chapter 3, the following contributions were secured:

Factor	Contribution
Educational Background	.00346
Job Training	.00289
Mental and Visual Effort	.00364
Physical Effort	.00198
Responsibility for Material or Product	.00240
Responsibility for Tools and Equipment	.00274
Responsibility for Safety of Others	− .00044
Work Surroundings	.00078
Unavoidable Hazards	.00502

A review of these contributions indicated that the range of values was narrower than the contributions secured at the time of the first multiple correlation. The regression weights indicated that the factors Responsibility for Safety of Others and Work Surroundings should be reduced in weight and that the factor Unavoidable Hazards should be increased. Weight assignments which then existed on these factors were as follows:

Factor	Total Points
Responsibility for Safety of Others	15
Work Surroundings	35
Unavoidable Hazards	25

In view of the results of the multiple correlation, it was decided to reweight the factors as follows:

Factor	Total Points
Responsibility for Safety of Others	10
Work Surroundings	25
Unavoidable Hazards	40

It was decided that no further changes would be made in the weight assignments in order that the effect of these changes could be carefully analyzed.

It is interesting to note that the results of the first multiple correlation indicated that the weight on the factor Unavoidable Hazards should remain approximately the same. As a result of adopting the weight on the Hourly Plan in Chapter 3, points on this factor were reduced from 56 to 25. The second multiple correlation using the same factor weights as those on the Hourly Plan in Chapter 3 indicated that more weight should be applied to this factor. A study of the intercorrelations between factors and between factors and rates indicated that Unavoidable Hazards had a correlation of .21 with rates. Although such a correlation is exceedingly low, it appears that the factor is a fairly independent predictor for this job sample.

In view of the decrease in range of the contributions, the high correlation coefficient, and the low standard error of estimate, further improvement in the predictive value of the factors could be secured by only minor changes in factor weights. It appears obvious that as far as this sample is concerned, the factor Responsibility for Safety of Others could be disregarded.

Step 6.   Analysis of Results of Step 5 and Computation of a Third Multiple Correlation

Description of Step 6. In order to secure a system of weights which would produce a more reliable prediction of rates, the results of Step 5 were analyzed. This analysis indicated that it would be desirable to increase the weight on Unavoidable Hazards and decrease the weight on Responsibility for Safety of Others and Work Surroundings. By using the adjustments indicated in Step 5, a third multiple correlation was computed. A least-squares trend line, standard error of estimate, and correlation coefficient were computed. The data covered in this step are presented in the following order:

1. Table presenting the points assigned each degree of each factor where changes were made.
2. Presentation of graphic information, Figure 15.
3. Summary of results obtained in Step 6.

25-Job Sample

Factor and Degree Weights the Same as Hourly Plan in Chapter 3 except as Follows

Factor	Degrees and Point Weights				
	A	B	C	D	E
Safety of Others	1	2	4	7	10
Work Surroundings	1	6	11	17	25
Unavoidable Hazards	2	10	18	27	40

Plotting of 25 Jobs Using Hourly Plan in Chapter 3,
Except for Weight on Responsibility for Safety of Others,
Work Surroundings, and Unavoidable Hazards

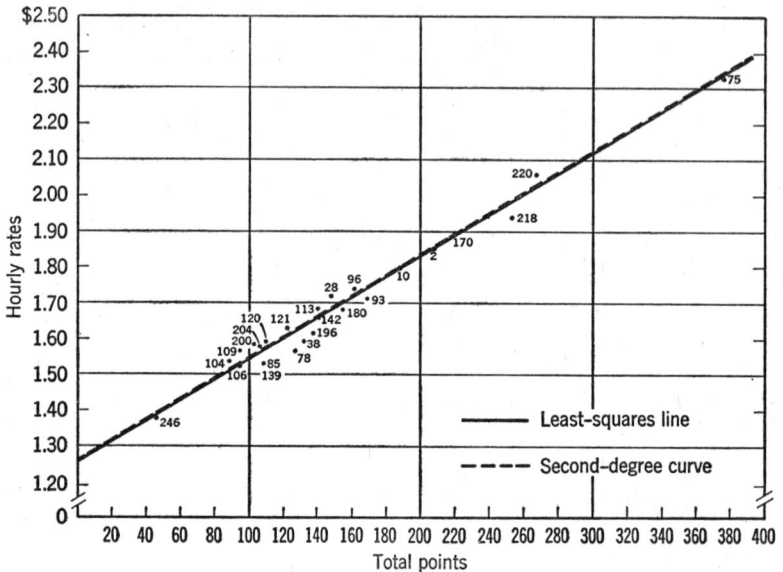

Figure 15

Summary of Results Obtained in Step 6. As a result of the multiple correlation study, the following weights were secured:

Factor	Contribution
Educational Background	.00355
Job Training	.00288
Mental and Visual Effort	.00368
Physical Effort	.00201
Responsibility for Material or Product	.00238
Responsibility for Tools and Equipment	.00265
Responsibility for Safety of Others	.00089
Work Surroundings	.00088
Unavoidable Hazards	.00293

A review of these contributions indicated that the range of values is narrower than the contributions secured at the time of the second multiple correlation. An analysis of the correlation coefficient and standard error of estimate indicated that there were only slight changes in these statistical measures. Although the multiple correlation indicated that a few minor changes could still be made in factor weights, it appeared doubtful whether these changes would improve appreciably the predictive value of the factors.

The table which follows indicates, in average cents per hour, the estimated variance from the least-squares trend lines resulting from the three multiple correlations.

Job Code No.	First Multiple Correlation (Step 4) Above	Below	Second Multiple Correlation (Step 5) Above	Below	Third Multiple Correlation (Step 6) Above	Below
2		$.085	$.005			
10		.040	.010		$.005	
28	$.145		.030		.035	
38	.005			$.025		$.025
75	.150			.025		.005
78		.055		.035		.035
85		.015		.025		.035
93		.050		.030		.030
96	.035				.010	
104	.070		.020		.020	
106	.005					
109	.045		.040		.035	
113		.010	.025		.015	
120	.010		.005		.005	
121	.020		.020		.020	
139		.055		.040		.035
142	.010				.005	
170		.040		.010	.005	
180		.210		.030		.020
196		.035		.030		.025
200			.020		.020	
204			.010		.015	
218	.025			.050		.045
220	.105		.040		.035	
246		.005				
	$.625	$.600	$.225	$.300	$.225	$.255

Average Dispersion in Cents

First multiple correlation $1.225 ÷ 25 = $.049
Second multiple correlation   .525 ÷ 25 =   .021
Third multiple correlation   .480 ÷ 25 =   .019

It will be noted that average dispersion decreased from $.049 to $.019. It is apparent from reviewing these figures that distortions in the wage structure can be substantially reduced as a result of reweighting factors. Trend lines throughout the steps in this study have considered each job as having equivalent weight. For greatest accuracy, particularly where trend lines are being established for cost purposes, a trend line weighted by the number of persons on each job should be calculated.

It may be observed that the correlation coefficient and standard error of estimate for the data have varied substantially from the analysis made under Step 4 when equal weights were applied to the factors. The correlation coefficients and standard errors of estimate for the three studies are as follows:

	Correlation Coefficient	Standard Error of Estimate
Study 1 (Step 4)	.9333	$.0705
Study 2 (Step 5 and Step 1)	.9912	.0260
Study 3 (Step 6)	.9917	.0252

As a result of computing the last multiple correlation, the correlation coefficient was increased to only a minor extent and the standard error of estimate was only slightly reduced. The results of the technique should be analyzed carefully to determine whether the weights allocated to the factors appear to be logical. In view of the small sample presented in this report, some of the weights which result do not appear logical. For example, the weight applied to Unavoidable Hazards appears to be too high in relation to the weight applied to the factor Work Surroundings. Use of a larger sample usually alters this weighting.

The utilization of various statistical techniques including multiple correlation has reduced the purely arbitrary effect that weighting of the factors has upon the wage structure. At the same time, these methods present logical substantiation for factor weights which are finally developed. A careful study of the results of using these statistical techniques reveals that the cost of installing the program is substantially reduced, since job classifications are grouped more closely around the trend line.

Upon completion of the multiple correlation studies, the jobs should be plotted on a chart having total evaluation points on the horizontal scale and present hourly rates on the vertical scale. Plotting the jobs on transparent overlays will save considerable time. The basic chart, having total points on the horizontal scale and wage rates on the vertical scale, may be drawn on cross section paper. Transparent paper may be laid over this scale and the jobs plotted as dots (or lines where a rate range is involved) properly identified by code numbers. Separate transparent sheets may be used to plot jobs from each operation or plant.

The chart prepared upon completion of the multiple correlation studies should be carefully reviewed to determine the possible effects which the evaluation plan may have upon the wage structure. Tentative pay grades should be established, and the effect which the plan will have upon rates for individual jobs should be studied. Where it is indicated that the plan will result in rate changes, these changes should be carefully reviewed in order to determine whether they appear logical. It may be found at this stage that certain jobs have been selected for the sample which appear to be unusual and are going either up or down in rate by a substantial amount as compared with other jobs in the sample. These jobs should be checked, possibly by re-analyzing them, in order to determine whether all facts have been obtained. Statistical studies based on large samples have indicated that a high percentage of the jobs do not change in rate and that about the same number will be going up as go down in rate. If the job sample has been properly selected, the plan properly developed, and the multiple correlation studies used effectively, the variation from present rates will usually not exceed 15 or 20 cents, and only a relatively few jobs will vary by this amount. A variation of this amount should be checked to make certain that the job has been properly evaluated. It may also be found that the present rate is out of line as compared with other rates. This situation may be checked by contacting members of production supervision who are acquainted with the job in question as well as with similar jobs within the organization.

If jobs were selected from the various operations performed in the company, comparisons should be made between the jobs performed in these different operations. Changes in rates should be reviewed to determine whether they appear to be consistent. The effect the evaluation system will have upon jobs with heavy populations should be carefully reviewed. The number of rate changes and individuals experiencing these changes at the time of installation will probably have a pronounced effect upon acceptance of the plan by management as well as by employees.

At the same time that internal comparisons are made, a preliminary area survey should be conducted in order to make comparisons between the rates paid for similar jobs at outside companies. This preliminary survey should be based upon the jobs selected for the statistical sample. Comparisons should be made between companies operating in competing labor markets. If other manufacturers in the area are producing products which are competitive, comparisons should also be made with these manufacturers. An analysis should then be made of the data secured from the outside survey. In all cases least-squares trend lines should be computed based upon the rates in outside companies and weighted by the population distribution existing on jobs within the company conducting the survey or the population distributions in the outside companies. The tentative trend line and pay grades established should be compared with those for the companies surveyed. A more complete explanation of area survey techniques is presented in Chapter 7.

Analysis of Existing Plans

The study outlined in this chapter has been primarily concerned with the application of statistical techniques to the development of an hourly evaluation plan. The same techniques may also be used to check the results of either hourly or salary plans being utilized within a company in order to determine whether the existing plan requires improvement. A summary of the results of such a study in connection with a salary evaluation plan is as follows.

The salary structure resulting from evaluation on a plan having over fourteen factors arbitrarily weighted was compared with the structure resulting from evaluation on an eight-factor plan weighted with the aid of statistical techniques. A sample consisting of several hundred typical jobs was evaluated on each plan, and various mathematical measures were computed. In addition salary ranges were developed to determine the number of persons outside (either above or below) the ranges.

The plan having in excess of fourteen factors resulted in a salary structure which was not linear. Since a straight line was forced through the structure, and since this line formed the basis for the salary grades, the actual salaries of many of the employees covered by the plan were outside the established ranges. This condition was complicated further by the inability of the plan to produce a structure with minimum dispersion of salaries from the trend line.

	Existing Plan Having in Excess of 14 Factors	New 8-Factor Plan
Correlation coefficient	.96	.98
Standard error of estimate	$23.65	$17.11
Percent of persons outside the ranges	31.0%	13.9%
	(based upon ranges varying between 35 and 40%)*	(based upon ranges of 35%)*

* The percentage width of the range is established by using the midpoint as a base. A 40% range, for example, would be equivalent to 20% on each side of the midpoint.

The relatively high correlation of .96 for the existing plan indicates a strong relationship between total evaluation points and present average salaries. Since the existing plan used only about 200 out of a possible 500 points, relatively small variations in points accounted for fairly sizable variations in dollar amounts. A better indication of the dispersion within the salary structure as a result of evaluation on the two plans is presented by the standard error of estimate. This measure indicates that approximately 67% of the average salaries are included within an area defined by one standard error of estimate on both sides of the trend line (an area having a total width in this instance of $47.30 for the old plan and $34.22 for the new plan and extending the length of the salary structure). Within three standard errors of estimate on both sides of the trend line (an area having a total width of $141.90 for the old plan and $102.66 for the new plan), about 99% of the average salaries would be included.

Where there is considerable dispersion within a salary structure, there is a tendency to define ranges so as to include most of the employees. Such action on the part of management tends to defeat one of the primary objectives in any job analysis and evaluation program—the proper control of salaries paid within the company. Moreover, continued use of a plan which has been improperly developed tends to contribute to inequities, since the control being exercised is somewhat arbitrary and does not reflect true market conditions. Attempts to obtain improved administration by reducing the number of salary grades are ineffective when considerable dispersion exists within the structure. In the study outlined above it is evident that proper development of the plan and weighting of the factors actually permit the establishment of narrower ranges and at the same time include more of the employees within those ranges. Reduced dispersion within the structure also has a tendency to permit the establishment of fewer pay grades to administer salary payments.

5

Analysis of Job Content

The effectiveness of applying any point evaluation plan to hourly jobs is directly dependent upon the accurate analysis of job content. Since the accumulation of reliable concise information is of primary importance to the success of the entire program, it is essential that persons gathering information be thoroughly informed as to the exact type of data desired. Before persons are actually assigned to the gathering of job data, procedures should be developed and forms designed to obtain complete information in an organized manner. It is necessary to expand the step by step outline presented in Chapter 2 and adapt it to conditions existing within the company installing the program.

Qualifications of Job Analysts

In addition to the development of procedures designed to promote efficient analysis of jobs, it will be necessary to select trained analysts or to train a group of personnel having the proper qualifications. Analysts for the program should be selected with extreme care. If the analytical force is to be very large, it will be desirable to secure personnel with different backgrounds. Individuals having analytical experience, personnel connected with the production organization, and individuals who have writing ability should be selected. If a certain phase of the operations involves a knowledge of foundry activities, it will be advisable to include analysts who possess a background in this type of work. Personnel having industrial engineering methods or time and motion study experience are of particular value in a job analysis program. It will frequently be found that it is exceedingly difficult to secure persons with writing ability. This qualification is essential, however, to the development of job descriptions and job specifications.

106

Training of Job Analysts

If trained job analysts are available, it will usually be found that considerable time will be saved by hiring such personnel. If trained analysts are not available, it will be necessary to develop a training program. In addition to covering job analysis methods and techniques, the training program should include a careful study of the procedure to be used in analyzing and evaluating jobs. Each analyst should be provided with a complete procedure manual as well as forms designed for use in obtaining the desired information. Throughout the training period, stress should be placed upon securing accurate, complete information. The obtaining and the recording of job information represent one of the major costs of the program, and it is essential that this phase of the work be done effectively.

In addition to the description of the nature of job analysis and evaluation and the procedure to be used, the analyst should be given an opportunity to analyze several different types of typical jobs. Meetings should be held to discuss the type of information which is desired as well as information which is of little or no value. It should be pointed out that broad general statements may be misleading and will offer little tangible value as far as the evaluation of a job is concerned.

The job analysis Survey Sheet A has been designed to obtain detailed information concerning each of the factors used in the Hourly Plan in Chapter 3. Analysts should be instructed to sift all facts with considerable care and enter only pertinent data on the form. It will be found essential that information be properly organized on this form at the time jobs are evaluated. During the early stages of the job analysis program, the forms designed for gathering information should be carefully tested, and where necessary, terminology and spacing should be revised.

There is a tendency during the initial stages of a job analysis program to move too rapidly and, as a result, it may be necessary to re-analyze certain jobs handled at the beginning of the program. Careful training of analysts during the early stages of the program will usually result in such effort being unnecessary.

As soon as several typical jobs have been analyzed, the analysts should be given an opportunity to evaluate these jobs on the plan being developed. By so doing, the analysts will have a complete picture of the analysis and evaluation process. During this time, every effort should be made to bring about consistent thinking among the analysts.

Hourly Job Analysis Program
Survey Sheet A

Date_____

Analyst_____

Location_____ Building_____ Dept. no._____

Present classification title_____ Code_____

Suggested title_____ Suggested code_____

Approx. no. employed on this classification within dept. Male____ Female____

Single rate_____ Merit range: Min._____ Max._____ Incentive_____

Analyze the Job Not the Man on the Job

I. *Educational Background*

(Basic mentality, intelligence, knowledge, or schooling required
to absorb training and exercise judgment.)

A. *Reading:* Give examples of material which must be read and understood:

____None	____Simple instructions	____Letters, non-technical reports	____Interpret tech. reports

B. *Writing:* Give examples of writing required:

____None	____Simple statements	____Complete prepared forms	____Letters, non-tech. reports	____Comprehensive tech. reports

C. *Mathematics:* Indicate type of and reason for computations:

____None	____Add, subtract whole nos.	____Decimals & fractions	____Shop math.	____Complicated formulas & calculations

D. *Trade or specialized knowledge:*

    1. Indicate operations or machines with which individual must be familiar:

    2. What knowledge of feeds, speeds, tools, jigs, and fixtures is required?

Hourly Job Analysis Program
Survey Sheet A—Continued

3. What measuring instruments are used:

____rule, square ____dial indicator ____pressure
calipers ____bevel protractor gauge
____micrometers ____vernier-height ____weigh scale
____fixed gauges, calipers ____shrink rule
plug, ring, snap ____volt, ohm, and ammeter
Others:_____

4. What type of drawings, diagrams, and blueprints must be interpreted?
_____

5. A period of ____ years of apprenticeship or trades training is required to perform this job.

6. What knowledge of office machinery (i.e., touch typing) is required?
_____

E. *Additional job details:*

_____

_____

_____

Circle degree: A   B   C   D   E

II. *Job Training*

(Necessary time required to acquire mental and manual skills.)

A. What specific types (if any) of on-the-job training in related work are essential for employees before they are assigned this classification?

Type of job or classification: Period of time:

_____   _____

_____   _____

_____   _____

B. Estimated time, in months, required to train an employee on all phases of the job after being assigned the classification: _____

C. *Mental skills:* What background of practical knowledge must be acquired from experience on the job in order to plan, visualize, and reason through job details?

_____

_____

_____

D. *Physical skills:* What coordination must be developed between sensory cues and physical response in order to maintain pace? Consider the independence of finger, hand, foot, and/or leg movements.

_____

_____

E. *Additional job details:*

_____

_____

Circle degree: A   B   C   D   E   F   G   H

III. *Mental and Visual Effort*

(Frequency and intensity of mental and visual application required to perform the job.)

A. *Mental effort:* Discuss the mental exertion involved, the routine or exacting nature of the work, the concentration, analysis, and reasoning which must be applied.

_____

_____

Frequency (avg. time per day)	Occasional up to 10% ☐	Frequent 10% through 50% ☐	Continuous over 50% ☐

B. *Visual effort:* Describe intensity and continuity of visual effort necessary to assemble parts, manipulate tools, set up machines, inspect materials, check records, record data, and perform service operations:

_____

_____

Frequency (avg. time per day)	Occasional up to 10% ☐	Frequent 10% through 50% ☐	Continuous over 50% ☐

C. *Additional job details:* _____

_____

Circle degree: A   B   C   D   E

Hourly Job Analysis Program
Survey Sheet A—Continued

IV. *Physical Effort*

A. *Working position:*

Primary:	Avg. % time	Secondary:	Check	% if other than occasional
Sitting		Bend-stoop		
Standing		Push-pull		
Mostly walking		Arms in unsupported position		
Unusual awkward positions				
Total	100%	Lift-handle		
		Ride		
		Shovel		
		Handle-tote boxes		

B. *Handle materials by:*
Hand_____
Truck_____
Crane or hoist_____

C. *Weight of materials or tools handled:*

Frequency of handling

	Occas. up to 10%	Freq. 10%– 50%	Cont. over 50%	List materials or tools handled
Up to and inc. 5#				
Over 5# through 15#				
Over 15# through 30#				
Over 30# through 60#				
Over 60#				

Hourly Job Analysis Program
Survey Sheet A—Continued

D. *Additional job details* (indicate frequency of cycle): _____

_____

_____

_____

Circle degree: A   B   C   D   E

V. *Responsibility for Material or Product*

A. What operations does worker perform that could cause scrap or rework (indicate probability)?

_____

_____

B. Where would it be discovered and by whom (indicate usual disposition of material)?

_____

_____

C. Estimated cost of single loss. Include number of pieces and approximate labor and material cost of each piece.
Substantiate estimates by actual cases if possible.

_____

_____

D. On clerical jobs indicate relationship of job to production activities, probability and degree of damage to materials or loss of labor through improper recording of data or routing of materials.

_____

_____

E. *Additional job details:* _____

_____

_____

Hourly Job Analysis Program
Survey Sheet A—Continued

Circle degree and amount:

A	under $25	B	$25.00	C	$25.00	D	$100.00	E	$100.00
			100.00		100.00		500.00		500.00
			500.00		500.00		1000.00		1000.00
		over	500.00	over	500.00		1500.00		1500.00
						over	1500.00	over	1500.00

VI. *Responsibility for Tools and Equipment*

A. List and describe briefly the exact types of tools and/or equipment involved (manufacturer, size, operating characteristics).

_____

_____

_____

B. Nature of damage (give actual examples, if possible).

_____

_____

_____

C. What degree of care is required to prevent damage?

_____

_____

D. Estimated cost of repair, labor, and material. Substantiate estimates by actual cases if possible.

_____

E. *Additional job details:* _____

_____

_____

_____

Circle degree and level:

A	B	Minor	C	Minor	D	Minor	E	Minor
		Intermediate		Intermediate		Intermediate		Intermediate
		Major		Major		Major		Major

Hourly Job Analysis Program
Survey Sheet A—Continued

VII. *Responsibility for Safety of Others*

(Appraise the care required to prevent injury to others.)

A. *Hazard causing injury*	Discuss who can be injured and how injury can occur. How near are other workers?
____Air hose ____Dropped tools ____Dropped work ____Electric shock ____Flying parts or chips ____Flying work ____Hot material ____Molten metal ____Wheel breakage	

B. *Additional job details* (discuss the possibility of injury, care required in preventing injuries, actual examples of accidents):

_____

_____

_____

_____

Circle degree: A   B   C   D   E

VIII. *Work Surroundings*

(Environment or physical discomfort surrounding the job.)

A. *Element*	Check time exposed			Intensity (cause or source, degree of discomfort)
	Occas. up to 10%	Freq. 10% to 50%	Cont. over 50%	
____Acid				
____Cold				
____Dust				
____Fumes				
____Glare				
____Grease				
____Heat				
____Noise				
____Oil				
____Respirator				
____Steam				
____Vibration				
____Water				
____Weather				
____				

B. *Additional job details* (i.e., Is job located in enclosed area? What protective clothing or devices are used?):

_____

_____

_____

_____

_____

Circle degree: A   B   C   D   E

Hourly Job Analysis Program
Survey Sheet A—Continued

IX. *Unavoidable Hazards*

(Frequency of exposure to accident and probability and severity of resulting injuries, assuming reasonable care is exercised in observing safety regulations.)

A. *Hazard*	Discuss cause, probability, severity, actual examples
____Abrasions	
____Back injury	
____Bruises	
____Burns, minor	
____Burns, major	
____Crushed fingers	
____Crushed toes	
____Cuts	
____Electric shock	
____Eye injury	
____Falls, ladder, etc.	
____Fatal accident	
____Fractures	
____Hernia	
____Loss toes, fingers	
____Loss arm, leg	
____Sprains & strains	
____	

B. *Additional job details:* _____

_____

_____

Circle degree: A   B   C   D   E

Additional information not specifically requested but of use in making determinations concerning consolidations of jobs, suitability of present classification titles, and evaluation of the classification:

At the meetings held with the analysts during the training period, an outline of the research and development work done by the nucleus group should be presented. Other discussions should be held concerning policies in connection with contacting production supervision and labor union personnel.

Steps in Analyzing Jobs and Preparing Job Descriptions

After the preliminary indoctrination and training program, the process of analyzing jobs throughout the company should be started. Basically, the steps involved in analyzing jobs and preparing job descriptions are as follows:

1. Before entering an area to prepare job descriptions, analysts should obtain a general idea of the operations involved on the basis of the existing rate sheets and any written information which is available. Further information on the operations may be obtained from production supervision or personnel representatives in the area, such as the labor relations representatives.

2. The supervising analyst should obtain necessary clearance and arrange for a meeting with production supervision in the area in which analysts are operating. At the time analysts enter the area they should be introduced to the labor relations representative, foremen, general foremen, and superintendents. As they proceed from department to department, analysts should arrange for a brief discussion with the individuals supervising the operations.

3. At the time analysts are ready to write job descriptions in a specific department, arrangements should be made with the supervisor involved to review the specific operations in the department. A discussion should be held with each foreman concerning the types of jobs he supervises.

4. In order to obtain accurate information concerning the various jobs performed, it may be necessary to arrange an interview with employees on the job. Arrangements for the interview with the employee should always be made with his immediate supervisor. In no case, however, should the analyst initiate an interview unless some member of the supervisory force, preferably the immediate supervisor, has first been informed of the analyst's presence in the department. The time chosen for such interviews should be the earliest possible time consistent with production requirements. Care should be taken to avoid undue postponement. If the supervisor advises that changes are being made in the job content or method, the supervising analyst should be informed immediately in order that the study may be

postponed. In most instances the analyst should be introduced to the employees by the employees' immediate supervisors. Although it is impossible to establish a definite outline for each job interview, certain generalizations can be made which may be of assistance to analysts.

In starting the interview, the analyst should become acquainted with the employee as a person before beginning the formal interview pertaining to his duties. If the employee is at all nervous or ill at ease, the analyst should not show any impatience. If, on the other hand, the employee is self-confident and willing to talk, he should be kept on the subject courteously but firmly. Even though the analyst may be entirely familiar with the details of the work involved, he should evidence a real interest in the employee's story. The analyst should indicate his desire to learn by encouraging the employee to speak more freely concerning other related subjects with which he is not so familiar. The analyst must be sure to get an adequate answer to every question, even though it may be necessary to leave that particular subject for the time being and return by another approach before the end of the interview.

Job analysts should not make suggestions to workers or production supervisors in connection with methods changes or the organization of the work. Analysts are primarily concerned with an analysis of the work as it is now being done and not with any efficiency studies in connection with the methods being used or the individuals employed to carry them out. The analyst should never create the impression of being critical of work methods, the employee, or the supervisory force. Such criticism is not within the jurisdiction of job analysis and may act adversely upon the entire program.

Questions in connection with the reasons for doing certain types of work or for doing work in a certain way should be phrased in such a manner that there can be no doubt that the analyst is seeking only indications of the importance of such operations and their relationships with other jobs. The analyst must always avoid formation of preconceived ideas as to job level or content. His mind should be open to instruction and information before, during, and after the interview. Job analysis and evaluation have merit and value only to the degree that their results are based on facts and the pooled judgment of a group of qualified individuals.

Although job analysis and evaluation are oftentimes considered a part of the industrial relations function, the job analyst, in conducting the interview, should studiously avoid discussion of grievances or conflicts of opinion concerning employer-employee relations. Matters of controversy and disagreements between employees and management are the particular field of the supervisory force and the labor relations office. The analyst's attention should be confined to the job, its contents, and its requirements.

If an analyst is asked the reason for the analysis program, he may state simply that the company is making a factual study of jobs to help in developing job descriptions. It is best not to enter into an explanation of the procedure or a discussion of the probable outcome of the study. Questions about the value or need for job analysis and evaluation or about the methods employed should be referred to the foremen, to the appropriate labor relations representative, or to the analyst's supervisor. If, in the extreme case, an employee refuses to cooperate, the analyst should not argue with him but should report immediately to the supervising analyst.

During the interview, the analyst should take notes of all significant information secured. Questions should be asked and the discussion guided along the logical lines of development required by the detailed survey sheet. It is important that notes made during the interview be complete and legible. All of the detail secured during the interview with the man on the job should not be transferred to the final job description. The notes taken during the interview, however, will provide valuable information for later review. These notes may have to be used by others at some later date when the analyst may not be available to interpret them. The analyst should not depend or make others rely on his memory for details or translation of obscure thoughts. He should remember that the notes taken will be part of a permanent file pertaining to the job.

During the entire interview, the relationship of the job to other jobs in the department should be considered. The analyst should have clearly fixed in his mind the primary purpose for which the job was created. The interview should not be completed until this has been well established. It is only in this way that the important features of the job can be separated from the unimportant, a satisfactory description prepared, and the job properly rated. The analyst should ask himself questions such as: "Assuming that the work being done is necessary, why was this job established? What is its relation and main contribution to the overall production cycle?"

During the course of the interview, the survey sheet may be completed in the presence of the employee. If the employee is interested, he should be permitted to see all questions and entries on the form.

At the close of the interview, the employee should be thanked for his time and cooperation. Analysts should try to develop the facility of remembering faces and names and connecting them with the job. This will aid in recalling job details and will enable the analyst to recognize and speak to employees previously interviewed.

5. In general, there are two types of hourly jobs:

a. The job which involves a specific cycle or sequence of operations performed by the employee.

When analyzing jobs of this type, the analyst should begin with the start of the operation cycle or the first element the employee is called upon to do at the beginning of the day and record successively the duties or work steps. For example, the elements for some machine-operating jobs may be arranged in the following order: (1) set up the machine, (2) operate the machine, (3) remove the work pieces, (4) maintain tools, (5) maintain machine. This type of description can usually be applied to jobs which are relatively simple or for which the skill involved is limited.

b. The job description which defines the functions of an employee. In this instance, no regular cycle of operations is evident.

This type of description is usually required for more difficult jobs with considerable variety or responsibility. The work of a hydraulic repairman or a maintenance electrician is a good example of a job for which the functional type of description may be used. Personnel working on these classifications may be called upon to cover a wide variety of repair jobs, and it would not be feasible for analysts to try to describe every individual job which employees on these classifications might be called upon to perform.

6. It will probably be unnecessary to contact all employees in the department concerning the work they are actually performing. In many instances, observation of the jobs performed will reveal that a sizable group of employees are performing identical work. In such instances, it is only necessary to cover a representative sample of the work performed.

7. The data developed at the time of the interview with the employee should be reviewed with his immediate supervisor to be certain that the information secured is accurate.

8. After the details have been developed concerning each job classification, the next step is to prepare a general description of the duties on a form such as Survey Sheet B. In the writing of job descriptions, considerable assistance may be obtained from descriptions written earlier in the program. Since there are oftentimes a number of jobs within a company which are similar in nature, it is important that descriptions for these jobs be written in a similar manner.

Hourly Job Analysis Program
Survey Sheet B

Date_____

Location_____ Building_____ Dept._____
Present classification title_____ Code_____
Suggested title_____ Suggested code_____
Approx. no. employed on this classification within dept. Male_____ Female_____
Single rate_____ Merit range: Min._____ Max._____ Incentive_____

General Description of Duties

The statement above reflects the general duties considered necessary to describe the principal functions of the job identified and shall not be construed as a detailed description of all work requirements which may be inherent in the job.

_____   _____
Analyst   Foreman

_____   _____
Checked by

Descriptions should be identical for those jobs in which the work content is the same. Careful review of the job descriptions by a central office editing group will tend to promote this overall consistency.

Analysts can help bring about consistency if they have access to job descriptions already prepared and on file at the central office. Where a worker performs more duties than are described in one of these descriptions, they should be added. Where the worker does not perform some of the duties described in the central office job description, these duties should be deleted. If the worker performs parts of several jobs, appropriate amendments must be made by using these data to prepare a new analysis. It should always be remembered that the information included in job descriptions at the central office is to be used primarily for reference purposes and not as data which can be copied in their entirety.

The general description of the duties should be a brief statement of the essential occupation or facts and characteristics of the work. Its primary purpose is to identify the job and point out the basic factors which differentiate the level of performance of the job from that of other jobs. It is to be written in a form which will immediately orient the readers with respect to the scope of the job. A well-written summary should provide readers with a general indication of the skill level of the work performed. Therefore, in summarizing a job, the analyst must be careful to indicate facts which are highly important for characterizing jobs.

When organizing a job description, the analyst may divide the occupational information into three categories:

a. *What the Worker Does.* The physical and mental responses of the worker to a given work situation comprise what the worker does. Physically the worker may carry, cut, bend, grind, assemble, repair, set up, disassemble, write, insert, regulate, clean, finish, or otherwise change the position, shape, or condition of the work by the expenditure of physical effort. Mentally a worker can plan, develop, judge, direct, control, compute, or otherwise govern the expenditure of his own physical effort and that of others by exercising mental effort. For any given job, the effort expended by the worker may be any combination of physical and mental effort. In summarizing the job, the analyst should decide on its complete scope and describe it accordingly with carefully selected terminology which conveys clearly and precisely what the worker does. Verbs chosen to impart this thought must be broad in meaning to identify the job but not so general as to include, by reference or otherwise, occupational information which does not pertain to the job. General terms, such as "operates," are to be avoided whenever possible because they do not give an accurate picture of the job. In many cases, such terms do not describe what the worker does. Instead, they describe the method by which an employee performs his job and thus relate to how the work is accomplished.

b. *How the Worker Does the Job.* The methods used by a worker to perform the job indicate how the work is done. Physically the methods include the use of machinery, tools, equipment, instruments, measuring devices, and materials. The following of procedures and routines, the use of the senses, physical movements required to do the job, and the job knowledge possessed by the worker and applied in the performance of the job also convey how the work is done. Methods may involve the application of judgment and decision, the selection of courses of action, or the relaying of thoughts to others. The worker may use a single method in the accomplishment of a job or he may have at his command several alternative methods, all of equal merit.

c. *Why the Worker Does It.* Why the worker performs a job is the purpose of the job and indicates its place in the organizational structure of the plant. Knowledge of the purpose of the job is necessary to understand the scope of the work and to justify the What and How of the job. The purpose of the job may be the conversion of materials from one form to another form. It may be the maintenance of conditions under which other jobs in the same or other departments can successfully be performed. Also, the purpose may be to solve problems, repair damages, detect or prevent errors, oversee quality of production, or control the quantity of production. Each job studied by the analyst will have its own particular purpose within the plant.

Job descriptions should not be written so specifically that they encroach upon work standards by describing methods or pace. It should be borne in mind that the information being secured is for the purpose of judging job characteristics and not for establishing incentives for the individuals working on the jobs. At the time the job descriptions are prepared covering each individual job, they should be written as specifically as possible. Later, consolidations with other jobs which are practically identical will result in job specifications being written so as to cover the general duties being performed by the classification.

It is probably advisable to analyze jobs in a complete department or plant before they are evaluated on the plan. In large companies, such a procedure will usually involve securing several hundred job analyses. During the time this information is being obtained, however, it should be carefully checked, and typical or benchmark jobs should be evaluated on the plan in order to be certain that all of the information required is being developed.

The information developed on the survey sheets used by the analyst should record sufficient identifying facts for locating the job at a later date. Space should be provided under each factor for recording information which is not called for in the form but which is believed to be pertinent. Survey Sheet A provides space for the analyst to give his opinion concerning the level of the job. These levels correspond to the degrees on each factor in the evaluation plan. The order of information on this form, as well as on all other forms relating to evaluations or specifications, should be in the same sequence. After all facts concerning a job have been recorded and the summary of job content prepared, these sheets should be filed in a job folder properly identified by the job title and location.

6

Evaluation of Jobs and the
Preparation of Specifications

Evaluation Procedure

When the analysis of jobs in a particular area has been completed, the jobs should be evaluated on the plan. It may be convenient to analyze jobs in a complete department or other organizational unit before that evaluation is begun. As explained in Chapter 4, individuals in the evaluation groups should first evaluate independently and then meet to reconcile their differences. In some instances, it may be necessary to secure additional facts concerning a job before it can be evaluated accurately. It will be recognized at this time that accurate evaluations on the plan will be directly dependent upon the adequacy of the information obtained. The Evaluation Sheet provides a convenient form for recording evaluations. Several columns have been designated for points, thereby facilitating statistical studies relating to the weighting and reweighting of factors and degrees of factors.

It may be desirable during this period to conduct an analysis to determine which analysts are the most consistent evaluators. Such a study may be conducted by selecting a sample group of about twenty-five jobs and having each analyst evaluate them on the plan. A criteria may be established by having the supervisors evaluate the same twenty-five jobs and reconciling differences. Each analyst's evaluations may then be compared with the evaluations made by the supervisory group and a correlation coefficient computed. Analysts having low correlation coefficients will usually be found to be interpreting the plan in a different way, or they may have failed to give careful consideration during evaluation to all of the job facts which were available.

Hourly Job Analysis Program
Evaluation Sheet

Classification title _____ Code no. _____ Dept. _____

Rate _____ Date _____

	Degrees									Points							
	A	B	C	D	E	F	G	H		1	2	3	4	5	6	7	8
1. Educational Background																	
2. Job Training																	
3. Mental and Visual Effort																	
4. Physical Effort																	
5. Responsibility for Material or Product									Amount								
6. Responsibility for Equipment and Tools									Minor ___ Intermediate ___ Major ___								
7. Responsibility for Safety of Others																	
8. Work Surroundings																	
9. Unavoidable Hazards																	
Average rate _____ Population _____									Total								

Plotting of Jobs

After the jobs in a certain area within a company have been evaluated and differences reconciled, they may be assigned code numbers for plotting purposes. Total evaluation points should be computed and the jobs plotted in order to show the wage structure in the particular area under consideration. Until differences in evaluation have been reconciled, no attempt should be made to determine total evaluation points. In many instances, it may be found desirable to let only the relatively small group of personnel concerned with the plotting of jobs and conducting of statistical studies know the points on the degrees of the factors. By so doing, any influence which the points might have on evaluators will be minimized.

The plotting can probably be done most effectively by preparing a basic chart having total points on the horizontal scale and present rates on the vertical scale. This basic chart may be prepared after observing the results secured from the typical jobs analyzed and evaluated during the development of the plan. The tentative pay grades established at that time should be indicated on the basic chart. The jobs for a particular department, plant, or operation may then be plotted on transparent paper after it has been laid over the basic chart. By using this method, it will be unnecessary to redraw the basic chart at the time each plant or operation is plotted. It will only be necessary to prepare a transparent overlay for each particular operation.

Reviewing Jobs

Upon completion of the job plotting, the results should be reviewed to determine which jobs appear substantially above or below the trend line. The statistical analysis conducted at the time the plan was developed should indicate the area in which most of the jobs will fall. If the job sample has been properly selected, the rates for practically all of the jobs in the company will fall within an area defined by three standard errors of estimate on each side of the trend line computed for the sample. Jobs which fall beyond this range should certainly be reviewed from the standpoint that they may have been improperly evaluated or that the present rate may be out of line with other rates in the company. If an area differential in rates exists, this fact will also cause distortion at the time jobs are plotted. Thus, if there are several separate operations, located in various parts of the country, they may have different wage structures varying with the rates paid in each locality. Jobs with the same total points will plot in different areas on the chart since their current wage rates vary. An analysis of these different plottings will reveal the extent of the differential.

Upon completion of the plotting and review of all jobs in a particular area or location, the jobs should be analyzed from the standpoint of consolidation. Job content should be carefully reviewed in order to determine similarities between the types of work performed. Such factors as management's desire for interchangeability of personnel, seniority provisions of the union contract, and the similarity of work performed should be considered at the time jobs are consolidated. Although it is usually desirable to administer rates with as few classifications as possible, it is essential that they remain clearcut; otherwise difficulties will be experienced in positioning individuals on the classifications.

Preparation of Job Specifications

After all consolidations have been made, it will be necessary to prepare job specifications covering the various types of work performed. A sample specification appears on pages 129–130. Job specifications are of vital importance since they provide the basis for the classification structure within a particular area. They represent a refinement and a condensation of all of the data secured during the course of the analysis and evaluation. As such they should provide a complete description of each job and substantiating data for the evaluation on each factor. Depending upon the purpose for which the description is intended, it is sometimes desirable to consider presenting the job duties in individual paragraphs rather than in one single paragraph. Job specifications are sometimes defined so as to exclude the factor evaluations and substantiating information.

If jobs in several areas or locations are being analyzed simultaneously, it will be necessary to set up a central clearing point for eliminating duplication in the writing of specifications. In any large company it will be found that certain jobs occur throughout the organization. Non-production classifications, such as cleaners, maintenance workers, and material handlers, will be found in many different departments. Usually it will not be desirable to write job specifications for each of these jobs.

Editing and Coding Job Specifications

In general, a central editing group should be responsible for editing all job descriptions prepared by analysts. They should code all

HOURLY EMPLOYEE   218
JOB SPECIFICATION

PLANT OR LOCATION

JOB TITLE   Die Maker   CODE NO. 1402
TOTAL POINTS: 254   PAY GRADE: 14   DATE:

GENERAL DESCRIPTION OF DUTIES

Builds, alters, and repairs blanking, forming, piercing, drawing, and other types of dies.

Studies die print to determine machining operations of component die parts. Draws sketches of die parts and designates machining operations, dimensions, tolerances, and finishes. Applies layout ink to surface of stock and scribes outline of machining operation on stock. Writes work order, attaches part sketch, and carries or hand-trucks work to clearance desk for distribution to machinists. Checks returned machined work, using precision instruments such as height gauge, micrometer, surface plate, and bevel protractor. Fits and assembles machined die components into die unit. Hand-scrapes, grinds, and files surfaces to obtain precision bearing surfaces. Checks contours, angles, and radii with templates, gauges, and other measuring instruments. Dismantles defective, broken, or worn dies to determine necessary repairs. Replaces broken die parts or requests welder to build up worn or cracked surfaces. Grinds, scrapes, and files re-built surfaces to required specifications. Observes performance of newly built or repaired dies.

The statement above reflects the general duties considered necessary to describe the principal functions of the job identified and shall not be construed as a detailed description of all work requirements which may be inherent in the job.

jobs, review incoming job descriptions in relation to job descriptions already written, consolidate and combine jobs where necessary, rewrite job descriptions in order to promote internal consistency, maintain necessary files, turn over job descriptions to the clerical unit for typing, control the preparation of specifications, and edit specifications upon their completion.

A job classification code manual should be developed as a basis for assignment and control of code numbers. This manual should include:

| JOB TITLE: Die Maker | | CODE NO. 1402 |
| PLANT OR LOCATION. | | PAY GRADE: 14 |

	DEGREE	POINTS
1. EDUCATIONAL BACKGROUND Requires a four-year apprenticeship or equivalent in die making.	E	35
2. JOB TRAINING 37 months through 60 months of practical experience in industrial tool room is required to become proficient with most phases of die making.	G	82
3. MENTAL AND VISUAL EFFORT Exercises concentrated mental and visual attention to plan work sequences and machining layouts of component die parts. · Checks machined work and fits die parts together to form die unit.	D	51
4. PHYSICAL EFFORT Light physical.effort. Lifts, tilts, and handles component die parts to check dimensions and to fit parts together.	B	11
5. RESPONSIBILITY FOR MATERIAL OR PRODUCT Exercises sustained high degree of care to prevent scrap or re-work of dies. Must plan sequence of machining operations, scribe machining layouts, and check machined work for tolerances and finish ESTIMATED COST: $500	D	43
6. RESPONSIBILITY FOR TOOLS AND EQUIPMENT Exercises considerable care and attention to prevent damage to precision measuring instruments and to machines when making set-ups or performing operations. ESTIMATED COST: Inter.	C	14
7. RESPONSIBILITY FOR SAFETY OF OTHERS Exercises ordinary attention to prevent injury to other employees when transferring dies or die components to and from work bench.	B	4
8. WORK SURROUNDINGS Works in factory building and is exposed to moderate degree of noise, grease, and oil.	B	8
9. UNAVOIDABLE HAZARDS Accident hazard moderate. Probable injuries consist of minor cuts and abrasions.	B	6
TOTAL POINTS		254

1. A description of the job classification code system.
2. Job families and code areas assigned.
3. Procedure for installing and controlling the job classification coding system.

A list of the individual plants and operations for which separate classification manuals would be issued may also be included. Typical information which would appear in such a manual follows.

1. *Description of Job Classification Code System.* This manual presents the occupational coding system applied to hourly job classifi-

cations within the company. Each job classification has a six-digit code number assigned as follows:

Digit Code	Interpretation
1–4	Job family
5	Job level (helper, leader, etc.)
6	Job pay grade

Based upon the types of work performed within the company, job families have been established. A list of job families and code areas assigned is presented in Part 2. The job level code is assigned as follows:

1—Leader
2—Apprentice
3—Helper
4—Machine setter
5—Utility and relief
6
7 } May be used for other
8 } special classifications
9 } or groups

The job pay grade is coded as follows:

Pay Grade	Evaluation Points	Tabulating Card Code*
1	Up to and including 35	1
2	36–52	2
3	53–69	3
4	70–86	4
5	87–103	5
6	104–120	6
7	121–137	7
8	138–154	8
9	155–171	9
10	172–188	11†
11	189–205	J
12	206–222	K
13	223–239	L
14	240–256	M
15	257–273	N
16	274–290	O
17	291–307	P
18	308–324	Q
19	325–341	R
20	342–358	12‡
21	359–375	A
22	376–392	B

* Where card columns on the tabulating card are at a premium, a code may be assigned which saves one column.
† X punch.
‡ High punch.

A master job classification manual covering all jobs within the company will be prepared and separate manuals will be issued for the individual plants and operations within the company.

2. *Job Families and Code Areas Assigned.* An example of this portion of the manual, which is usually prepared in alphabetical order, follows.

	Code Area
Metal-finishing	
Filers, grinders, buffers, polishers, sanders, burring operations	7101–7500
Metal-forming other than machining	
Sheet metal work, stamping, powdered metallurgy	6601–7100
Metal-machining	
Grinders	8801–9025
Lapping machines	9026–9060
Multi-purpose machines	9061–9090
Milling machines	9091–9190
Combination machines	9191–9250
Hobbing machines	9251–9350
Gear shavers	9351–9375
Boring machines	9376–9470
Chamfering machines	9471–9490
Saws	9491–9510
Threading machines	9511–9545
Setup men	9546–9595
Turning machines	9596–9620
Bullards	9621–9641
Honing machines	9642–9654
Drill presses	9655–9780
Burnishers	9781–9820
Gear shapers	9821–9840
Broaching machines	9841–9900
Lathes	9901–9980
Screw machines	9981–9999
Paint production and application other than maintenance	1501–1700

If this code system is to be used in conjunction with tabulating machines, consideration may be given to using an alphabetic code in the first position. If code letters such as A through I are used instead of numbers in the first position to designate certain specific groups, cards for all highly skilled classifications, for example, could be separated from the remaining cards in one sort.

3. *Procedure for Installing and Controlling the Job Classification Coding System.* In order to install and properly control the job classification coding system, the following procedure is outlined:

(1) Secure the rough draft (prior to typing) edited copies of the job specifications at the time they are processed through central editing.

(2) Sort the job specifications into job families.

(3) Assign the proper four-digit code number as outlined in Part 2 of this manual.

(4) Type one copy each of Form 101, 101-A, 102 and 102-A (see Figures 16, 17, 18, and 19). All four copies are to be prepared simultaneously.

(5) Two types of files are to be prepared for centralized control: (a) master company job classification file, (b) individual plant or operation file.

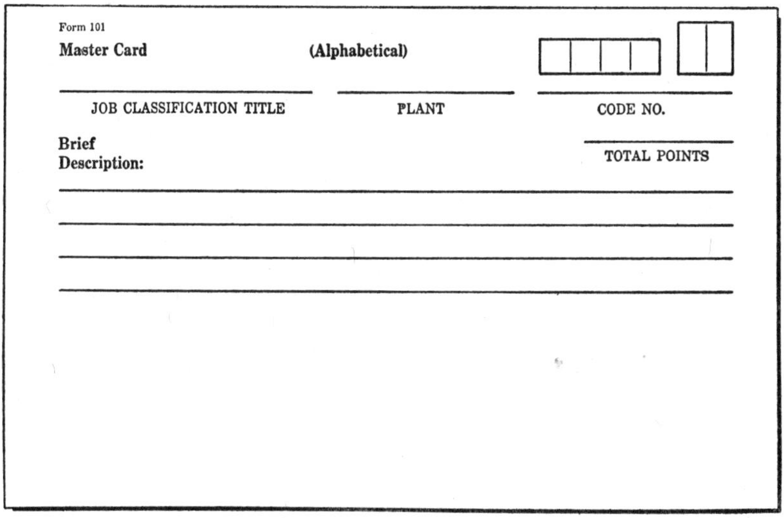
Form 101

Master Card (Alphabetical)

JOB CLASSIFICATION TITLE | PLANT | CODE NO.

Brief Description:

TOTAL POINTS

Figure 16

Form 101 is to be filed alphabetically and Form 101-A is to be filed numerically in a master company file. Form 102 is to be filed alphabetically and Form 102-A is to be filed numerically in a plant file. The code number in the upper right corner of these forms provides two spaces for the pay grade. Form 102-A has been designed to facilitate keypunching for tabulating card studies.

If jobs which have been prepared in a certain area of the company are being activated in another area, it is unnecessary to complete Forms 101 and 101-A. Forms 102 and 102-A should be completed, and the name of the plant where the specification is being activated should be recorded on Form 101-A.

Forms 101, 101-A, 102, and 102-A will provide a complete index to both the alphabetical and numerical specification files for the entire company as well as to the individual plants and operations. Under

Form 101-A

Master Card   (Numerical)

JOB CLASSIFICATION TITLE   PLANT   CODE NO.

Brief
Description: TOTAL POINTS

Operations or Plants using Classification:

Figure 17

certain conditions, it may be desirable to maintain these records on interpreted punched cards. These cards may then be used in the preparation of rate schedules or as header cards for rate and classification runs. The forms or cards will also provide a control upon the assignment of code numbers.

Form 102

Plant Card   (Alphabetical)

JOB CLASSIFICATION TITLE   PLANT   CODE NO.

Brief
Description: TOTAL POINTS

Superceded Job Title or Titles: Classification Active in
                                         Following Departments:

Figure 18

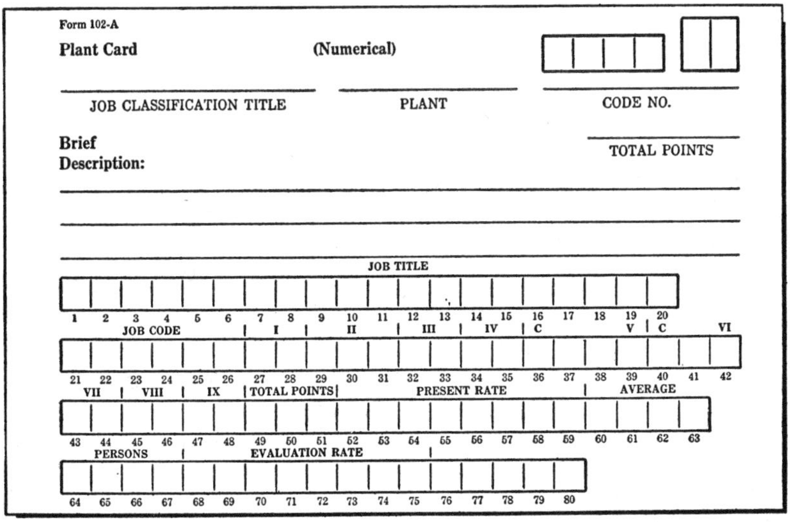
Form 102-A

Plant Card (Numerical)

JOB CLASSIFICATION TITLE — PLANT — CODE NO.

Brief Description: — TOTAL POINTS

JOB TITLE

1 2 3 4 5 6 7 8 9 10 11 12 13 14 15 16 17 18 19 20
JOB CODE | I | II | III | IV | C | V | C | VI

21 22 23 24 25 26 27 28 29 30 31 32 33 34 35 36 37 38 39 40 41 42
VII | VIII | IX | TOTAL POINTS | PRESENT RATE | AVERAGE

43 44 45 46 47 48 49 50 51 52 53 54 55 56 57 58 59 60 61 62 63
PERSONS | EVALUATION RATE |

64 65 66 67 68 69 70 71 72 73 74 75 76 77 78 79 80

Figure 19

Upon receipt of job descriptions covering a complete department or other unit, the central editing group should proceed as follows:

(1) All jobs should be coded in accordance with the coding system adopted.

(2) Individual job descriptions should be checked against the library of job descriptions to determine whether any duplication exists between the incoming job and jobs already written.

(3) If duplication does exist, the incoming job description should be edited to conform with the existing job description. It should be noted that the job description should not be made to conform to the description which currently exists unless the job content is the same or very similar to the job description on file.

(4) If duplication does not exist, the incoming job description should be edited to conform to the established pattern.

(5) In all instances the central editing group should check to be certain that the first sentence of the job description provides a general statement of the duties and that the following paragraphs provide greater detail concerning the job performed.

(6) All job descriptions should be edited for clarity of expression, completeness, consistency, and grammatical errors. Sentences should begin with action verbs and all words not imparting necessary information should be omitted.

(7) If in the rewriting or editing of a job description it becomes evident that the information given on Survey Sheet A (see pages 108–116) is inadequate, the job folder should be returned to the supervisor with notations concerning the material which appears to be lacking. Job descriptions returned to supervisors should be given special handling

to make sure that the required information is obtained; then the folders should be reprocessed immediately. It is not anticipated that a large number of job folders will be returned to supervisors. All job descriptions should be reviewed by supervisors before they are sent to the central editing group. This review of job descriptions should include the careful checking of substantiating information on Survey Sheet A so that it will

---

Hourly Job Analysis Program
Specification Check Sheet

1. Job title_____ Date_____

                                            Present   Total

    Plant or operation_____ rate_____ points_____

2. A review of Central Editing files indicates that the following jobs should be checked prior to preparation of specifications:

                Job Title   Job Code No.

    1.

    2.

    3.

    4.

3. Specification not on file. Suggest you contact_____ group where similar specification is being written.

4. Central files have been checked and specification should be written

_____

_____

                                   Central Editing

---

be unnecessary to gather additional information at a later date. It should be recognized by both supervisors and the central editing group that the information contained in job description folders must be sufficient for job evaluation purposes and the preparation of job specifications.

(8) The central editing group should maintain two files of job descriptions. One file may be alphabetical by job title and the other file may be numerical by job code. In large companies with multiplant operations, it is usually desirable to maintain individual plant files in addition to the central company file.

(9) The central editing group should be responsible for the editing of all job titles.

(10) Upon completion of the review and editing of material in each job folder, job descriptions are sent to the clerical unit for typing. To

make sure that individual job descriptions will not be lost, it is suggested that descriptions be held until a complete department has been edited. After the material has been typed, necessary copies should be placed on file at the central office and remaining copies returned to the supervisor concerned.

(11) To facilitate tracing and returning of job descriptions, it is suggested that the name of the analyst who wrote the job description and the name of his supervisor be included on all job folders. A rubber name stamp may be provided for each supervisor so that he can stamp the folders with his name at the time descriptions are being reviewed and forwarded to the central editing group.

(12) The central editing group should authorize and control the preparation of all job specifications. The Specification Check Sheet is suitable for controlling the preparation of specifications by different groups of analysts. Following their preparation by the analysts, specifications should be returned to central editing for review and final editing.

Procedure for Salaried Positions

The procedure which has been outlined is designed primarily for use in connection with a job analysis and evaluation program for hourly employees. Where salaried employees are involved, there are some differences in both the forms and procedures. In the past, typical programs for salaried personnel have involved increased employee participation, particularly in regard to the supplying of job information. In many instances, employees have been asked to complete job analysis forms describing their work in detail. This information is then reviewed and approved by supervision in the area being studied. More recently, there has been a tendency to gather information by discussion with the employee in a manner similar to the way in which hourly jobs are analyzed. The latter method is preferred since the quality of the end result is not impaired and the speed of accomplishment may be substantially increased. A questionnaire based upon the factors being used in the salaried plan may be developed and used by the analysts to guide the discussion. When descriptions have been gathered for a specified area or from all company locations, they are analyzed and grouped so as to provide the basis for development of position specifications. A sample specification form is presented on page 138.

After this portion of the program has been finished, the basic steps in analyzing and evaluating jobs may be considered completed. Two very important phases remain, however—the establishment of administrative controls and the installation of the new wage system. These final phases are discussed in the chapters which follow.

Salaried Employee Position Specification

Position title Clerk, shipping and receiving		Position code and salary grade 1546–3	
Staff or division manufacturing	Department 4339	Approved by	Date
Section 17	Unit		

Summary: Prepares and processes various shipping and receiving forms to maintain records of material movements.

Typical duties: Compiles records of materials received and shipped by posting such information as shipping and receiving form numbers, dates issued, received, or shipped, types and quantities of materials, destination, and carrier number. Files and distributes copies of shipping and receiving forms to various departments. Prepares shortage and discrepancy lists. Requests traffic or transportation department to furnish proper type of carrier for material to be shipped.

The statement above reflects general details necessary for performance of the job and is not to be construed as being all-inclusive.

Note: On the reverse side of the position specification, statements are frequently included concerning education and experience required, equipment used, and unusual physical or working conditions. Depending upon the purpose for which the specifications are intended, a decision can be made as to the value to be derived from including substantiating information and evaluations on each factor.

7

Establishment of
Administrative Controls

Statistical Basis for Establishing Wage Structures

The establishment of administrative controls for a wage structure can be greatly facilitated by calculating various statistical measures. In addition to computing a weighted (by population on each job) least-squares trend line, standard error of estimate, and correlation coefficient for the wage structures in individual plants and operations, it is necessary to compute these same statistics covering all data for the entire company. The weighted least-squares trend line is actually a cost line and has a pivot point around which the line can be rotated in such a manner that costs will remain constant. This pivot point is the point where the weighted average of the points for the jobs intersects with the weighted average of the rates for the jobs. The computed trend line will usually provide the basis upon which the final trend line is established. It is important to realize that job analysis and evaluation do not establish the level of wages to be paid by a company. They merely establish the relative worth of each job in relation to all other jobs and are of assistance in the equitable allocation of funds provided for wages.

It is usually desirable in establishing the final trend line to secure some sort of an anchor point. This anchor point can be the pivot point of the trend line, or a low-rated highly populated job can be selected at the lower end of the scale and used as a point through which the trend line is drawn. In practically all cases it will be necessary for the final trend line to closely approximate the weighted least-squares line. It should be remembered that usually the intention of the entire job classification program is to equalize or nearly equalize present payrolls rather than to increase or decrease payrolls over a long-range period.

139

Procedure for Conducting Area Wage Rate Surveys

At the time that a least-squares trend line is adopted, an area survey should be conducted to secure factual information concerning the real income received by a company's employees so that this income may be compared with the earnings of employees performing comparable jobs in other companies. All elements entering into the compensation of employees should be considered at the time the survey is conducted. Since the results of the analyses will have an important bearing upon management decisions concerning the wage structure, it is exceedingly important that the data obtained be accurate and complete. Every effort should be made to check the validity of the data at the time it is secured.

These studies usually involve the securing of information for a selected group of typical jobs from companies competing in the same labor market. The jobs must be reviewed from the standpoint of job content and evaluated on the plan. In comparisons of this nature, it is essential that representative jobs be included in the sample. They may be plotted on a chart, using the rates for the particular company where the survey is being conducted. A trend line should be computed and weighted (if figures are available) by the population distribution on the jobs in the survey. The least-squares trend lines may then be compared in order to determine whether the wages in any particular plant as represented by the trend line are higher or lower than in another plant.

In conducting an area wage rate survey, the following information is desired:

1. General information pertaining primarily to important management policies, such as holiday pay, vacation pay, shift differentials, and incentives, is required. A questionnaire such as the Area Wage Rate Survey Sheet, General Information (see pages 141–144), may be used to secure this information. In conducting the survey, it is usually advisable to complete this form upon arrival at the company. Such information provides a general background of knowledge and will be useful in securing the specific information required later.

2. Specific information concerning a selected group of comparable jobs should also be obtained. A form similar to the Area Wage Rate Survey Sheet, Detail Information (see page 145), may be used in securing this data. In most instances, the classifications being surveyed will be jobs in which the company is primarily interested from the standpoint of establishing or comparing rates. Accurate comparisons of job content are essential to the development of reliable wage surveys. If after discussion it is apparent that individual jobs at the company being surveyed are not comparable to jobs listed for survey purposes, information for those jobs should not be secured. Only those jobs which are comparable should be studied and included in the survey.

Area Wage Rate Survey
General Information
Hourly Employees

Name of Company _____

Address _____

Products manufactured _____

Person contacted _____ Title _____ Date _____

1. *Approximate number of employees:*   Hourly   Salary

    Male _____   Male _____

    Female _____   Female _____

The following information refers to hourly employees only:

2. *Are employees organized?*   Yes _____   No _____

    By what Union? _____

3. *Minimum hiring rates:*   Male _____

    Female _____

4. *Payment for holidays:*   Indicate whether the following holidays are observed:

	With Pay (check one)	
New Year's Day	No	Yes
Lincoln's Birthday	No	Yes
Washington's Birthday	No	Yes
Memorial Day	No	Yes
Independence Day	No	Yes
Labor Day	No	Yes
Armistice Day	No	Yes
Thanksgiving Day	No	Yes
Christmas Day	No	Yes
Good Friday	No	Yes
Election Day	No	Yes
Others	No	Yes

What are employees paid for working on holidays?

Time and a half	No	Yes
Double time	No	Yes
Other time	No	Yes

5. *Shift differential:*   What is the shift differential policy?

_____

_____

6. *Overtime payments:*   Is plant normally operating on a 40-hour week? _____
   If not, approximately what percentage of employees and what types of operations are working overtime?

_____

_____

7. *Bonuses:* Are bonuses, other than incentive, paid in addition to regular earnings?

	No	Yes
Profit sharing	_____	_____
Christmas	_____	_____
_____	_____	_____

Please explain: _____

_____

8. *Administration of wage rates:* Do jobs have a:

	Yes	No
Single rate?	_____	_____
Rate range?	_____	._____

What method of progression through a rate range is used?

Merit increase only	_____	_____
Automatic increase only	_____	_____
Combination of merit and automatic	_____	_____

What is the relationship of the hiring rate to the rate for the classification?

_____

Is a job analysis and evaluation plan used?_____ (Secure sample if possible.)

9. *Benefit plans:* What employee benefit plans do you have excluding those required by law?

			Contributed by	
			Company	Employee
	Yes	No	%	%
Death	_____	_____	_____	_____
Accident	_____	_____	_____	_____
Sickness	_____	_____	_____	_____
Hospitalization	_____	_____	_____	_____
Pension	_____	_____	_____	_____
Savings	_____	_____	_____	_____
_____	_____	_____	_____	_____
_____	_____	_____	_____	_____

_____

_____

10. *Guaranteed annual income or supplemental unemployment benefits:* Are employees guaranteed an annual income or supplemental unemployment benefits? Yes_____ No_____
If yes, please explain_____

_____

_____

11. *Incentive plan:* What type of incentive plan is in operation? _____

_____

_____

_____

In what operations of the company is a plan currently in effect? Indicate the approximate percentage of makeout.

_____

_____

_____

_____

12. *Vacation policy:* Indicate periods of time.
Service required _____ for annual vacation of _____

_____

_____

13. *Clothing:* What work clothing is furnished employees and how often?

_____

_____

14. *Tools:* What tools are employees expected to furnish? _____

_____

_____

15. *Separation allowance:* Are payments made when service terminates?
                                    Yes_____   No_____
If so, explain_____

16. *Payment for absence:* Are employees paid for

	Yes	No
a. Sick leave	_____	_____
b. Death in family	_____	_____
c. Absence for personal reasons	_____	_____
d. Absence caused by layoff	_____	_____

Where answers are yes, explain policies:

_____

144 Industrial Wage and Salary Control

17. *Lunch periods:* Is employee paid during lunch period?   Yes＿＿   No＿＿
How much time is granted with pay?   ＿＿＿＿＿＿＿＿＿＿＿＿

18. *Clean-up time:* Is employee paid for clean-up time at end of shift?
Yes＿＿＿＿   No＿＿＿＿
How much time is granted with pay?   ＿＿＿＿＿＿＿＿＿＿＿＿

19. *Paid rest periods:* Are employees granted paid rest periods?
Yes＿＿＿＿   No＿＿＿＿
How much time is granted with pay?   ＿＿＿＿＿＿＿＿＿＿＿＿

20. *Union committeemen:* Are Union committeemen paid for time devoted to presenting grievances and attending meetings?   ＿＿＿＿＿＿＿＿＿＿＿

＿＿＿＿＿＿＿＿＿＿＿＿＿＿＿＿＿＿＿＿＿＿＿＿＿＿＿＿＿＿＿＿＿

Additional comments:

Area Wage Rate Survey Sheet
Detail Information
Hourly Employees

Company_____   Date_____

Job Classification	Single Rate or Rate Range	No. Persons on Classification	Approx. Pres. Avg. Rate	For Jobs on Incentive Indicate Approx. Average Earnings	Minor Variations in Job Content

Contact should always be made with the individuals at the company being visited in advance of the time of arrival so that definite arrangements can be made to see the proper personnel. In some instances, companies will be reluctant to release data concerning the number of persons on each job classification. If the plant is relatively large, these figures may not be readily available without considerable computation. Usually, however, there are individuals in the organization who are sufficiently familiar with the rate structure to provide accurate estimates as to the approximate number of persons on the classifications and the approximate average rates. Unless the companies volunteer information, no pressure should be exerted to secure rate information. If it is apparent that they will have to conduct extensive studies at their expense, it is unwise to press them for the information. Before the survey is made, individuals representing the company conducting the survey should have complete information pertaining to its own operations, particularly in regard to the number of individuals and average rates on the classifications being studied. When companies request this information, it should be given to them.

The time required to conduct a survey at a particular plant will vary with the number of jobs which are to be compared and the adequacy of the data available from the company. Normally it takes approximately one hour to complete the general information sheet. To secure complete information for 50 jobs may require from two to three hours. In all instances sufficient time should be allowed in order that personnel at the company being visited will have ample time to read the job descriptions and compare them with jobs performed within their company.

Presentation of Area Wage Rate Survey Information

The presentation of data obtained at the time of an area wage rate survey may be divided into five sections:

1. *Summary and Conclusions.* This section is primarily concerned with a summary of all the data secured at the time of the area wage rate survey. It will point out broad overall significant relationships between the rates and policies of the company conducting the survey and the companies visited.

2. *Presentation of General Information for the Area Surveyed.* This section should summarize in tabular form the general information secured at the time of the survey. Conclusions should be stated

concerning the fringe benefits provided by the companies visited in relation to those provided by the company conducting the study.

3. *Presentation of Wage Rates for Companies Surveyed.* In this section, specific rate information may be presented in tabular form for the classifications included in the survey. Separate tabulations should be made for plants having incentive rates. When a company is conducting the survey prior to the establishment of a new plant in a particular area, comparisons may be made with rates paid by the company at a plant in some other location. A similar operation or the main plant of the company may be selected for comparison purposes.

Example of Weighted Wage Trend Lines for Individual Plants Included in Survey Based upon 50 Typical Jobs

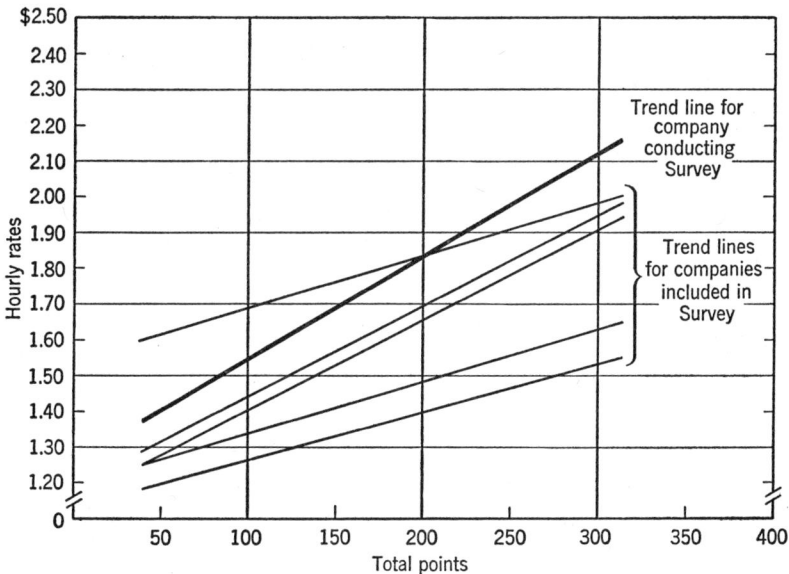

Figure 20

4. *Presentation of Wage Trend Lines.* In order to summarize the specific rate information presented in Section 3, wage trend lines indicating the relationship between total evaluation points (the points may be derived from the evaluation plan being used by the company conducting the survey) and existing wage rates should be computed for each plant. These lines, weighted by the number of persons on each job, may be compared with the wage structure of the company conducting the survey. Figure 20 presents an example of computed

trend lines. Where companies have incentive plans in operation, two trend lines should be computed: one on the basis of guaranteed rates and the other on the basis of estimated actual earnings, including incentive. Consolidated trend lines, including all of the companies surveyed, may be computed to secure an indication of the overall level of payment within the community.

5. *Recommendations Concerning Wage Trend Line and Rates to Be Established Based upon Job Evaluation.* The recommendations made in this section will be based primarily upon an analysis of the data developed during the study. If the area survey is being conducted as the basis for establishing the wage structure for a new plant, specific recommendations should be made concerning the trend line to be established and rates to be paid. If the survey is being conducted preparatory to union negotiations, job rates which should be revised may be indicated. In addition, a table may be presented which will indicate the estimated annual cost of increasing or decreasing rates by fixed amounts. Such a table, which takes into consideration the number of employees on the jobs, is extremely valuable during negotiations.

Specifications covering the jobs surveyed may be presented at the end of the survey for reference purposes.

It is interesting to note that in recent years more and more companies operating in a particular area have agreed to exchange periodically information concerning wages. Sometimes an abbreviated evaluation plan with typical benchmark jobs is used as the basis for such comparisons, with trend lines being computed to indicate the relative wage levels of the companies participating. Resort to this method of conducting wage surveys results in a significant improvement in their accuracy.

In establishing a pay structure, management personnel have been too prone to look at individual rates or average rates from a variety of different companies within the area, whereas it is probably more important for them to be observing overall trend lines. The result is that management personnel have been unable to measure accurately differences in the level of payment within the community or industry. Unions have faced similar problems with the result that negotiations in regard to this particular topic have oftentimes been confused.

It should be pointed out, however, that if a wage structure is being negotiated with a union, it is important that information be available concerning rates paid for specific key jobs in the area. Questions concerning specific rates paid for comparable jobs are almost certain to arise during the negotiations. When incentive plans are prevalent in the area, it is important to consider both base rates and incentive earnings during the course of conducting area rate surveys. Where there are variations in the fringe benefits given by different companies, some evaluation of these differences may be necessary. Oftentimes, accurate cost figures for some of these benefits are not available, thereby contributing to the inaccuracy of the survey.*

Establishment of the Final Wage Trend Line

Final determinations concerning the positioning of the trend line will be dependent upon policies defined by top management. If it is decided to set the trend line below the area rates, it should be recognized that union or employee opposition will undoubtedly be encountered. Setting rates below area rates sometimes results in less-qualified workers applying for employment. If it is decided to set the final trend line so that rates are above area rates, it should be recognized that there may be a competitive disadvantage. If such a policy is adopted, however, the company should make every effort to hire workers who are actually above average in order to compensate for the higher rates paid.

If the company is dominant in a particular area or location, some consideration should be given to smaller local firms and the rates being paid by these companies. Adoption of a wage scale which is out of line with local conditions may lead to a number of problems in community relations. It should be remembered, however, that the local standard of living will be largely dependent upon rates paid by the company. If it is the objective of the company to promote a high standard of living among its workers, it will be necessary to establish a high wage scale.

Establishment of Pay Grades

After establishment of the basic wage trend line, the next step is to establish pay grades. There are no mechanical methods which may be rigidly followed in determining these grades. The increments between grades must be sufficiently large to be meaningful. On the other hand, increments which are too large will have a tendency to bring dissimilar jobs together. The number of pay grades to be used will depend upon the range of jobs being covered. In general, the

* For further information concerning computation of fringe benefit costs see *Studies in Personnel Policy No. 128,* 1952, National Industrial Conference Board, Inc., New York.

wider the range of jobs and the greater the monetary differential between low jobs and high jobs, the larger the number of grades which will be required. A careful review of the entire wage structure is essential in order to reveal jobs which are being grouped as a result of evaluation on the plan and the establishment of pay grades. Historical relationships must be taken into account and the influence of applying different point intervals should be investigated. For example, the application of a uniform 17-point interval between pay grades will result in a structure which groups certain classifications together. An 18-point interval would result in the grouping of somewhat different classifications. For certain wage structures, it may be desirable to adopt point intervals which increase progressively as rates rise. From an administrative standpoint, production type jobs where there is little variation in the work performed should probably be assigned single rates. Jobs where more skill is required are frequently given rate ranges. These ranges should be sufficiently wide to permit the granting of perceptible increases to employees.

Rate ranges may be established in different positions in relation to the trend line. For example, the trend line may bisect the ranges, be at the bottom of the ranges, or be at the top of the ranges. The philosophy of payment, tradition within the industry, and the type of workers involved are some of the factors to be taken into consideration when establishing ranges. In most companies, ranges are usually established to control salary payments. They frequently vary in width from 30% to 40% (15% to 20% on each side of the midpoint), with about 35% recommended. There is more of a tendency in salary structures to establish pay grades with point ranges which increase progressively as they rise.

Preparation of Cost Studies

At the time that administrative controls are established, it will be necessary to prepare a complete cost study covering the various plants and operations as well as a consolidated cost study covering the entire company. Such a cost study requires careful planning, since it is necessary to secure accurate population counts on the various classifications. These population counts can usually be obtained through tabulating lists, manpower rosters, payroll lists, contacts with production supervision, or actual on-the-job observations. Insofar as possible, the cost study should be conducted simultaneously in all locations in order that the figures will be secured at approximately the same time. The cost study should be prepared in such a manner

Summary Sheet*

Cost Analysis for _____
(Plant or operation)

	Per hour	Per month	Per year
A. *Estimated straight-time earnings excluding leaders, machine setters, and utility men:*			
Estimated present average rate per hour A-13b for A-12a persons.	A-13a	A-14a	A-14b
B. *Estimated immediate cost of installing job evaluation:*			
1. Estimated immediate cost to raise all employees on single-rate jobs which are below the standard rate to the standard rate.	B-1f	B-1g	B-1h
2. Estimated immediate cost to raise all employees on jobs with a rate range to same relative position in evaluated ranges as they now have in present ranges.	B-2i	B-2j	B-2k
3. Estimated immediate cost of installation.	B-3a	B-3b	B-3c
4. Estimated cost immediately after installation excluding leaders, machine setters, and utility men.	B-4a	B-4b	B-4c
Estimated average rate per hour B-4d for A-12a persons.			
C. *Estimated long-range cost after installation of job evaluation:*			
1. Estimated reduction in payroll as a result of turnover and upgrading, assuming all persons above the standard rate are lowered to the standard rate (single-rate jobs only).	C-1f	C-1g	C-1h
2. Estimated reduction in payrolls as a result of reducing† all persons on jobs with rate ranges to same relative position in evaluated range as they now have in present ranges.	C-2i	C-2j	C-2k
3. Total estimated long-range reduction in payroll.	C-3a	C-3b	C-3c
4. Estimated net future payroll after initial cost of installation and long-range savings.	C-4a	C-4b	C-4c
Estimated average rate per hour C-4d for A-12a persons.			

*Code numbers on this summary sheet refer to the detail sheets on the following pages.
†Reductions may be accomplished through normal turnover and do not refer to reductions in individual rates.

Cost Analysis Detail Sheet

_____
(Plant or operation)

A. *Estimated straight-time earnings, excluding leaders, machine setters, and utility men.*

1. Payroll by months*	2. Total straight-time earnings	3. Actual hours worked	4. Average rate $\dfrac{\text{Col. 2}}{\text{Col. 3}}$	5. Average weekly employment
Year____				
January				
February				
March				
April				
May				
June				
July				
August				
September				
October				
November				
December				

Year ——

January	
February	
March	
April	
May	
June	
July	
August	

Totals

A-2a   A-3a   A-5a

*A period of 20 months is illustrated here for cost-estimating purposes. Other suitable periods may also be used.

Calculations to obtain estimated straight-time earnings, excluding leaders, machine setters, and utility men.

Description of data	Obtain data described as follows:					Code number assigned
	Add	Subtract	Multiply	Divide	Other source	
Total straight-time earnings	Column A-2					A-2a
Total actual hours worked	Column A-3					A-3a
Total of average weekly employment	Column A-5					A-5a
Average hourly rate				A-2a by A-3a		A-6a
Average employment per month				A-5a by 20 months in sample		A-7a
Cost of operating per hour			A-6a by A-7a			A-7b
Average actual hours worked per month				A-3a by 20 months in sample		A-8a
Average straight-time earnings per month				A-2a by 20 months in sample		A-9a
Annual straight-time earnings			A-9a by 12 months per year			A-10a

Number of leaders, machine setters, and utility men				Personnel records	A-11a
Average hourly rate, leaders, machine setters, and utility men				Personnel records	A-11b
Cost of operation per hour, leaders, machine setters, and utility men		A-11a by A-11b			A-11c
Average hours worked by leaders, machine setters, and utility men per month*		A-11a by A-8a	Divide result by A-7a		A-11d
Actual hours worked per month by personnel excluding leaders, machine setters, and utility men	A-11d from A-8a				A-11e
Number of persons excluding leaders, machine setters, and utility men	A-11a from A-7a				A-12a
Average hours worked per person per month excluding leaders, machine setters, and utility men			A-11e by A-12a		A-12b
Straight-time earnings per hour excluding leaders, machine setters, and utility men	A-11c from A-7b				A-13a
Average rate excluding leaders, machine setters, and utility men			A-13a by A-12a		A-13b
Straight-time earnings per month excluding leaders, machine setters, and utility men		A-13a by A-12b			A-14a
Straight-time earnings per year excluding leaders, machine setters, and utility men		A-14a by 12 months per year			A-14b

*Assumes that the hours worked by this group to the total hours worked by all employees is in the same ratio as the number of employees in the group to the total employment.

B. *Estimated immediate cost of installing job evaluation.*

1. Estimated immediate cost to raise all employees on single-rate jobs which are below the standard rate to the standard rate.*

(a) Standard hourly rate	(b) No. persons below standard rate	(c) No. persons (Col. b) × Standard hourly rate (Col. a)	(d) No. persons (Col. b) × Present rates	(e) Immediate cost of installation (Col. c − Col. d)
$1.32				
1.37				
1.42				
1.47				
1.52				
1.57				
1.62				
1.67				
1.72				
1.77				
1.82				
1.87				
1.92				

1.97

2.02

2.07

2.12

2.17

2.22

2.27

2.32

2.37

Total cost per hour _____ B-1f

Cost per month   B-1f × A-12b =   _____ B-1g

Cost per year   B-1g × 12 months per year =   _____ B-1h

*Basic figures for this sheet may be secured from the Cost Study by Pay Grade, Figure 21.

2. Estimated immediate cost to raise all employees on jobs with a rate range to same relative position in evaluated ranges as they now have in present ranges.

(a) Present range		(b) Pres. avg. rate	(c) % Relation of avg. to max. of range $\left(\dfrac{\text{Col. b}}{\text{Col. a2}} = \%\right)$	(d) Evaluated range		(e) Estimated new average rate (Col. d2 × Col. c)	(f) Difference in avg. rates (Col. e − Col. b)	(g) Number persons	(h) Estimated cost difference × No. persons (Col. f × Col. g)
(1) Min.	(2) Max.			(1) Min.	(2) Max.				

Total cost per hour B-2i

Cost per month B-2i × A-12b = ... B-2j

Cost per year B-2j × 12 months per year = ... B-2k

3. Estimated immediate cost of installation.

(a) Per hour
B-1f + B-2i = B-3a

(b) Per month
B-3a × A-12b = B-3b

(c) Per year
B-3b × 12 months per year = B-3c

4. Estimated cost immediately after installation, excluding leaders, machine setters, and utility men.

	(a) Per hour	(b) Per month	(c) Per year
Straight-time earnings	A-13a	A-14a	A-14b
Immediate cost of installation	+B-3a	+B-3b	+B-3c
Cost after installation	B-4a	B-4b	B-4c
Estimated average rate per hour	B-4a ÷ A-12a = ...		

C. *Estimated long-range cost after installation of job evaluation.*

1. Estimated reduction in payroll as a result of turnover and upgrading, assuming all persons above the standard rate are lowered to the standard rate (single-rate jobs only).*

(a) Standard hourly rate	(b) No. persons above standard rate	(c) No. persons × Standard hourly rate (Col. b × Col. a)	(d) No. persons (Col. b) × Present hourly rate	(e) Estimated eventual reduction in cost as a result of installation (Col. d − Col. c)
$1.32				
1.37				
1.42				
1.47				
1.52				
1.57				
1.62				
1.67				
1.72				
1.77				
1.82				

*Basic figures for this sheet may be secured from the Cost Study by Pay Grade, Figure 21.

	(a)	(b)	(c)	(d)	(e)
1.87					
1.92					
1.97					
2.02					
2.07					
2.12					
2.17					
2.22					
2.27					
2.32					
2.37					

Total cost per hour _____ C-1f

Cost per month   C-1f $\times$ A-12b = _____ C-1g

Cost per year   C-1g $\times$ 12 months per year = _____ C-1h

2. Estimated reduction in payrolls as a result of reducing all employees (through turnover) on rate range jobs to same relative position in evaluated ranges as they now have in present ranges.

(a) Present range		(b) Pres. avg. rate	(c) % Relation of avg. to max. of range $\left(\dfrac{\text{Col. b}}{\text{Col. a2}} = \%\right)$	(d) Evaluated range		(e) Estimated new average rate (Col. d2 × Col. c)	(f) Difference in avg. rates (Col. b − Col. e)	(g) Number persons	(h) Estimated cost difference × No. persons (Col. f × Col. g)
(1) Min.	(2) Max.			(1) Min.	(2) Max.				

Total cost per hour ———— C-2i

Cost per month C-2i × A-12b = ———— C-2j

Cost per year C-2j × 12 months per year = ———— C-2k

3. Total estimated long range reduction in payroll.

(a) Per hour
C-1f + C-2i =
C-3a

(b) Per month
C-3a × A-12b =
C-3b

(c) Per year
C-3b × 12 months per year =
C-3c

4. Estimated net future payroll after cost of installation and long-range savings.

	(a) Per hour	(b) Per month	(c) Per year
Cost after installation	B-4a	B-4b	B-4c
Long-range decrease in cost	− C-3a	− C-3b	− C-3c
Estimated long-range cost	C-4a	C-4b	C-4c

Estimated average rate per hour   C-4a ÷ A-12a = ———— C-4d

that the basic work sheets will be flexible in nature. The basic information required to calculate the cost of installing a job analysis and evaluation program may be derived from the work sheet presented in Figure 21. In a large company, information entered on this form should be prepared by tabulating machines. The form provides for the calculation by pay grade of the number of employees and hourly cost for personnel below, on, or above the evaluated rate. The form may be expanded either horizontally or vertically, depending upon the existing job rates on classifications evaluating in the pay grade and the point width of the pay grade. The sample personnel and cost figures entered in the form for demonstration purposes indicate the speed with which the number of hourly employees and the hourly cost can be derived under different conditions. If the plan is being negotiated with a union, this flexibility will permit rapid calculation of cost differences as a result of changes at the time of negotiations. A summary sheet and detailed work sheets to develop cost information for the installation of an hourly evaluation plan are presented on pages 151 to 161. These forms assume that leaders, machine setters, and utility men are not included in the evaluation program and that separate cost records for this group do not exist. Similar forms may also be developed to indicate the cost of installing a salary evaluation plan.

It will usually be found that unless substantial inequities exist, only a few cents per hour for each employee will be required to raise the wages of personnel being paid below standard to the standard rates (raising all jobs below the trend line to the line). In most instances, the amount will be under 2% or 3% of the average base hourly rate. Since most salaried personnel are paid within salaried ranges, introduction of a job analysis and evaluation program can proceed gradually, without necessitating immediate increases. Where the salaries of personnel are below the ranges being established, consideration should be given to raising such salaries to the minimums of their respective grades. In most instances, this group constitutes a minor portion of the salaried work force.

Upon completion of the cost study, the results should be presented graphically to management. It is important that management be acquainted with the overall wage structure as well as detailed information concerning the influence of the program on each plant or operation. For example, Figure 22 is one method of presenting the overall wage structure resulting from introduction of job analysis and evaluation. A similar chart (Figure 23) may be used to indicate the influence of the program on each major organizational unit.

Cost Study by Pay Grade — Job Analysis and Evaluation Program

Pay Grade 8
Date

Points	No. Employees Cumulative ↓	↑	No. Employees and Hourly Cost below Evaluated Rate						No. Employees and Hourly Cost on Evaluated Rate		No. Employees and Hourly Cost above Evaluated Rate							Hourly Cost Cumulative ↑	↓
Rates →			Below 1.61	1.61	1.62	1.63	1.64	1.65	1.66	1.67	1.68	1.69	1.70	1.71	1.72	1.73	Above 1.73		
→					2			7		9			13		16				
←					16			14		9			7		3				
138																			
139																			
140	2	16			2 3.24													26.79	3.24
141	4	14								2 3.34								23.55	6.58
142																			
143																			
144																			
145																			
146	8	12											4 6.80					20.21	13.38
147																			
148																			
149																			
150	13	8						5 8.25										13.41	21.63
151																			
152	16	3													3 5.16			5.16	26.79
153																			
154																			
Hourly Cost Cumulative →					3.24			11.49		14.83			21.63		26.79				
Hourly Cost Cumulative ←					26.79			23.55		15.30			11.96		5.16				

Figure 21

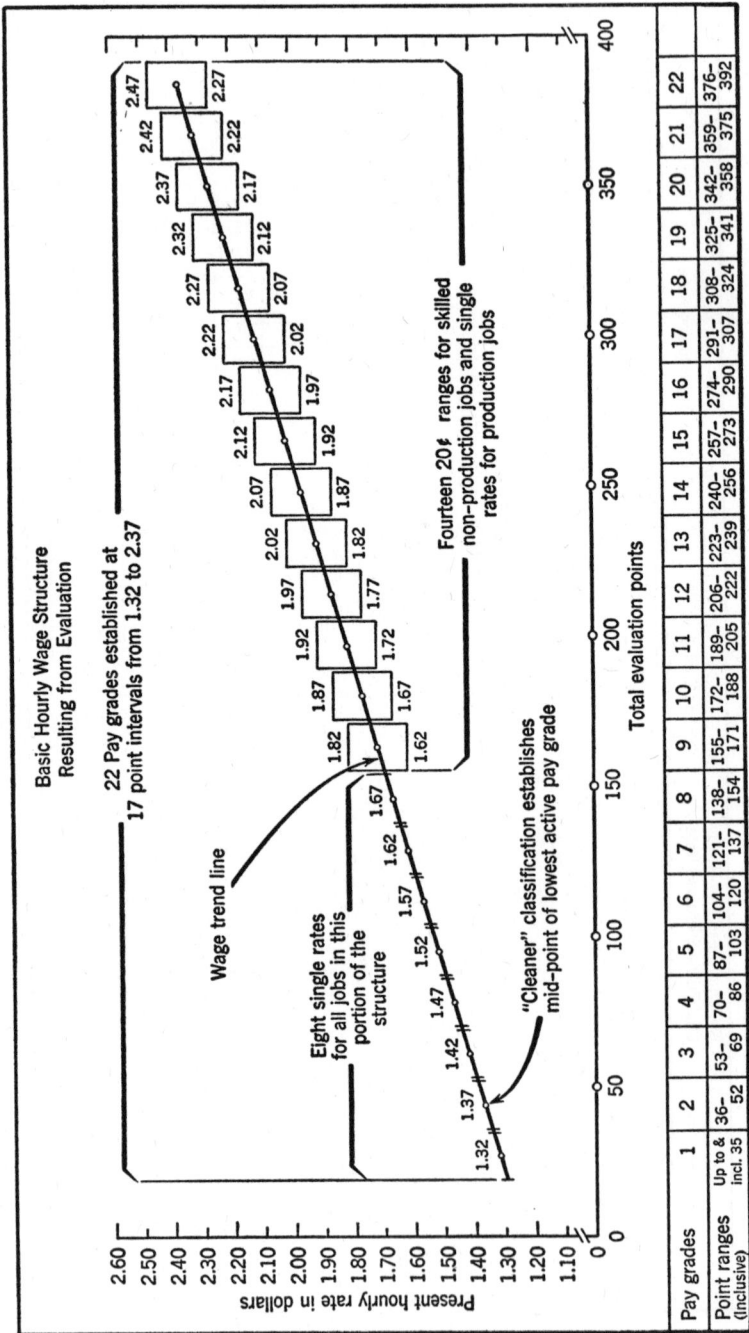

Figure 22

Basic Hourly Wage Structure
Resulting from Evaluation

22 Pay grades established at
17 point intervals from 1.32 to 2.37

Wage trend line

Eight single rates
for all jobs in this
portion of the
structure

"Cleaner" classification establishes
mid-point of lowest active pay grade

Fourteen 20¢ ranges for skilled
non-production jobs and single
rates for production jobs

Present hourly rate in dollars

Total evaluation points

Pay grades	1	2	3	4	5	6	7	8	9	10	11	12	13	14	15	16	17	18	19	20	21	22
Point ranges (inclusive)	Up to & incl. 35	36– 52	53– 69	70– 86	87– 103	104– 120	121– 137	138– 154	155– 171	172– 188	189– 205	206– 222	223– 239	240– 256	257– 273	274– 290	291– 307	308– 324	325– 341	342– 358	359– 375	376– 392

These charts would include wage trend lines for each operation, supplemented by the detailed analysis, mentioned above, indicating the cost of installation. Estimates may also be made concerning the gradual reduction in payroll costs by years, assuming turnover and upgrading percentages based upon experience (see page 167). The width or uniformity of pay grades and ranges in Figures 22 and 23 should not necessarily be considered as examples to be followed when introducing an evaluation plan. As was pointed out earlier in this chapter, numerous factors must be taken into account when establishing these controls, and no uniform system exists which can be applied with equal success in all companies.

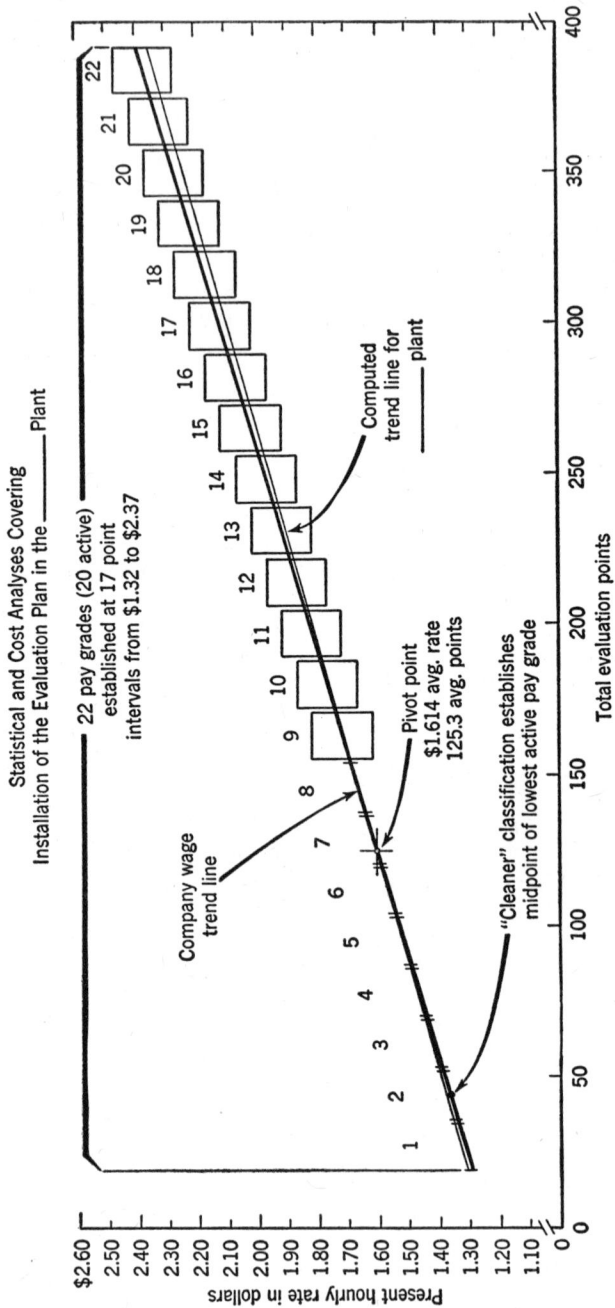

Statistical and Cost Analyses Covering
Installation of the Evaluation Plan in the———Plant

22 pay grades (20 active)
established at 17 point
intervals from $1.32 to $2.37

Computed
trend line for
———plant

Company wage
trend line

Pivot point
$1.614 avg. rate
125.3 avg. points

"Cleaner" classification establishes
midpoint of lowest active pay grade

Present hourly rate in dollars

$2.60
2.50
2.40
2.30
2.20
2.10
2.00
2.00
1.90
1.80
1.70
1.60
1.50
1.40
1.30
1.20
1.10

Total evaluation points

0 50 100 150 200 250 300 350 400

Figure 23

Cost Analysis for _____
(plant or operation)

	Per Hour	Per Month	Per Year
A. *Estimated straight-time earnings excluding leaders, machine setters, and utility men.*			
Estimated present average rate per hour $1.6366 for 3602 persons.	$5,895.077	$1,012,077.43	$12,144,929.16
B. *Estimated immediate cost of installing job evaluation.*			
1. Estimated immediate cost to raise all single-rate jobs which are below the standard rate to the standard rate.	57.949	9,948.79	119,385.48
2. Estimated immediate cost to raise all employees on jobs with a rate range to same relative position in evaluated ranges as they now have in present ranges.	10.508	1,804.03	21,648.36
3. Estimated immediate cost of installation.	68.457	11,752.82	141,033.84
4. Estimated cost immedately after installation excluding leaders, machine setters, and utility men.	5,963.534	1,023,830.25	12,285,963.00
Estimated average rate per hour $1.6556 for 3602 persons.			
C. *Estimated long-range cost after installation of job evaluation.*			
1. Estimated reduction in payroll as a result of turnover and upgrading, assuming all persons above the standard rate are lowered to the standard rate (single-rate jobs only).	94.171	16,167.45	194,009.40
2. Estimated reduction in payrolls as a result of reducing all persons on jobs with rate ranges to same relative position in evaluated range as they now have in present ranges.	.726	124.64	1,495.68
3. Total estimated long range reduction in payroll.	94.897	16,292.09	195,505.08
4. Estimated net future payroll after initial cost of installation and long-range savings.	5,868.637	1,007,538.16	12,090,457.92
Estimated average rate per hour $1.6293 for 3602 persons.			

D. *Estimated gradual reduction in payroll by years assuming turnover and upgrading of 25% per year up to range classifications and 10% per year in range classifications.*

Years After Installation	Est. Annual Payroll Beginning of Year	Reduction During Year	Est. Annual Payroll End of Year	Est. Average Rate End of Year
1	$12,285,963.00	$47,623.20	$12,238,339.80	$1.6492
2	12,238,339.80	35,841.00	12,202,498.80	1.6444
3	12,202,498.80	26,994.60	12,175,504.20	1.6407
4	12,175,504.20	20,346.36	12,155,157.84	1.6380
5	12,155,157.84	15,373.08	12,139,784.76	1.6359

8

Installation of the New
Job Classification System

Summarizing and Presenting Results of the Program

Installation of the new job classification system represents one of the most important phases of a job analysis and evaluation program. It is essential that top management personnel, supervisors, union representatives, and employees be acquainted with the results of the studies which have been conducted.

During the period when the job analysis and evaluation program is in process, periodic progress reports relating to individual analysts and the program in different areas of the company should be presented to top management. As the program nears completion, management personnel will be interested in:

1. A progress report indicating the number of jobs analyzed, jobs evaluated, and job specifications written. The number of persons assigned to the program and the cost of developing the new system should also be presented.

2. A summary of the steps taken during the job analysis and evaluation program, including a description of the existing wage structure, the influence of the new job classification system on the existing structure, and the cost of installing the program.

Presentation of Progress Report and Development Costs

The progress report summarizing the program may include a graphic presentation of the three major types of activity: job analysis, job evaluation, and the preparation of specifications (see Figure 24). A chart (see Figure 25) may also be presented to summarize the manpower and expense devoted to the program. In addition to the graphic presentation, a brief description of some of the highlights of the program as well as other pertinent data should be presented to top management.

Progress of Analysis, Evaluation, and
Specification Phases of Job Analysis
and Evaluation Program

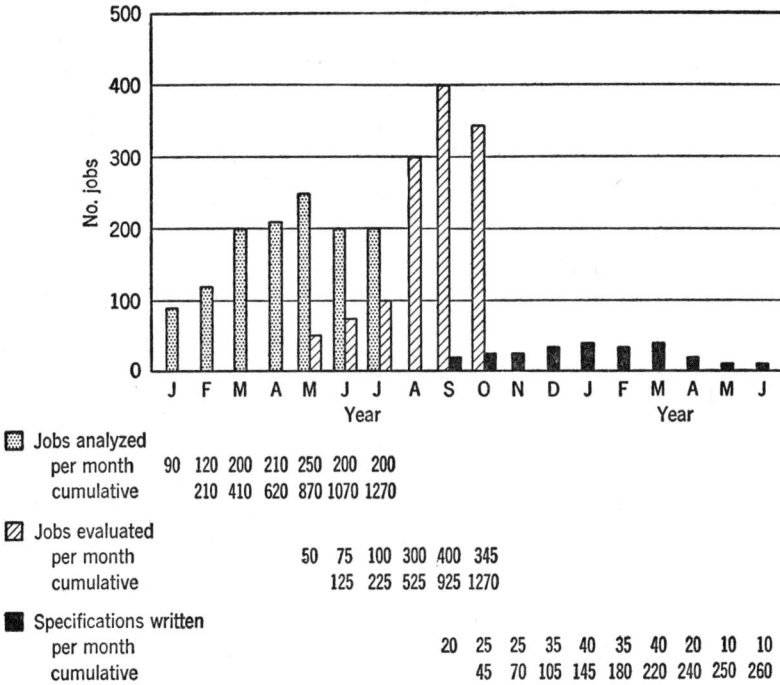

	Jobs analyzed										
per month	90	120	200	210	250	200	200				
cumulative		210	410	620	870	1070	1270				

	Jobs evaluated						
per month	50	75	100	300	400	345
cumulative	125	225	525	925	1270	

	Specifications written									
per month	20	25	25	35	40	35	40	20	10	10
cumulative	45	70	105	145	180	220	240	250	260	

Figure 24

Sample Management Presentation Summarizing Program

Summarizing the results of the entire job classification program is undoubtedly one of the most significant phases of the entire study. Careful consideration should be given to the development of graphic information which may be presented by means of slides, strip film, visual cast, or with the aid of large charts. Normally, a presentation of this nature should not take more than twenty-five or thirty minutes. New charts or graphs should be presented on the average of at least one per minute. In many instances, the backgrounds of the management personnel to whom the presentation is being made will determine the nature of the information to be presented. A question and answer period following the presentation can serve as a means of providing any detailed data which might be requested.

The first slide should indicate the title of the presentation, such

Manpower and Expense Devoted to Job Analysis and Evaluation Program

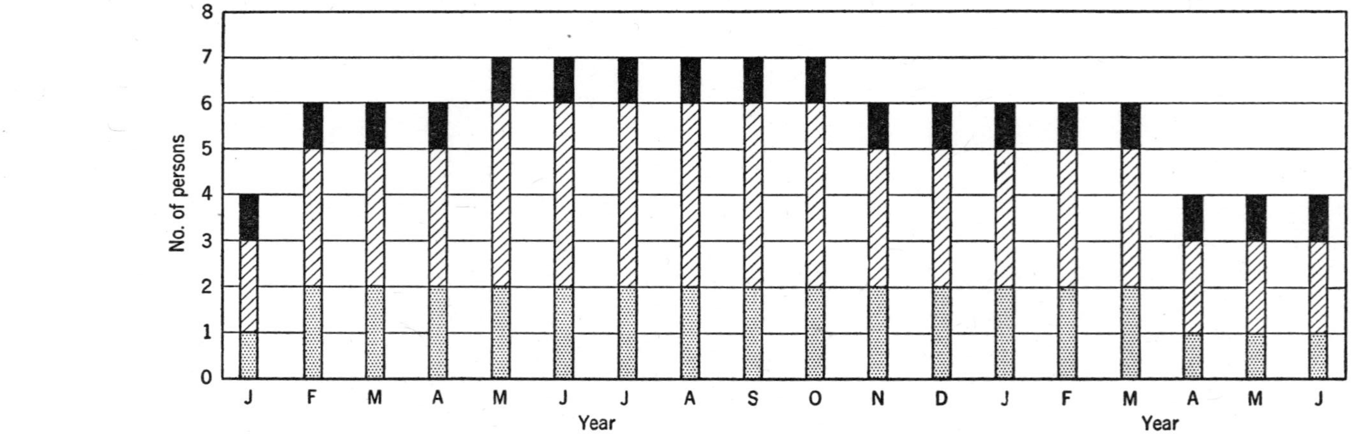

	J	F	M	A	M	J	J	A	S	O	N	D	J	F	M	A	M	J
No. supervisors	1	1	1	1	1	1	1	1	1	1	1	1	1	1	1	1	1	1
No. analysts	2	3	3	3	4	4	4	4	4	4	3	3	3	3	3	2	2	2
No. clerical	1	2	2	2	2	2	2	2	2	2	2	2	2	2	2	1	1	1
Payroll ($)	1700	2300	2300	2300	2800	2800	2900	2900	2900	2900	2500	2500	2500	2500	2500	1800	1800	1800
Other* expense ($)	100	100	100	200	200	200	200	200	100	100	100	100	100	100	100	100	200	200
Total expense ($)	1800	2400	2400	2500	3000	3000	3100	3100	3000	3000	2600	2600	2600	2600	2600	1900	2000	2000
Total expense cumulative ($)		4200	6600	9100	12100	15100	18200	21300	24300	27300	29900	32500	35100	37700	40300	42200	44200	46200

*Miscellaneous supplies, not including heat, light, space, and other similar overhead expenses.

Figure 25

as Job Classification Program or Job Analysis and Evaluation Program and the organizational unit responsible for conducting the study. The text might start as follows:

> For several years, we have been aware of our need for written job descriptions and a systematic method of establishing hourly rate differentials within and between the company's various operations. This report reviews the background of wage payment within the company, the progress of the job analysis and evaluation program, the proposed company wage structure, and the cost of installing the plan.

If the company where the study has been conducted is large, it may be advisable to devote the next several slides to a brief history of the company's rate and classification structure. For example, if the structure was established through negotiation with the union, slides might be developed on the procedure used at that time, the companies selected for comparison purposes, and important characteristics of the wage structure or the wage provision as stated in the contract. Any area differentials which existed between plants located in different geographical areas should be summarized. Employee and union reactions at the time the wage schedule was introduced may also be discussed.

Another slide might summarize the rate changes or revisions in wage payments which have taken place since the structure was established. If several general increases have been given, these should be indicated. Any influence which War Labor Board decisions have had upon the wage structure should be explained. If several general increases have been granted to all classifications, it may be well to point out the influence of such increases on unskilled, semi-skilled, and skilled classifications. It is important to recognize these changing relationships within the wage structure from the standpoint of long-range administrative policies.

After presenting several slides pertaining to the history of rates within the company, the existing wage structure should be reviewed in greater detail. Many companies, for example, have both single rates and rate ranges within their pay structures. In general, single rates are applied to unskilled production classifications or to jobs subject to incentive payments. Rate ranges are oftentimes applied to skilled or non-production classifications.

A slide may be presented concerning the company's single-rate structure, indicating the number of different single rates and the differences between these rates (see Figure 26).

A similar chart may be developed for the different rate ranges (see Figure 27).

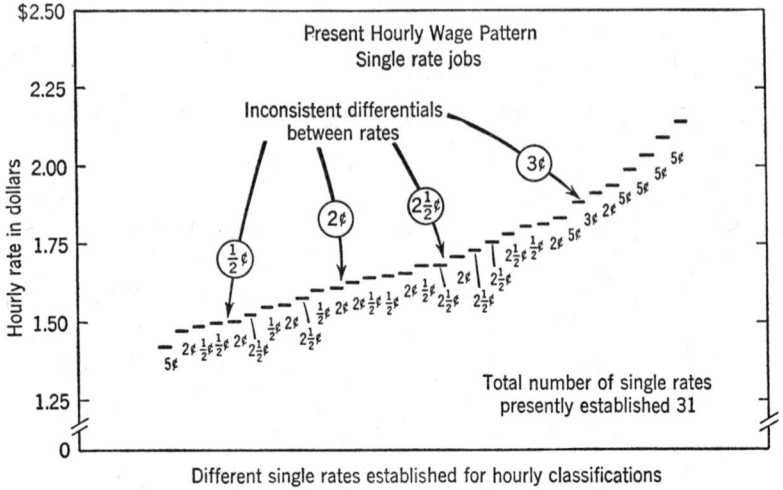

Figure 26

At the time that new wage structures are established, there is usually a consistent interval, such as five cents, between rates. Over a period of years, numerous forces act to destroy this uniformity. The tendency is to establish rates at levels in between the uniform

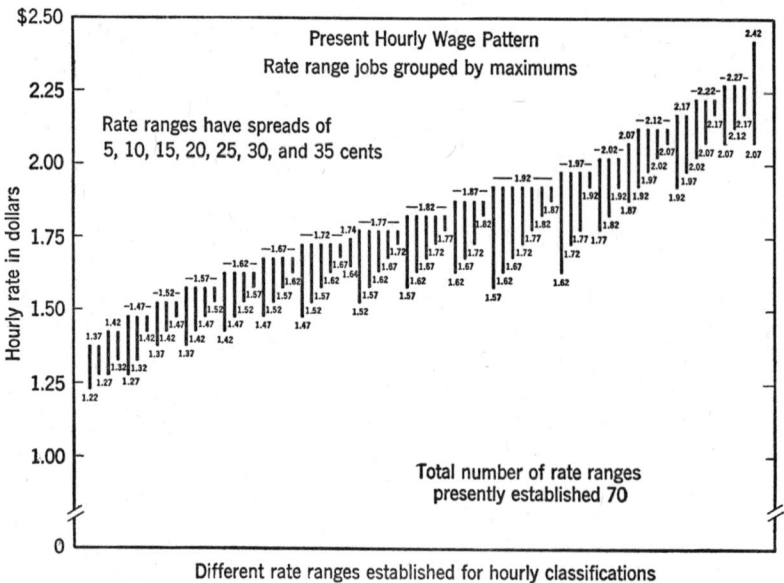

Figure 27

intervals. When the differences between two classifications become as small as half a cent, management is, in effect, saying that one job is worth four cents a day more than the other. From a practical standpoint, it is impossible to determine rates on different jobs with this degree of accuracy.

After presenting certain broad characteristics of the wage structure, information may be presented concerning conditions which lead to administrative problems or inconsistencies within the wage struc-

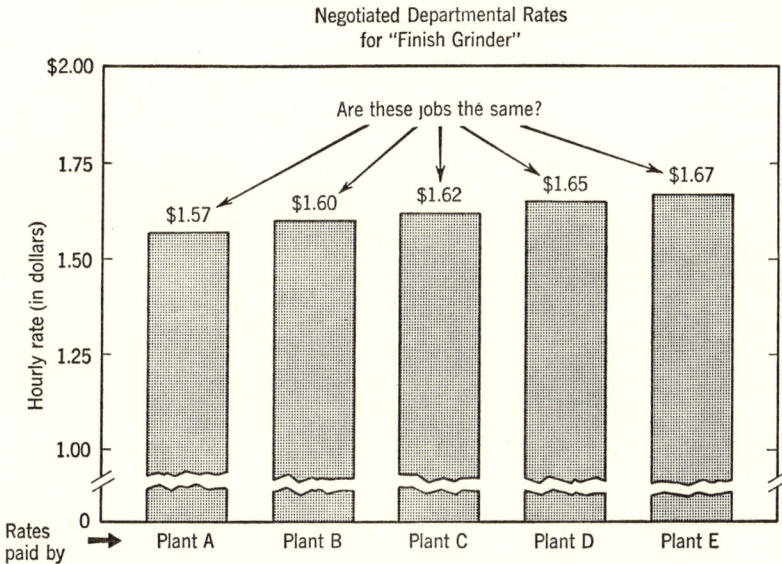

Figure 28

ture. For example, there may be instances where jobs with the same title but different rates occur in several operations of the company (see Figure 28).

In many instances, the jobs are probably different, but without job analysis and evaluation there is no systematic basis for establishing the differences. Moreover, the problem of selecting and defending hourly rates for new classifications with similar job content in other plants becomes exceedingly difficult.

The next slide, Figure 29, indicates the lack of consistency in the assignment of some rate ranges and single rates to job classifications.

Inconsistencies in classification assignment owing to lack of job descriptions or other undesirable administrative practices may also be developed for presentation purposes.

After these slides have been shown, it may be advisable to summarize some of the characteristics of the existing wage structure (see Figure 30). The conclusion may be stated that many of these problems result from the lack of job descriptions and a systematic wage determination plan.

Use of Rate Ranges in the Present Wage Structure

In some instances, the assignment of a single rate or a rate range is inconsistent.

Rate ranges have been assigned at all levels of skill. There is no consistent relationship between the skill used and the width of the range.

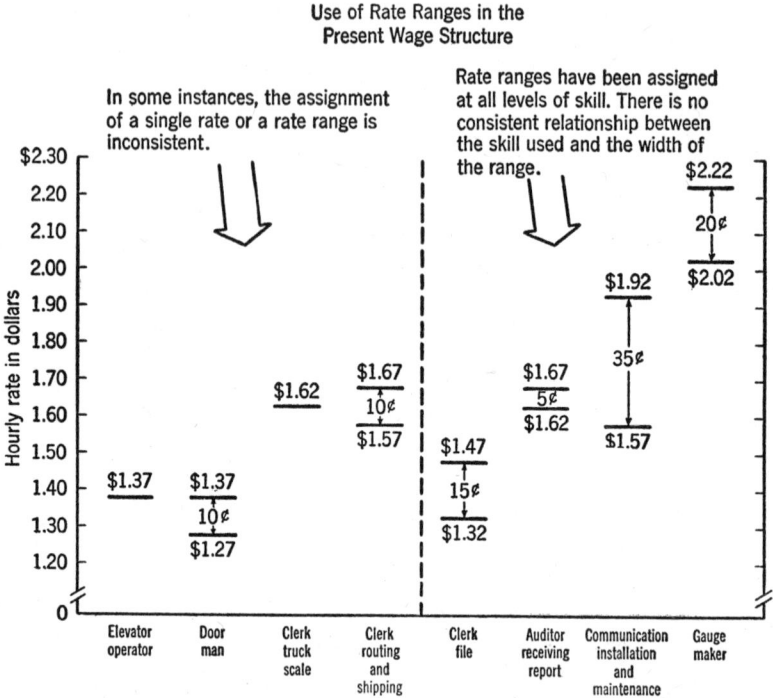

Figure 29

The prime purpose of the slides and text up to this point has been to present a brief history of wage rates within the company and to summarize some of the administrative problems which are being experienced. The next major phase of the presentation should involve a discussion of the significant steps taken during the wage analysis program and the influence which adoption of the program could have on the wage structure. As an initial step in any such program, and in order to obtain firsthand information concerning wage administration policies adopted by other concerns, many companies have their representatives visit other organizations. A slide may be developed to indicate the companies which were visited or the plans which were studied and the basic characteristics of their wage administra-

In Summarizing Our Present Wage Structure . . .

(1) We pay on 101 different single rates and rate ranges.

(2) We have inconsistent differences between rates, varying from $\frac{1}{2}$ cent to 5 cents.

(3) In some instances, jobs with similar characteristics are paid on either single rates or rate ranges.

(4) The width of existing ranges has no definite relationship to job skill.

Figure 30

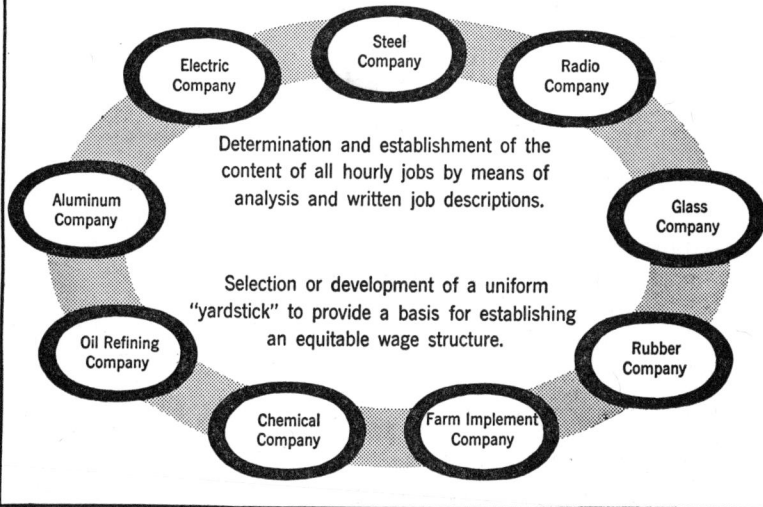

Basic Features of Wage Programs Developed and Installed by Other Companies

Electric Company

Steel Company

Radio Company

Aluminum Company

Glass Company

Oil Refining Company

Rubber Company

Chemical Company

Farm Implement Company

Determination and establishment of the content of all hourly jobs by means of analysis and written job descriptions.

Selection or development of a uniform "yardstick" to provide a basis for establishing an equitable wage structure.

Figure 31

tion programs (see Figure 31). Representatives of companies having job analysis and evaluation programs are usually in agreement that these methods provide the most reliable basis now known for establishing equitable rate relationships and effective administrative controls.

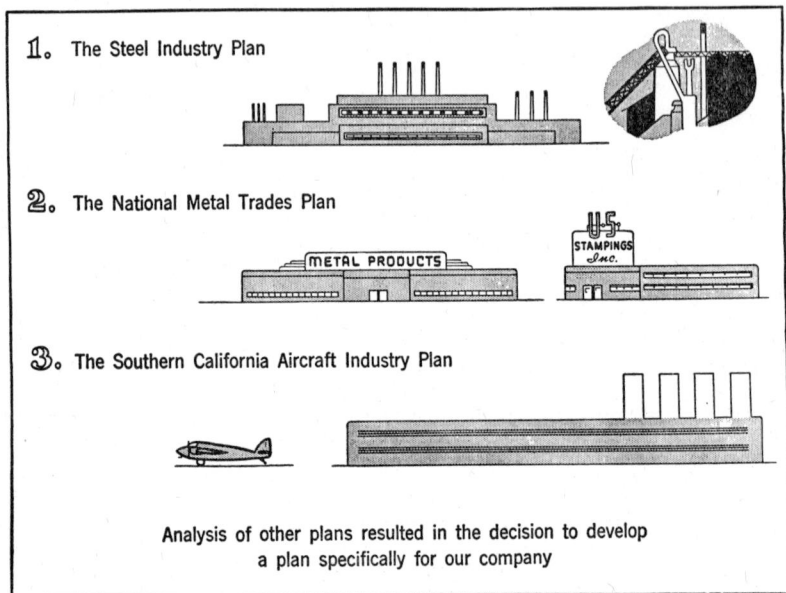

1. The Steel Industry Plan

2. The National Metal Trades Plan

3. The Southern California Aircraft Industry Plan

Analysis of other plans resulted in the decision to develop a plan specifically for our company

Figure 32

As the research progresses, several recognized plans are usually selected for further study (see Figure 32). Oftentimes, the conclusion may be reached, after reviewing plans such as these and their possible influence on the company's structure, that it will be necessary to develop an evaluation plan specifically adapted to the company's own requirements. Development of such an evaluation plan involves:

1. Selection and definition of factors and degrees of factors which will cover the various characteristics of the hourly jobs and at the same time facilitate the evaluation of these jobs on the degrees of the factors.

2. Utilization of appropriate statistical techniques to weight factors and degrees of factors to produce a straight-line structure and eliminate the purely arbitrary effect which weighting of the factors and degrees of the factors has upon the final evaluations of the jobs involved (see Figure 33).

A slide may be developed to indicate the factors which were finally selected for inclusion in the plan.

After selection of factors and development of the evaluation plan, further steps in the program include those on this slide (Figure 34). A slide should be developed to indicate the scope of the job analysis phase of the program (see Figure 35).

It may be pointed out that all jobs which were analyzed were evaluated on the plan which was developed. This slide, Figure 36, provides an opportunity to indicate that each job was evaluated by

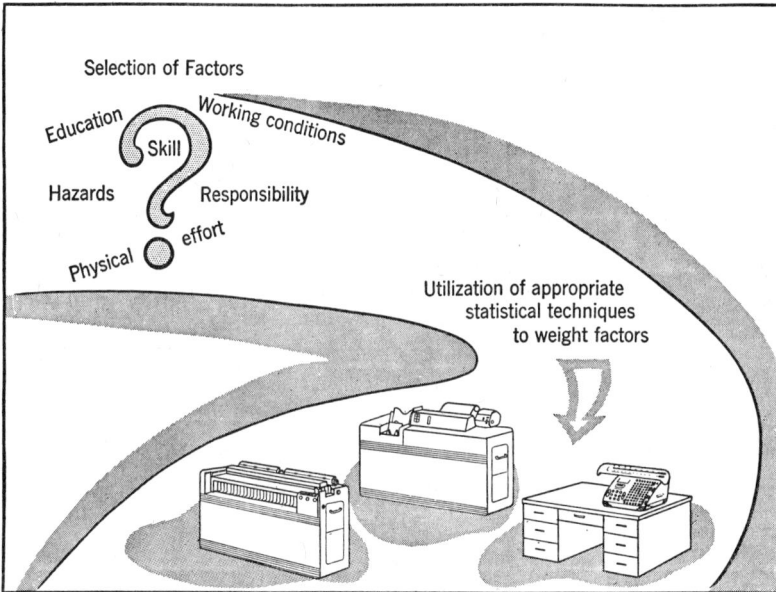

Figure 33

a committee consisting of three or more persons in order to have the benefit of group judgment. Percentage weights based upon the maximum points allowed each factor in the plan may also be indicated.

Questions may arise concerning the clearance of job descriptions with production supervision and steps taken in this connection may be presented (see Figure 37).

In order to present an example of the finished product, a typical job specification may be shown. This slide, Figure 38, shows the front of the specification which gives the job title, the code number, and the job description.

The back of the specification gives substantiating information covering evaluation on the degrees of each factor. Space is provided for evaluation points (see Figure 39).

Basic Steps in the Job Analysis and Evaluation Program

(1) Analysis of job content

(2) Preparation of job descriptions

(3) Clearance with immediate supervision

(4) Evaluation of all jobs

(5) Review and consolidation of job classifications

(6) Preparation of job specifications

(7) Clearance with plant management

Figure 34

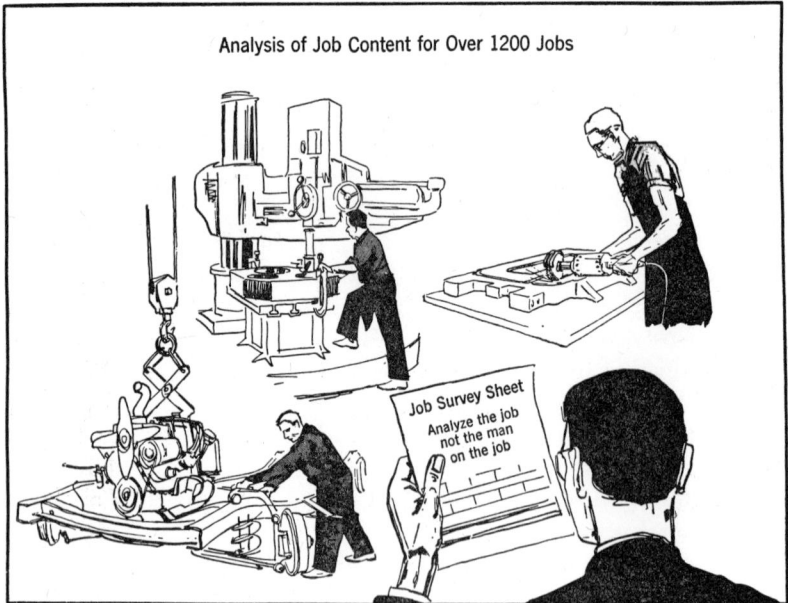

Analysis of Job Content for Over 1200 Jobs

Job Survey Sheet
Analyze the job
not the man
on the job

Figure 35

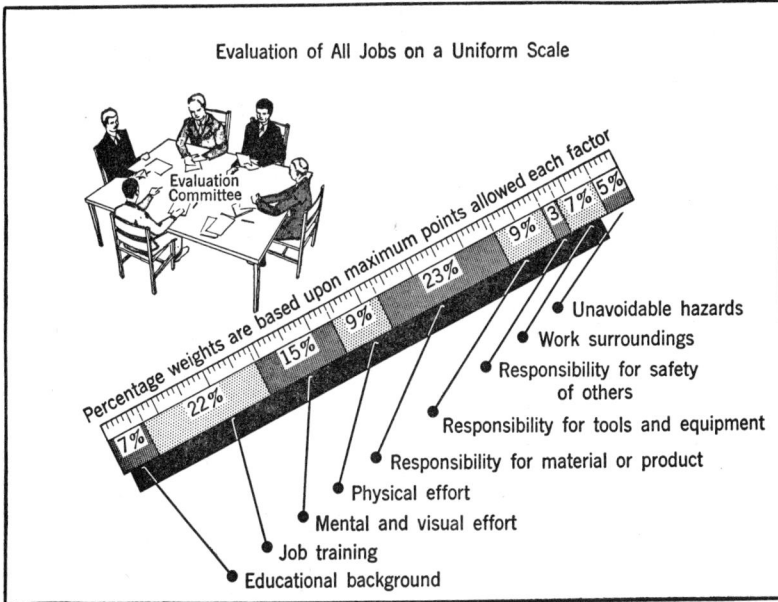

Evaluation of All Jobs on a Uniform Scale

Evaluation Committee

Percentage weights are based upon maximum points allowed each factor

7%
22%
15%
9%
23%
9%
3%
7%
5%

• Unavoidable hazards
• Work surroundings
• Responsibility for safety of others
• Responsibility for tools and equipment
• Responsibility for material or product
• Physical effort
• Mental and visual effort
• Job training
• Educational background

Figure 36

Job Content has been Cleared with Production Supervision

Figure 37

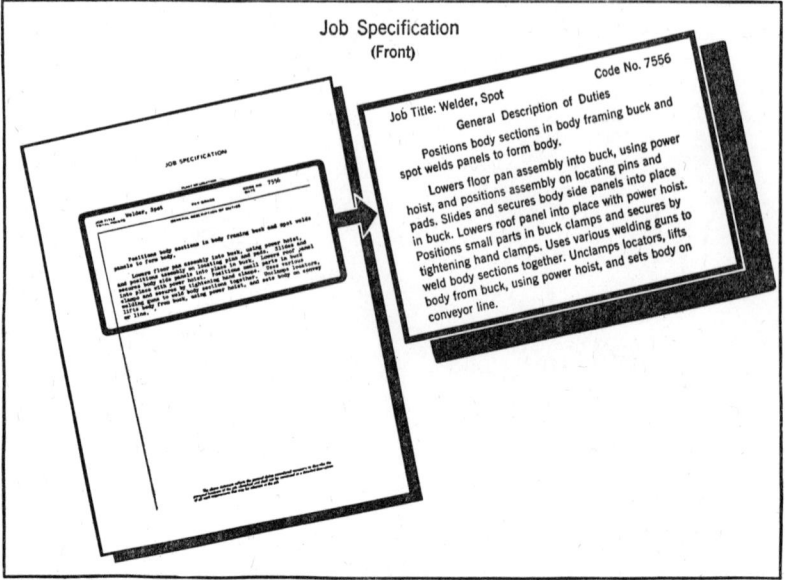

Figure 38

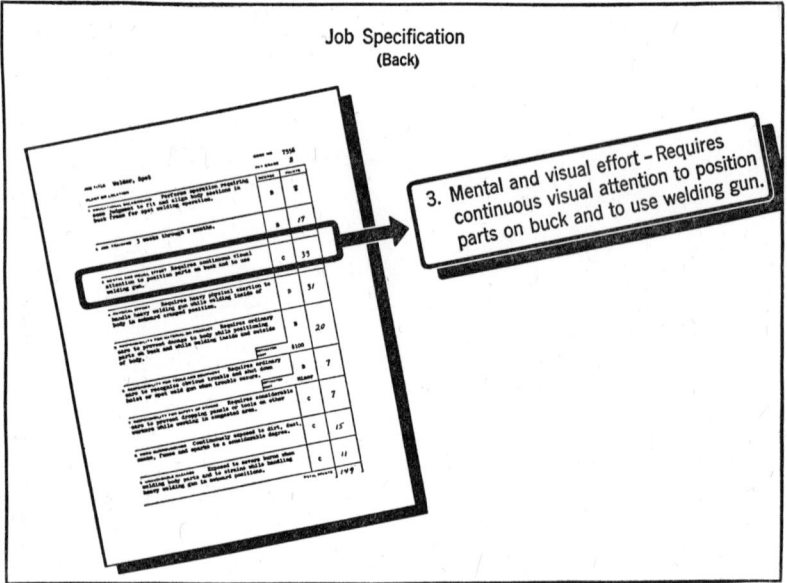

Figure 39

In order to maintain the information which has been developed on a current basis and expedite installation of the program, reference manuals may be developed (see Figure 40).

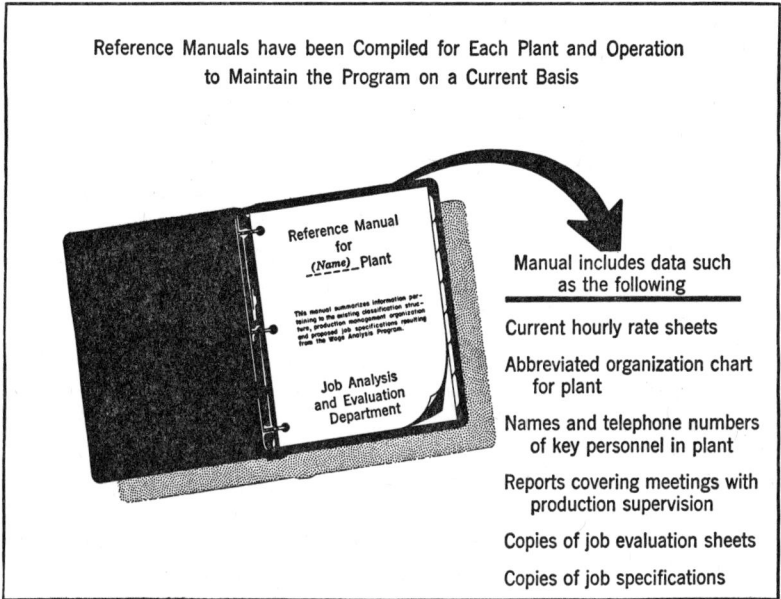

Reference Manuals have been Compiled for Each Plant and Operation to Maintain the Program on a Current Basis

Reference Manual for (Name) Plant

This manual summarizes information pertaining to the existing classification structure, production management organization and proposed job specifications resulting from the Wage Analysis Program.

Job Analysis and Evaluation Department

Manual includes data such as the following

Current hourly rate sheets

Abbreviated organization chart for plant

Names and telephone numbers of key personnel in plant

Reports covering meetings with production supervision

Copies of job evaluation sheets

Copies of job specifications

Figure 40

After summarizing the company's existing wage structure and the scope of the job analysis and evaluation program, information should be developed concerning the influence on the wage structure of introducing the plan within the company. At this stage, it may be well to indicate, by means of an example, how jobs are evaluated (see Figure 41).

After being evaluated, jobs are plotted on a graph having total evaluation points on the horizontal scale and present hourly rates in dollars on the vertical scale. The sample job evaluated above is indicated in Figure 42.

The plotting of all jobs comprises the hourly wage structure resulting from evaluation on the plan. In order to administer this structure, a wage trend line and pay grades must be established. In most instances, the wage trend line is based upon a mathematically computed line of best fit passing through the plotting of evaluated jobs.

In the following slide, Figure 43, the "cleaner" classification establishes the midpoint of the lowest active pay grade where jobs are

Evaluation of Sample Job: "Welder, Spot"

Factors	Job evaluates in following degrees of factors	Points for each factor
1 Educational background	B	8
2. Job training	B	17
3. Mental and visual effort	C	33
4 Physical effort	D	31
5. Responsibility for material or product	B	20
6. Responsibility for tools and equipment	B	7
7. Responsibility for safety of others	C	7
8. Work surroundings	C	15
9. Unavoidable hazards	C	11
	Total points	149

Figure 41

presently evaluated. To administer the structure, 22 pay grades were developed at 17 point intervals. Pay grades increase progressively from $1.32 to $2.37. Listed across the bottom of the chart are the

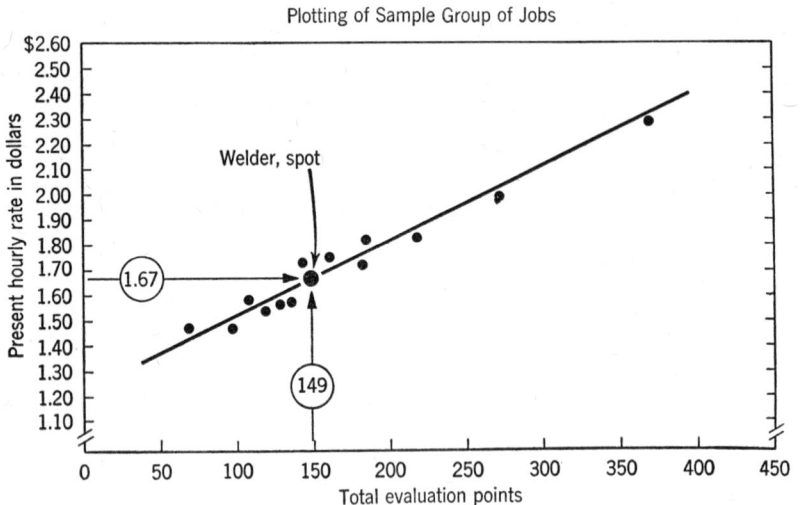

Figure 42

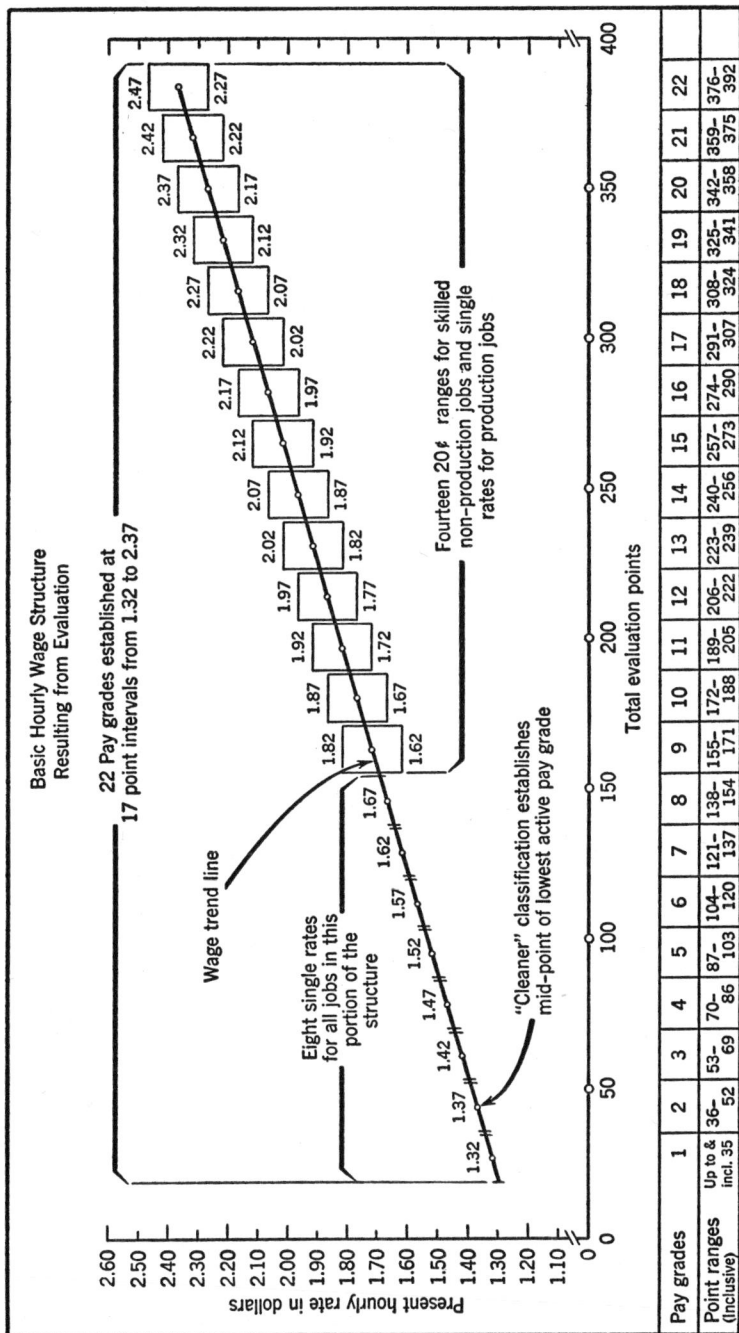

Basic Hourly Wage Structure
Resulting from Evaluation

22 Pay grades established at
17 point intervals from 1.32 to 2.37

Fourteen 20¢ ranges for skilled
non-production jobs and single
rates for production jobs

Wage trend line

Eight single rates
for all jobs in this
portion of the
structure

"Cleaner" classification establishes
mid-point of lowest active pay grade

Present hourly rate in dollars

Total evaluation points

Pay grades	1	2	3	4	5	6	7	8	9	10	11	12	13	14	15	16	17	18	19	20	21	22
Point ranges (Inclusive)	Up to & incl. 35	36– 52	53– 69	70– 86	87– 103	104– 120	121– 137	138– 154	155– 171	172– 188	189– 205	206– 222	223– 239	240– 256	257– 273	274– 290	291– 307	308– 324	325– 341	342– 358	359– 375	376– 392

Figure 43

pay grades and point ranges included in each grade. For example, pay grade 8 includes all jobs evaluated between 138 and 154 points. The evaluated rate for these jobs is $1.67. In the future, new jobs evaluating within this point range would receive the same rate. Superimposed on pay grades 9 through 22 are 14 uniform 20-cent ranges for skilled, non-production classifications. Production jobs falling in this area would receive single rates. Eight single rates have been established for all classifications in the lower portion of the

Characteristics of the New Hourly Wage Program Resulting from Job Evaluation	
1. Simplicity	The number of single rates and rate ranges we pay on will be reduced from 101 to 36.
2. Elimination of internal inequities	Jobs which are the same or very similar will pay the same rate.
3. Elimination of rates ending in $\frac{1}{2}$ cent	Uniform rate schedules will be established with all rates ending in $\frac{1}{2}$ cent eliminated.
4. Basis for elimination of inconsistent ranges	The basis will be established for a uniform system of ranges. Lower level jobs will be paid on single rates.
5. Improved administrative control	Job descriptions will provide a sound basis for accurate classification of hourly personnel. Rates for new jobs will be established uniformly.

Figure 44

structure. Obviously, the wage structure which is finally established within an organization depends to a large extent upon the history of rates within the company and the relationships between classifications after evaluation. It is possible, for example, that rate ranges for non-production jobs with the highest skill might be more than 20 cents. In some companies, single rates might be established for all jobs.

Some of the important characteristics of the hourly wage program resulting from job analysis and evaluation are presented on this slide, Figure 44.

In addition to these basic characteristics, installation of the program will provide other supplementary benefits shown on this slide, Figure 45.

Management is certain to be interested in the cost of installing the program. Estimates should be prepared to summarize the effect on hourly payrolls (see Figure 46). Detailed forms and procedures required to develop this cost study are presented in Chapter 7.

When this type of program is installed, there is universal agreement among authorities in the field of job evaluation that no attempt should be made to reduce rates paid individuals. When their existing rates are above evaluated rates, it is common practice to isolate these

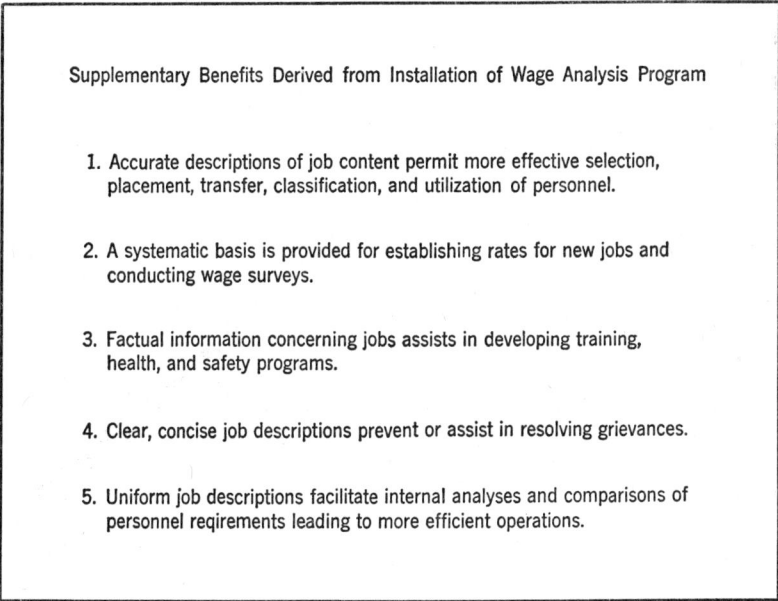

Supplementary Benefits Derived from Installation of Wage Analysis Program

1. Accurate descriptions of job content permit more effective selection, placement, transfer, classification, and utilization of personnel.

2. A systematic basis is provided for establishing rates for new jobs and conducting wage surveys.

3. Factual information concerning jobs assists in developing training, health, and safety programs.

4. Clear, concise job descriptions prevent or assist in resolving grievances.

5. Uniform job descriptions facilitate internal analyses and comparisons of personnel reqirements leading to more efficient operations.

Figure 45

so-called "red circle" jobs and pay the incumbents their present rates as long as they remain on the same job. New employees and persons transferred to these jobs are paid the evaluated rates. Normal turn-over and effective utilization of transfer and promotional opportu-nities tend to eliminate these "red circle" rates over a period of time.

Near the end of the presentation, a few statements such as the following may be included about the necessity for properly maintain-ing the program.

The wage analysis program has been designed to provide an equitable basis for effective long-range administration of hourly rates throughout all company operations. Although the systematic methods which have been developed provide a sound basis for administration, they do not

Estimated Effect on Hourly Payroll of Installing Wage Analysis Program

	Average rate per hour	Annual payroll
1. Straight-time earnings, excluding leaders, machine setters, and utility men (based on period_____through_____).	$1.6376	$3,063,380
2. Immediate increase in hourly payroll as a result of installing wage analysis program.	0.0137	25,750
3. Straight-time earnings immediately after installation of program.	1.6513	3,089,130
4. Long-range decrease in hourly payroll as a result of eliminating "red circle" jobs.	0.0146	27,290
5. Straight-time earnings after all inequities are eliminated.	1.6367	3,061,840

Figure 46

comprise an automatic process which will solve all problems concerning hourly rates. The experience of companies utilizing job evaluation has proved that installation of the program is only the beginning. The primary aim of all job analysis and evaluation plans is equitable assignment of rates to jobs as they exist when they are studied. Regardless of the type of organization in which such a program is installed, jobs do not remain static. Over a period of years, as we build new plants, revise methods, introduce technological changes, and vary the size of our work force, we shall be constantly confronted with changes in job content. Just as we are required to revise our work standards as a result of such changes, it will be equally essential for us to revise our specifications describing the jobs. Effective future administration of the program is certain to involve constant observation and careful management in order to maintain a high performance level.

Recommendations presented at the conclusion of the presentation will be primarily dependent upon conditions existing within the company. If a union is involved, it might be appropriate to recommend discussions with their representatives in order to

1. Review the characteristics of the existing wage structure and promote a better understanding of mutual classification problems.

2. Present results of the wage analysis program as a basis for providing an equitable wage structure.

Information developed for management may be adapted for presentation to other groups within the company. Since first-line supervision will undoubtedly be called upon to answer numerous questions in regard to the job classification program, they should be thoroughly indoctrinated concerning any changes which are contemplated. Where a union is not involved, the company should inform their employees as to the exact nature of the program and the effect it will have upon them. Booklets, employee newspapers, conferences, and other forms of internal communication may be utilized for this purpose.

Union Acceptance of the Program

It is assumed, where a union is involved, that clearance for the study is to be secured before work on the program is begun. As was pointed out in Chapter 2, this clearance should include a statement of the company's plans as far as the analysis is concerned.

When a company experiences difficulty in obtaining union acceptance of the results of a job analysis and evaluation program, it may be advisable to utilize these techniques only in establishing rates for new or changed jobs. Assuming successful negotiation of these evaluated rates, the wage structure which evolves will gradually acquire more and more of the desired characteristics. At some future date complete introduction of the program may be facilitated as a result of a conscientious effort to introduce evaluated rates.

In the past, management has sometimes used job analysis and evaluation as a tool for reducing labor costs. This misapplication of the technique has resulted in considerable skepticism on the part of unions. Actually the objective of any well-developed job analysis and evaluation program should be equitable determination of rates in order that the amount of money allocated for wages may be effectively administered. If a large number of rates are found to be decreasing and a relatively few increasing, it may be that the plan has not been properly developed or that the trend line has not been established in the correct relationship to the rate structure. The results of such a program will, of course, be extremely difficult to sell to any union. Where the reverse is true, the program may be difficult to sell to management.

Whereas job analysis and evaluation do not have as an objective the cutting or the increasing of rates from a long-range standpoint, they do involve an initial expenditure by the company at the time of installation. Although this cost is usually not high in relation to the total payroll, it will sometimes take several years before payrolls again return to the level which existed before installing evaluation. The length of time will depend almost entirely upon the extent of personnel turnover.

Oftentimes companies have adopted a job evaluation program in which they do not have complete confidence. The plan may or may not be suitable for the particular types of jobs being analyzed. Results secured may be somewhat illogical, and numerous rates may shift up or down. Where the entire plan has not undergone thorough study and when company personnel are not completely sold upon the methods used in the development of the plan, questions are certain to arise concerning the weighting of factors and degrees of factors. When a union raises these questions, they will be exceedingly difficult for company representatives to answer on any logical basis. It should be realized by the company that the union is not only interested in the immediate influence which the program will have upon the wage structure but that it is also interested in the long-range effects. Naturally, the union will be primarily concerned with those classifications receiving rate increases or decreases. It should be borne in mind that unions are faced with selling the program to their membership. If the results are not logical they will experience considerable difficulty in securing approval of the program by the rank and file.

One effective way of presenting the program to the union is to show union personnel the effects of the plan upon a group of typical jobs. Many of these typical jobs can be selected from the sample group which formed the basis for the statistical studies. At the same time that these jobs are presented, the characteristics of the plan can be discussed, including the positioning of benchmark jobs on the degrees of the factors. Resort should be made to graphic presentation where it is believed that such methods will promote a better understanding of the problems being discussed.

The important element as far as union personnel are concerned is that they have an adequate basis for judging the probable effects of the program on the company's wage structure. They should be on the alert for area differentials in wage rates. From their standpoint, the extent and nature of these differentials should be analyzed in order that the union may be in a position to bargain for the highest wage level currently paid within the company. Some companies with multiple plant operations have consciously avoided discussing job analysis and evaluation with the union because they are not willing to risk the possibility of having to negotiate the highest level of rates in their organization for all company locations.

Unfortunately, job analysis and evaluation have sometimes been used by management as a device for consciously altering the level of payment without notifying union representatives. Although such action may go unnoticed at the time the program is installed, eventually the workers become aware of the change. If the adjustment made by management is not sanctioned by the union, the entire program may be discredited.

When job evaluation is being discussed with a union, it is advisable to have information available concerning the mathematical techniques used during the development of the plan. Although most union members are usually interested primarily in the results secured, research personnel may be concerned with the basis for weighting factors and degrees of factors. If agreement with the union can be reached about the plan, the benchmark jobs, and the effect which the plan has on the typical jobs, it will then be necessary to reach agreement about the steps to be used in the installation of the program throughout the company. Reference manuals summarizing the results of the program in a specific organizational unit will prove of substantial value in the actual introduction of the revised system within a plant or operation. Since these manuals include information pertaining to the old and new classifications active in a specified area, they will facilitate the completion of individual status change forms.

During the period when the plan is being negotiated, management teams consisting of production supervisors familiar with the job content and job analysts who prepared the descriptions and evaluations should work in conjunction with union personnel. Both union and management personnel should assure themselves that the jobs are being evaluated consistently. At various stages of the discussion with the union it will be necessary to prepare written agreements concerning the wage classification plan and the procedures to be used in the installation of that plan. This process is time consuming, but it is probably the only adequate solution to successful introduction of the program. Even though the process tends to delay installation, it provides both management and the union with a mutual understanding of specific problems relating to classification assignment and rate determination. From the standpoint of future administration, it provides rank and file personnel with information concerning details of the wage plan. As a result of this further understanding, future grievances will, in many cases, be eliminated.

The introduction of job analysis and evaluation plans for salaried personnel is usually preceded by a presentation to top management which summarizes the results of the program. Although the presentation outlined earlier in this chapter pertained to hourly personnel, similar information would also be required for an evaluation plan covering salaried personnel. After the approval of top management has been obtained, supervisors throughout the organization should be acquainted with the new classification system. In many instances, conferences may be held with small groups of supervisors to outline and discuss the program. Questions should be encouraged and individual problems discussed. In large companies, booklets summarizing the new system may be prepared and distributed to all employees. Each supervisor should be sufficiently acquainted with the program to discuss it intelligently with his personnel. At the time of installation, supervisors should be provided with lists of their employees which indicate their old classifications, present salaries, new classifications, new salary ranges, and any adjustments required as a result of the program. Automatic adjustment policies or other policies relating to payment within the ranges should be explained. Oftentimes, the long-range effectiveness of a job evaluation program for salaried personnel is directly related to the confidence of supervisors in the program and their ability to relay their thinking to the employees under them.

If a salaried union is involved, it will be necessary to discuss the program with its representatives. Many of the same considerations mentioned previously in connection with unions representing hourly personnel would also apply to salaried unions.

9

Administration of the Job Classification System

Central Staff and Field Organization to Administer Job Classification Program

In order to administer the job classification system, the central staff office should be made responsible for coordination of the overall program and administration of rates throughout the company. In

Recommended Wage Administration Organization Chart*

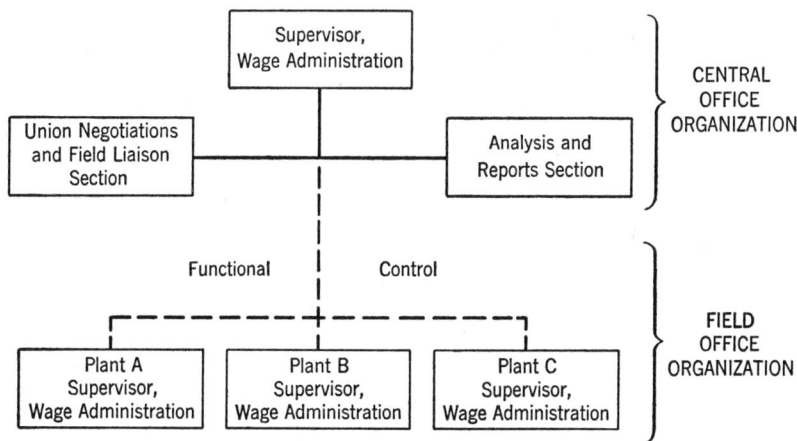

```
                    ┌─────────────────┐
                    │   Supervisor,   │
                    │Wage Administration│          ┐
                    └─────────────────┘           │   CENTRAL
                             │                     │   OFFICE
┌──────────────┐            │      ┌──────────────┐│   ORGANIZATION
│Union Negotiations│        │      │              ││
│and Field Liaison │────────┼──────│ Analysis and ││
│    Section       │        │      │Reports Section││
└──────────────┘            │      └──────────────┘┘
                            │
              Functional    │    Control            ┐
                            │                       │   FIELD
         ┌──────────────────┼──────────────────┐    │   OFFICE
┌────────────┐  ┌────────────┐  ┌────────────┐ │   ORGANIZATION
│  Plant A   │  │  Plant B   │  │  Plant C   │ │
│ Supervisor,│  │ Supervisor,│  │ Supervisor,│ │
│Wage Administration│Wage Administration│Wage Administration│┘
└────────────┘  └────────────┘  └────────────┘
```

*In many organizations, it may be desirable to consolidate wage administration and salary administration functions under one supervisor.

Figure 47

addition, decentralized field offices located in the various plants and operations should be made responsible for administration of the program in their respective areas. Figure 47 presents a recommended organization chart for administration of the program. At the staff

191

level two sections are required, one for union negotiations and field liaison and a second group for analyses and reports concerning wages. Staff personnel will exercise functional control over individuals in the field offices.

The central staff office should be responsible for the development of policies relating to wages, union negotiations, the preparation and maintenance of wage administration and specification manuals, control over records indicating the types of jobs existing within the company and where they are active, and the preparation of various statistical reports and analyses.

Decentralized field offices may be established in the various plants and operations of the company. Such offices are directly concerned with administration of wages in the particular areas over which they have jurisdiction. The decentralized offices may include a supervising analyst and a group of wage and classification analysts. Their responsibilities include the classification of personnel in their respective areas, the review of classification changes, analysis and evaluation of new jobs in their areas, the clearance of such jobs with the central staff office, and the answering of questions from production supervision concerning classifications and rates.

Field office personnel are usually responsible for processing status change forms for employees within their areas. A consolidated form designed for processing all major types of transactions for both hourly and salaried personnel is presented in Figure 48. The line containing "New Data" is suitable for posting to a status card, which gives a chronological history of changes occurring during an employee's service with the company. In companies where a large number of personnel status change forms are typed in central processing units, this form may be adapted to equipment which will prepare a tabulating card or perforated paper tape simultaneously with the typing of the form.

Job Specification and Wage Administration Manuals

To help administer the program, job specification manuals and wage administration manuals should be distributed to all offices responsible for wage administration. These two manuals should probably be compiled separately, since wider distribution will usually be given to the job specification manuals. Wage administration manuals will usually be distributed to personnel directly connected with the administration of rates and classifications, whereas job specification manuals are frequently distributed to employment represent-

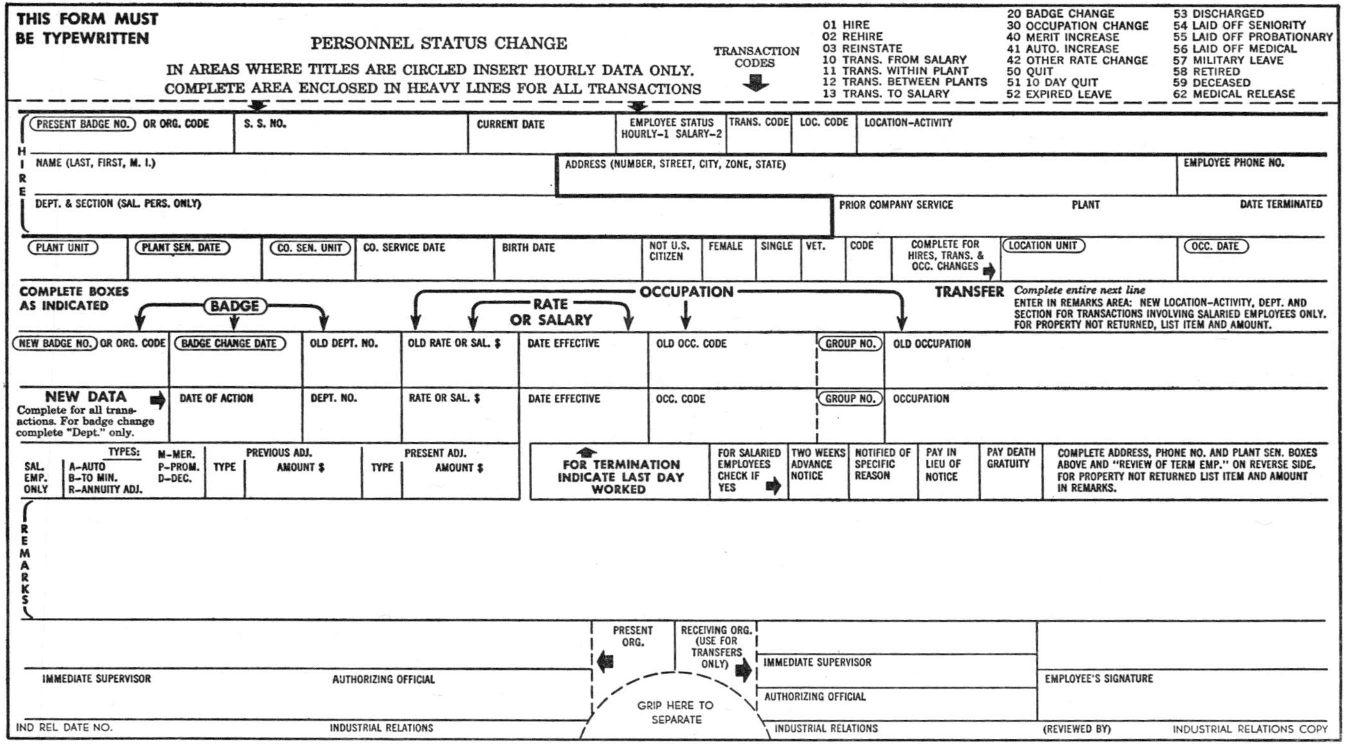

THIS FORM MUST BE TYPEWRITTEN

PERSONNEL STATUS CHANGE

IN AREAS WHERE TITLES ARE CIRCLED INSERT HOURLY DATA ONLY.
COMPLETE AREA ENCLOSED IN HEAVY LINES FOR ALL TRANSACTIONS

TRANSACTION CODES

01 HIRE
02 REHIRE
03 REINSTATE
10 TRANS. FROM SALARY
11 TRANS. WITHIN PLANT
12 TRANS. BETWEEN PLANTS
13 TRANS. TO SALARY
20 BADGE CHANGE
30 OCCUPATION CHANGE
40 MERIT INCREASE
41 AUTO. INCREASE
42 OTHER RATE CHANGE
50 QUIT
51 10 DAY QUIT
52 EXPIRED LEAVE
53 DISCHARGED
54 LAID OFF SENIORITY
55 LAID OFF PROBATIONARY
56 LAID OFF MEDICAL
57 MILITARY LEAVE
58 RETIRED
59 DECEASED
62 MEDICAL RELEASE

HIRE

PRESENT BADGE NO. OR ORG. CODE | S. S. NO. | CURRENT DATE | EMPLOYEE STATUS HOURLY-1 SALARY-2 | TRANS. CODE | LOC. CODE | LOCATION-ACTIVITY

NAME (LAST, FIRST, M. I.) | ADDRESS (NUMBER, STREET, CITY, ZONE, STATE) | EMPLOYEE PHONE NO.

DEPT. & SECTION (SAL. PERS. ONLY) | PRIOR COMPANY SERVICE | PLANT | DATE TERMINATED

PLANT UNIT | PLANT SEN. DATE | CO. SEN. UNIT | CO. SERVICE DATE | BIRTH DATE | NOT U.S. CITIZEN | FEMALE | SINGLE | VET. | CODE | COMPLETE FOR HIRES, TRANS. & OCC. CHANGES | LOCATION UNIT | OCC. DATE

COMPLETE BOXES AS INDICATED — BADGE — RATE OR SALARY — OCCUPATION — TRANSFER

TRANSFER *Complete entire next line*
ENTER IN REMARKS AREA: NEW LOCATION-ACTIVITY, DEPT. AND SECTION FOR TRANSACTIONS INVOLVING SALARIED EMPLOYEES ONLY. FOR PROPERTY NOT RETURNED, LIST ITEM AND AMOUNT.

NEW BADGE NO. OR ORG. CODE | BADGE CHANGE DATE | OLD DEPT. NO. | OLD RATE OR SAL. $ | DATE EFFECTIVE | OLD OCC. CODE | GROUP NO. | OLD OCCUPATION

NEW DATA
Complete for all transactions. For badge change complete "Dept." only.
DATE OF ACTION | DEPT. NO. | RATE OR SAL. $ | DATE EFFECTIVE | OCC. CODE | GROUP NO. | OCCUPATION

SAL. EMP. ONLY | TYPES: A-AUTO B-TO MIN. R-ANNUITY ADJ. M-MER. P-PROM. D-DEC. | PREVIOUS ADJ. TYPE | AMOUNT $ | PRESENT ADJ. TYPE | AMOUNT $

FOR TERMINATION INDICATE LAST DAY WORKED | FOR SALARIED EMPLOYEES CHECK IF YES | TWO WEEKS ADVANCE NOTICE | NOTIFIED OF SPECIFIC REASON | PAY IN LIEU OF NOTICE | PAY DEATH GRATUITY | COMPLETE ADDRESS, PHONE NO. AND PLANT SEN. BOXES ABOVE AND "REVIEW OF TERM EMP." ON REVERSE SIDE. FOR PROPERTY NOT RETURNED LIST ITEM AND AMOUNT IN REMARKS.

REMARKS

IMMEDIATE SUPERVISOR | AUTHORIZING OFFICIAL | PRESENT ORG. | RECEIVING ORG. (USE FOR TRANSFERS ONLY) | IMMEDIATE SUPERVISOR | AUTHORIZING OFFICIAL | EMPLOYEE'S SIGNATURE

GRIP HERE TO SEPARATE

IND REL DATE NO. | INDUSTRIAL RELATIONS | INDUSTRIAL RELATIONS | (REVIEWED BY) | INDUSTRIAL RELATIONS COPY

Figure 48. Multi-part carbon-interleaved status change form suitable for filing in a 5- by 8-inch employee jacket.

atives, safety representatives, or members of production supervision.

Job specification manuals should be prepared to meet the requirements of various offices within the organization. Manuals may be compiled for departments or for entire plants, depending upon the personnel to be served and the ease with which the manuals can be maintained. Since these manuals and their contents are usually subjected to extensive use, a durable binder should be considered for the cover, and multiple punching for the job specification sheets. Five holes are convenient, since the specifications may also be placed in either a three-ring or two-ring binder. A preface letter similar to the sample on this page should be included at the beginning of the manual. This may be followed by a condensed statement of wage administration policies and a rate schedule indicating the rates or rate ranges for different pay grades. Next there should be an index listing all jobs alphabetically by job classification title, followed by a cross reference index listing all jobs in code number order. The individual job specifications for the area or operation concerned will complete the manual.

Sample Preface Letter to be Used in Specification Manual

To_____:

This manual has been prepared to assist in the administration of hourly wage rates within the _____(Your)_____ Company. The basis for wage rates within the Company is the evaluation plan agreed to by Management and the Union and included in an agreement negotiated between the Company and the Union dated _____.

The Job Analysis and Evaluation Program which has been installed is designed to eliminate internal inequities in wage rates. The effectiveness of the entire program will depend to a large extent upon the judgments made by personnel responsible for the classification of employees.

This Manual includes a description of the procedure to be used in the classification of personnel. Job specifications covering the types of duties currently being performed have been compiled for reference purposes and should be used by all persons connected with classification of hourly personnel. An alphabetical index by job title and numerical index by job code number are provided for cross reference.

Questions concerning the classification of personnel or the administration of wage rates should be referred to the Wage Administration Department.

_____(Signature)_____

Industrial Relations Manager

The wage administration manual should include information such as the following.

Wage Administration Policies

Production supervisors are charged with the responsibility for proper administration of wage rates in the areas over which they have jurisdiction. Wage administration personnel are responsible for the development of wage policies for the company, consistent administration of wages throughout the company, and checking to be certain that classifications are assigned accurately. The procedure governing the classification of hourly personnel is as follows:

1. *Classification Procedure for New Hires, Rehires, and Reinstatements.* When an employee is hired, rehired, or reinstated, the responsible production supervisor and a representative of the employment office will determine the nature of the job to be performed and the job specification which covers the activities of the employee being hired. The classification will be assigned to the new employee, subject to review by a wage analyst. If no specification currently active in the area covers the duties of the employee being hired, supervision will contact the local wage administration office. A wage analyst will analyze the job of the new employee and classify him on an existing classification if available. If no suitable classification is available, the job will be analyzed and evaluated and a new specification will be prepared. Before the specification is made active or the rate becomes effective, it will be necessary for the central wage administration office to approve the specification and rate. (Where the program is negotiated with a union, their concurrence would probably be required.)

2. *Transfers Involving Classification Changes.* Transfers involving changes in classification are of two types: (a) permanent transfers extending beyond 3 days, (b) temporary transfers of 3 days or less. In the case of permanent transfers, the responsible production supervisors will process the necessary personnel form to show the transfers and classification changes. These changes will be reviewed by the wage analyst assigned to the area. It is unnecessary to change an employee's classification when the change is for a temporary period of 3 days or less. If the temporary transfer extends beyond 3 days, production supervision should immediately process the necessary change in classification.

3. *Change in Classification as a Result of Promotion or Demotion.* If an employee is promoted to a job carrying a higher classification than the one he has now, it will be necessary to process a change in classification form indicating the old classification and the new classification. If an employee is demoted to a job carrying a different classification, it will also be necessary for supervision to process a change in classification form indicating the old and new classifications. Wage analysts will be responsible for on-the-job checking of these classification changes.

4. *Transferring Overpaid Employees.* As a result of the installation of the wage analysis program, a number of employees are presently receiving rates in excess of the standard rate for the classification. The company has reached an agreement with the union whereby these individuals will not be reduced in rate and if they are transferred it will be to jobs having a rate equivalent to or higher than their present rate. It

is the intention of management to reduce to a minimum, as soon as possible, the number of employees receiving rates in excess of the standard rate for the job. Supervisors are encouraged therefore to make every attempt to transfer these personnel in accordance with the agreement reached with the union.

5. *Revision of Rate for a Job.* As a result of changes in job content and disagreement with the present evaluation on a job, supervision may be called upon to revise the rate for a particular type of work performed. If, in the opinion of supervision, the case merits consideration, the local wage administration office should be called and a wage analyst will review the job content. If significant changes have occurred in the job, it will be re-analyzed and evaluated. Unless it is believed, however, that the changes in evaluation will result in an increase in evaluation by one full pay grade, supervision should not call upon wage administration personnel to re-analyze the job. In most instances, minor changes in job content will not involve the re-analysis of the job.

Numerous other company wage administration policies may be included in the manual. Many of these policies will depend upon the philosophy of payment adopted by the company and administrative decisions which have been made over a period of years.

In addition to the administrative regulations included in the wage administration manual, wage analysts should have a job specification manual for the area over which they have jurisdiction and access to reports and periodic analyses pertaining to classifications and rates.

Procedure for Establishing Rates at New Plants

From time to time, central office personnel assisted by field personnel will have the responsibility for establishing wage structures for new plants and operations. The following steps outline the general procedure which may be followed in establishing hourly wage rates at a new plant by the job evaluation method.

Steps	Purpose
1. Area wage rate survey.	This survey is designed to determine the wage level in the community and to offer guidance in establishing the wage level to be paid by the new plant in the area. Rate comparisons with industrial companies in the area are made on the basis of a selected group of jobs representing the company's basic wage structure. Wage trend lines for the various companies in the area are computed and compared in order that rates for the new plant may be set in line with the area pattern. Refer to Chapter 7, page 140.

Steps	Purpose
2. Select copies of job specifications from the central office which describe jobs to be performed at the new plant.	Through selection and careful study of job specifications from the central office, information can be obtained as to the characteristics of jobs currently being performed within the company which are similar to the jobs contemplated for the new plant.
3. Carefully check the job specifications secured in Step 2 above with the content of hourly jobs in the new plant. These specifications should be compiled in the form of a manual.	It is extremely important that the job specifications be carefully checked in order to determine whether the new job is identical to the job outlined in the job description and evaluation. Whenever possible, this checking process should be done before personnel are hired, and specifications should be verified again after workers are on the job. Necessary changes should be made in the job specifications in order that they will accurately describe the jobs as they are performed. Any changes in evaluations should be carefully checked to determine the influence upon rates.
4. The job specification manual including all revisions in job content should be carefully checked with the central office.	The cross checking of local job information with information available at the central office will insure consistency in evaluation and specifications throughout the company. The central office maintains a record of all locations where each specification is active. It will be necessary, therefore, to inform this office of the specifications being used. When a change in evaluation is made, one copy of the revised specification will be required by the central office.
5. Establish a rate on each job.	A wage rate will be established on each job classification in accordance with a conversion table (total evaluation points converted to rate). The conversion table is prepared by the wage administration office based upon a review of the results obtained in Step 1 (area wage rate survey).
6. After specifications have been corrected or, when necessary, developed, administration of wages should be in accordance with the wage administration manual.	Administration in accordance with definite prescribed policies will lead to consistent application of the classification system throughout the company.

Steps	Purpose
7. Prior to negotiation of rates with the union, a second area wage rate survey should be conducted. (It is assumed that negotiations with the union will not take place until several months after the plant is in operation.)	This survey will provide up-to-date information concerning rates paid for classifications in the area. The data secured will serve as a basis for negotiations with the union.

Establishment of Wage and Salary Policies

Policies influencing wages will be dependent to a certain extent upon the philosophy of management concerning the level of payment they desire within their operations. Decisions will be based upon the financial ability of the company to pay a certain level of wages as well as their competitive position in the industry. Some companies have adopted the policy of paying rates equal to, or in excess of, the wage level in a particular area or industry, with individual rates to be established on the basis of job analysis and evaluation. When such a policy is adopted, definitions of how comparisons will be made and the companies to be used in the comparisons are usually not decided upon, with the result that the policy becomes nothing more than the statement of a management desire or interest.

If merit rate ranges have been established for certain job classifications, it will be necessary to establish policies governing the granting of increases within these ranges. In his book entitled *Salary and Wage Administration*, Ralph W. Ells discusses various factors affecting payment within rate ranges.

The effectiveness of a merit increase program depends to a large extent upon supervision. In general, a group of supervisors are in a position to act as an effective control if they are:

1. Thoroughly familiar with the work of employees being considered for increases.
2. Assisted by some sort of a formal employee-rating program.*
3. Governed by well-defined policies pertaining to increases.
4. Provided with periodic comparative reports summarizing classifications and rates.
5. Limited as to the total amount which can be spent over a period of time by a carefully developed budget.

* Although a discussion of merit- or performance-rating programs is beyond the scope of this book, it should be pointed out that the granting or withholding of an increase should probably not depend upon the individual receiving a specific

Obviously, if company policies provide for automatic adjustments based upon length of service, the importance of some of these administrative controls is minimized. On the other hand, if a merit increase policy does exist and a union is present, it is even more important that the controls be well defined. The tendency in many companies has been to establish ranges without simultaneously defining administrative regulations. Within a relatively short period of time, the ranges are no longer effective since practically all employees are receiving the maximum rate. Employees, union representatives, and, quite frequently, members of supervision exert pressures for increases particularly during periods of labor scarcity.

In addition to the granting of rate changes on an individual basis, policy decisions must be made concerning the nature of general adjustments influencing all job classifications. Once a job analysis and evaluation program is installed, adjustments are usually of two types:

1. A single amount granted to all classifications regardless of their relative position in the wage structure.

2. A percentage type increase using as a basis the rates currently being paid. When this type of increase is given, the policy results in the granting of an increasing amount to higher classifications. In actual practice, to avoid fractions an increasing increment between pay grades is usually granted.

In each instance, the minimum and maximum of each range, if any, would be altered in accordance with the type of increase granted. For obvious reasons, under a job analysis and evaluation program, the granting of spot increases to certain job classifications is to be avoided.

In recent years, companies not having job analysis and evaluation programs have had a tendency to segregate certain job classifications within their wage structures and grant them amounts such as 5, 10, 15 or 20 cents in excess of any amounts granted other classifications. These differentials have usually been granted to skilled or highly skilled jobs. The continued granting of increases of this type has a tendency to create breaks within the wage structure. For example, if a 10-cent increase is given to all classifications above a certain rate, a 10-cent interval will occur in which no classifications are paid. Since job classification rates as reflected by labor market conditions usually rise on a smooth basis, depending upon such factors as in-

---

rating on the plan. Where a sound rating plan is in operation, however, administrative policies should discourage the granting of increases to personnel receiving low ratings.

creasing skill, creation of a break in a company's wage structure is unrealistic. Moreover, within a large company job demands vary from the low classifications to the high classifications by a gradually increasing amount. Under such conditions, there should be no areas within the rate structure which are in conflict with both external and internal job demands as they currently exist. From the standpoint of equity, classifications immediately below those granted the increase can be considered neglected. These borderline jobs provide an excellent basis for union demands. Management, which frequently acts as the guardian of equitable relationships within the rate structure, is in the position of losing one of its strongest arguments when this type of union pressure can be used against it. Continued granting of specific amounts to certain classifications will tend to force companies into overhauling their wage structures.

Although the granting of specific increases to certain classifications may bring about a rapid settlement with a union, the practice certainly cannot be condoned on this basis. A far more equitable way of granting larger increases to skilled jobs where rates are not evaluated is to establish rate groups and apply an increasing increment to these groups. For example, all jobs paying over $1.90 up to and including $2.00 might be granted 5 cents, jobs over $2.00 up to and including $2.10, 6 cents, and so forth throughout the wage structure. Oftentimes, companies where jobs are not evaluated have structures consisting of a large number of rates with inconsistent differentials between these rates. This condition tends to complicate the granting of a graduated or percentage type increase.

The recent experience of several leading industries in the United States indicates that the continued granting of uniform or flat adjustments cannot proceed indefinitely without eventually necessitating an increasing increment or percentage type adjustment. It appears obvious that excessive use of either one type of adjustment or the other over a prolonged period is not in the best interests of either labor or management.

In the administration of a rate structure, a problem almost always arises concerning increases to be granted long-service employees. In general, length of service increases are relatively easy to administer. If a policy of longevity pay is adopted, the ground rules should be clearly outlined and adherence to them should be automatic. Under any conditions, it should be clearly understood that increases granted for long service consist of recognition for the service rendered and in no way influence job rates. Discarding this principle can easily lead to other deviations. In most cases, service increases should be established on the basis of total company seniority and not on the basis of service rendered in a particular job or organizational unit of the company.

The granting of annual wage guarantees to employees has an influence on wage payment practices somewhat opposite to that of length of service increases. Most annual wage programs provide additional security to personnel with relatively low seniority. In most instances, the employee with long service gains less from an annual wage guarantee than a person with short service, since the likelihood of a long-service employee's being laid off is not particularly great. It might be advisable when considering an annual wage plan to supplement such a program by length of service increases.

It should be evident to management that the union's major objective in demanding a GAW* is to obtain employee security during periods when work does not exist. There is no conceivable way that companies can guarantee continuous employment. Interruptions, some of which are beyond the control of the employer, are certain to occur. Unions emphasize the inability of many of their members to set aside a sufficient amount of money to provide for necessary expenditures during these periods of layoff. In a sense, the union desires security for employees with low seniority in much the same way as they have demanded, and in many cases received, a pension plan for retired workers.

Unions have placed increasing emphasis upon the inadequacy of employer-financed unemployment compensation systems regulated and administered by state governments. Although the benefits under these plans are undergoing gradual improvement, the possibilities of obtaining a uniform national pattern acceptable to state legislatures, labor, and management appear remote. By negotiating supplemental unemployment compensation plans, which have relatively few of the characteristics of a guaranteed annual wage, unions tend to focus attention upon the inadequacy of existing state benefit schedules. As state legislatures act to liberalize these benefits, all eligible workers, and not just those covered by benefit plans, will gain additional security during periods of layoff. From economic and social standpoints, legislative methods of meeting the basic needs of the unemployed appear to be far superior to the results achieved through collective bargaining.

Nevertheless, union pressures to liberalize plans which have been negotiated will undoubtedly be exerted in the future. One possible

---

* Guaranteed Annual Wage, a term which appears to be acceptable to neither management nor labor.

solution to future demands, which will still provide management with certain essential safeguards from a financial and administrative standpoint, may be in the establishment of company-financed security funds in which each employee has a vested interest. Employees would have the right to draw on this fund under certain conditions, such as when they are laid off. Certain incentives could be built into the plan, such as interest accrual, separation allowances, and increased pension benefits, which would tend to encourage an employee to leave his fund intact unless it becomes absolutely essential that he have the money. Integration with pension plans would provide a gradually increasing pension benefit as workers with more and more service under the plan retired. Such a plan could be financed on the basis of a negotiated amount for straight-time hours paid until an individual employee's fund reached a predetermined maximum, thereby limiting company liability and simplifying the administrative aspects of the program. The establishment of definite financial limitations is an absolute necessity in any plan to provide greater security for employees. Obviously, workers can receive little benefit from becoming the creditors of their bankrupt employers. Since an employee would have a choice as to whether he wanted to use his fund or not, the entire plan would be somewhat similar to a savings account. As such, unemployment compensation funds could be used without raising questions concerning dual payments and possible ineligibility under some state laws. By establishing the fund on an individual basis, long-service employees and salaried employees, who are not as subject to frequent layoffs, could also benefit from the program.

Regardless of the types of guaranteed wage plans which are adopted, the additional administrative control which a job analysis and evaluation plan provides should act as a strong incentive for companies to install and maintain such programs. In the future, management will require improved control over manpower in order to minimize costs which might be incurred under an unemployment benefit plan. A comprehensive knowledge of job duties in addition to greater flexibility in the movement of manpower will be essential. The supplemental unemployment compensation benefit plans as well as most of the guaranteed wage plans currently in existence establish a direct relationship between the amount of money paid during periods of layoff and an employee's hourly rate or earnings during a specified period. This relationship makes it even more important to develop and maintain an equitable base rate structure.

Although pressure by unions to obtain greater security during periods of layoff has been directed primarily toward additional stability of earning power, demands relating to 40-hour pay for 30 hours worked are essentially an attempt to gain a wage increase. The demand for equivalent pay for fewer hours worked has several rather far-reaching implications. Probably the most important characteristic of this demand is not the increase in wages but the possible restriction which could be placed upon a company's production facilities.

For example, it is conceivable that an agreement might be reached whereby employees would work five 7-hour days for a total of 35 hours, and, in turn, receive 40-hour pay. There appears to be potential danger in such an agreement, since productive hours would be scheduled over a 5-day period. Under a normal work schedule of 35 instead of 40 hours, there would be 5 fewer hours of production per week over which to allocate overhead costs. Potential solutions to the union demand in this area appear to lie not in reducing but in substantially increasing the use of production facilities. This objective can probably be accomplished through the scheduling of two complete shifts during the week rather than one—an arrangement which might be identified as the dual shift system.

If 40-hour pay were to be granted for 32 hours worked, a schedule might be developed whereby one shift of employees worked Monday, Tuesday, and Wednesday for 8 hours on each day turn and on Thursday for 8 hours on the afternoon turn. A similar schedule could be developed for another shift which would work Thursday, Friday, and Saturday for 8 hours on the day turn and for one other day, probably Tuesday, for 8 hours on the afternoon turn. From the standpoint of scheduling employees on continuous operations, shift schedules in multiples of eight are extremely desirable.

Although some questions would undoubtedly be raised by unions if companies were to schedule shifts as outlined above, there would, nonetheless, be many strong points for both management and labor from a bargaining standpoint. Management might use the proposal as a means of securing the elimination of shift differential payments, except for those employees assigned permanently to afternoon or midnight shifts. Unions could point to the substantial decrease they had achieved in hours worked while still maintaining base rates. With the increasing automation in industry, more complete utilization of facilities would result in fixed charges being prorated over a larger number of hours worked, a factor which would tend to counterbalance, or possibly more than counterbalance, the increased direct labor cost. If a plan giving 40-hour pay for 32 hours worked were adopted, with the assumption that it would be possible to work 8-hour days without payment of premium time for hours less than 40, the percentage increases in direct labor costs at different operating levels would be as they appear in the chart on page 205. If a company were to be scheduled for a 64-hour week instead of the 40-hour week normally scheduled, direct labor costs attributable to the increase in rates only, not taking into account other fringe benefits, would increase between 5% and 7%.

A further analysis of the dual shift system reveals that almost infinite variations in work schedules can be established in the range of 64 hours up to approximately 100 hours. The variations can be developed by scheduling additional 8-hour increments or 9-hour days or both. Additional benefits might be achieved during the vacation period when personnel replacement problems exist. These schedules could be far more sensitive to market demands than the prevailing system based on forty hours. Insofar as this is the case and management might be in a position to develop increased employment stability under the dual shift system, benefits might accrue to companies having some form of a guaranteed annual wage plan. Obviously, in the granting of any concessions of this type to hourly employees, management would have to consider the cost of granting compensating benefits to its salaried personnel.

It should be noted that there are several factors which could contribute to reducing the flexibility of scheduling under the dual shift system. For example, if the government should pass legislation requiring the payment of time and a half for hours in excess of thirty-five, it would not be as advantageous for companies to schedule hours for which premium payment would be required. Thus, insofar as federal legislation had a tendency to reduce the flexibility of manpower scheduling, it might act as a deterrent to those companies attempting to bring about additional employment stability. Companies negotiating agreements with the union whereby premium payments are provided for Saturday work, regardless of the number of hours worked during the week, should realize that they may be creating another condition which might reduce flexibility in scheduling of employees.

In companies where strong unions exist, management should always be on the alert for demands which could result in major revisions to existing wage and salary policies. Negotiation of changes which might eventually lead to encroachment upon the rights of management to administer and control rates and classifications could lead to serious long-range consequences.

Cost Relationship between Existing 40-Hour Single Shift System and Dual Shift System at Different Operating Levels
(Assumed labor cost per hour $1.00)

Work Schedule	40-Hour Pay with Present Overtime Provisions	40-Hour Pay for 32 Hours Worked No Overtime for Hours Worked up to 40 in Any One Week	% Increase in Labor Cost
40-Hour week	40 hours @ $1.00 = $40.00	40 Hours @ $1.25 = $50.00	25.0%
60-Hour week	40 hours @ $1.00 = $40.00 20 hours @ 1.50 = 30.00 $70.00	Instead of a 60-hour week, a 64-hour week would probably be worked. If, however, it is possible to have two shifts, each working 30 hours: 60 hours @ $1.25 = $75.00	7.1%
64-Hour week	It is doubtful whether an operation would be scheduled for any substantial period of time at 64 hours. Consideration would probably be given to scheduling two shifts. 40 hours @ $1.00 = $40.00 24 hours @ 1.50 = 36.00 $76.00	Assuming dual shifts: 64 hours @ $1.25 = $80.00	5.2%
80-Hour week	Assuming two shifts with 5-cent afternoon shift premium: 40 hours @ $1.00 = $40.00 40 hours @ 1.05 = 42.00 $82.00	Assuming dual shifts with no shift premiums: 80 hours @ $1.25 = $100.00	22.0%

Factors Influencing Wage and Salary Control

Although both centralized and decentralized offices share the responsibility for administering wages and salaries, the effectiveness of their efforts is directly dependent upon four factors, not all of which are under their control.

1. Determination of the proper number of persons to perform the required work.
2. Establishment of the proper classifications to staff the operation or assignment.
3. Development of the proper relationship between classifications within the wage or salary structure.
4. Control of individual compensation on established rates or within established rate ranges so as to provide for an equitable distribution of available funds.

Control of Hourly Personnel Expense

With the rapid increase in automation during the last several years, management's opportunities to exercise more effective controls over manpower on hourly jobs have increased. In the building of new plants, the months and sometimes years of advance planning concerning the machines to be installed and the methods to be used have made possible accurate forecasts concerning the number of persons required to occupy work stations and the skill or backgrounds which these individuals should possess. As these changes occur, management should reappraise the adequacy of their existing classification structure. In operations not as subject to automation, manpower requirements can be secured with the help of studies conducted by work standards or industrial engineering personnel. Variable manpower schedules can be established based upon anticipated production requirements. Thus, the numbers of persons required to perform a production operation as well as the classifications involved are frequently the by-products of intensive studies conducted over a period of time. The results of these studies, accompanied by rapid internal reports which would provide such information as the number of hours worked by classification in each cost unit, could form the basis for a system of manpower control substantially better than many currently in existence. Controlling manpower by relating the number of employees, rather than man-hours worked, on each classification to established standards does not appear to be sufficiently refined to provide management with a sound basis for making decisions, since it does not account for borrowed and loaned personnel, vacations, and employee absences for other reasons. Within the next few years, considerable attention will undoubtedly be devoted to the construction of mathematical models relating to the number of employees, their classifications, and their wage rates for various production levels. Mathematical programing techniques, the theory of probability, and various other statistical methods have some definite applications in this area. Job requirements and the number of employees required to staff an operation will undoubtedly change as a result of some of these studies.*

In recent years, unions have taken an active interest in the establishment of work standards and the determination of classifications required to staff an operation. There is a growing tendency for unions to share in the development of an equitable relationship between classifications within a wage structure. The merger of the AF of L and CIO will stimulate further interest in this area. Pressure will be exerted to increase rates of skilled personnel in CIO unions to enable them to obtain earnings which will approximate the earnings of skilled workmen in the AF of L. In companies where both unions are recognized, management is almost certain to be faced with demands for equivalent pay where similar work is involved. Obviously, the highly skilled jobs will not be the only ones included in such a controversy. Rates for many semi-skilled jobs might also require revision.

Some unions have indicated an interest in revising existing rate structures to reflect changes brought about by increased automation within industry. In this regard, neither management nor union personnel should be deceived by the size, complexity, or productivity of automatic equipment. The important factor in determining the relationship between rates continues to be relative job requirements. In some instances, new classifications should undoubtedly be established. If the job demands are significantly greater, evaluation on a suitable plan will reflect this difference and a higher rate may result. As far as evaluation plans are concerned, in those plants where substantial automation exists, there will be more of a tendency to apply additional weight to factors relating to Responsibility for Material or Product and Responsibility for Tools and Equipment. As modernization progresses, weight applied to factors such as Physical Effort, Work Surroundings, and Unavoidable Hazards will probably decrease. The overall influence of these changes on resulting wage

---

* For a description of such a study, see *An Introduction to Probability Theory and Its Applications*, William Feller, Volume I, John Wiley & Sons, New York, 1950, page 379.

structures should be beneficial. Where it is obvious that individual job demands are not significantly greater as a result of installing automation, management should resist attempts by the union to obtain rate increases on individual classifications. Unions should be quick to recognize that one of the direct benefits of installing more automatic equipment is a change in the relative number of employees in skilled versus unskilled classifications. Proper planning on the part of management to train and upgrade existing personnel should go a long way in satisfying union demands for a greater share in the benefits to be derived from automation.

Management's recourse, when there are demands relating to substantial changes in the wage structure or job to job relationships, might be to indicate that a systematic study should be undertaken for all jobs in order to develop a plan for the elimination of any existing inequities. In many instances, joint union management agreements relating to classifications and rates have led to rather long periods of relative stability as far as the relationship between jobs in the wage structure is concerned. If the first three out of the four conditions mentioned above have been accomplished satisfactorily, loss of administrative control from a cost standpoint is not likely to arise in connection with hourly employees, since single rates or relatively narrow rate ranges tend to restrict the area of payment.

Control of Salaried Personnel Expense

Effective administrative control over salaried expense presents certain difficulties not experienced in the control of hourly rates. Careful planning concerning the methods and procedures to be used by salaried personnel is oftentimes lacking. Consequently, the number of persons required as well as the classifications necessary to staff the operation are not accurately predetermined. Without this advance planning, management's ability to control expense is limited. The development of an equitable salary structure and control of salaries within the ranges cannot compensate for the failure to establish efficient methods and correct classifications.

Top management in many companies has been too prone to accept existing methods of conducting office functions without subjecting them to the same critical analysis given production operations. It is becoming more and more evident that many of the functions performed by salaried personnel can be accomplished by more efficient methods. Classifications required to staff an operation as well as the number of persons necessary to perform the work have oftentimes reflected the ability of a supervisor to sell his particular ideas rather than a careful evaluation of the benefits to be derived for the company.

Despite the fact that systems and procedures may be practically identical in several organizational units within a company, variations exist in the number of persons needed to accomplish the required work. Some of these variations are a result of differences in:

1. *Work load.* In addition to variations in the total work load, unpredictable increases or decreases also occur in the individual items comprising the total work load.

2. *Ability of Personnel.* The ability and qualifications of personnel vary and are directly reflected in work output.

3. *Quality Standards.* In some locations the quality standards are not as high as in others.

4. *Physical Layout and Facilities.* Available physical facilities may influence the quantity and quality of work performed as well as manpower required.

5. *Organization and Allocation of Work Assignments.* Lack of well-defined responsibilities or improper work distribution may contribute to inefficiencies.

6. *Efficiency.* Some locations may be doing unnecessary or marginal work, with the result that methods and procedures may need alterations.

In view of the many variables, it is difficult to establish standard manpower budgets. Another problem in developing staffing standards and manpower expense controls involves the establishment of a system whereby operating personnel can judge periodically the relationship between the actual number of persons employed and an established standard. Obviously, such comparisons can only be made if the standard can be recalculated at periodic intervals to reflect changing activity. Internal communications, particularly in larger companies, have a tendency to impede the obtaining of data for calculations as well as delaying the return of information to persons responsible for taking action.

In one organization having multiplant operations, research personnel confronted with the problem of developing staffing standards for field offices used the multiple correlation technique in evaluating the relative difference in manpower at different locations. The study involved the establishment of staffing standards at more than twenty assembly and manufacturing plants for the following personnel functions relating to hourly employees:

1. Employment of hourly personnel including interviewing, completion of the hiring forms, counseling, placement, exit interviewing, and terminating personnel. Medical activities, such as the induction physical examination, were not included.

2. Administration of wages for hourly employees including checking of employees on the job, assisting in the processing of status change forms, and analyzing new jobs.

3. Maintenance of hourly records including the checking and posting of status changes, the filing of these forms in a personnel jacket, and the checking of unemployment compensation claims.

Analyses indicated that there were certain factors which had a relationship to the number of persons required to perform these hourly personnel functions. The following factors were chosen to help establish the standards:

1. Number of Hourly Employees Served (number of hourly rated employees in the plant).
2. Number of Accessions.
3. Number of Transfers.
4. Number of Rate Changes.
5. Number of Separations.

The first factor provided a general measure of the activity in hourly personnel functions. Some of the remaining factors had a tendency to predict activity in specific portions of the function. For example, the number of accessions and terminations had special significance for hourly employment, whereas transfers and rate changes influence wage administration activities. All of these factors had a direct bearing upon work loads in the records functions. The factors chosen were common to all hourly personnel activities being studied, and it was possible to obtain historical data for each one selected.

From a statistical standpoint, the problem to be solved involved the periodic estimating or forecasting of the standard man-hours required to perform a constantly changing work load comprised of several different variables which could be measured. In addition, there was a need to develop a system whereby field personnel could perform simple arithmetic calculations and be able to determine the relationship of their actual man-hours to standard man-hours.

In order to accomplish these objectives, a manpower evaluation plan was developed with individual factors weighted with the aid of multiple correlation. Using their current experience, field personnel could evaluate their performance on each factor, add the total points, and by means of a simple formula or conversion table obtain the estimated number of man-hours needed to perform the work. A manpower calculation sheet may be completed comparing the estimated standard and actual man-hours of personnel performing the work.

A question might be raised concerning the establishment of standards based upon current experience, since the standard times which are derived might be inflated by inefficient procedures and methods in existence at certain locations. When it is apparent that such a condition exists, the results of the technique would tend to indicate where systems studies should be conducted first in order to maximize savings. Meanwhile, the remaining operations might use the results as a tentative standard until such studies could be conducted throughout the organization.

This system has the advantage of permitting current comparisons of actual to standard manpower. For example, information concerning the variables may be obtained at the end of a month, calculations performed to derive an estimated standard, and immediate comparisons made with the actual manpower performing the work. A suitable number of measurable variables, usually not more than ten, which have a relationship to work load and manpower required, may be taken into consideration, and actual historical experience from numerous locations of varying sizes may be used in establishing the standards. The nature of the sample used to develop the standards tends to limit the locations which can benefit from the information developed. If the calculations were made on the basis of plants ranging in size from 1000 to 5000 employees, the data should not be used for deriving standards for plants outside this range. Estimating beyond observed ranges is extremely hazardous since relationships in the data may vary. In some instances, the number of personnel transactions (accessions, transfers, rate changes, or separations) at an individual plant may fluctuate, with the result that they may exceed the normal range and evaluate in the highest degree. Such a condition should occur only at infrequent intervals. If it should persist, however, the accuracy of the calculated standard for the location should probably be questioned.

To provide a better understanding of the system, an example including instructions and forms relating to the functions in hourly personnel activities is presented. The evaluation system requires the completion of a Manpower Calculation Sheet (see page 212) as follows:

1. Calculate the actual man-hours applied during the month to hourly personnel activities.

    a. Enter 173.3 hours for each regular full-time employee in Column 1 of the Manpower Calculation Sheet. For part-time employees, 173.3 hours should be prorated in accordance with the hours worked in the activity. Include vacation time, time off for illness, and personal time off as hours worked.

    b. Enter the number of hours worked by employees borrowed from other departments or activities in Column 2 of the Manpower Calcula-

Manpower Calculation Sheet

Location _____

Year _____

Month	Man-hours							Number of Employees			
	Actual Full-time Employees 1	Actual Borrowed Personnel 2	Actual Overtime 3	Total Actual 4	Total Estimated Standard 5	Actual over Standard 6	Actual under Standard 7	Total Actual 8	Total Estimated Standard 9	Actual over Standard 10	Actual under Standard 11
Jan.	519.9	121.3	107.6	748.8	769		20	4.3	4.4		.1
Feb.											
Mar.											
Apr.											
May											
June											
July											
Aug.											
Sept.											
Oct.											
Nov.											
Dec.											

tion Sheet. Time worked by personnel borrowed to replace employees on vacation or absent because of illness or personal time off should not be included.

c. Enter the number of overtime hours worked in Column 3 of the Manpower Calculation Sheet.

d. Add the number of hours in Columns 1, 2, and 3. Enter the total in Column 4. Convert total man-hours to actual number of employees by use of the Conversion Table for Total Points, Man-hours and Employees (see page 215). Enter Column B, man-hours, and read the equivalent in Column C, man-hours converted to employees. Enter the amount found in Column C in Column 8 of the Manpower Calculation Sheet.

2. Calculate the estimated standard number of employees as follows:

a. The Manpower Evaluation Plan (pages 216–217) should be used to obtain the points which are equivalent to the monthly activity for each factor. For example, if the number of hourly employees served during the month was 3310, read across under this factor to obtain the equivalent number of points, 74. Obtain the equivalent points in the same manner for the other variables.

b. Add the points for the factors to obtain total points for the location. In Column A of the Conversion Table, find these total points, obtain the equivalent man-hours in Column B, and enter this amount in Column 5 of the Manpower Calculation Sheet. Then obtain the equivalent number of employees from Column C and enter this amount in Column 9 of the Manpower Calculation Sheet.

3. Calculate the variance.

a. Calculate the variance between the actual man-hours and estimated standard man-hours. If the actual man-hours are more than the standard, enter the difference in Column 6. If the actual man-hours are fewer than the standard, enter the difference in Column 7.

b. Calculate the variance between actual number of employees, Column 8, and standard number of employees, Column 9. If the actual number of employees is more than the standard, enter the difference in Column 10. If there are fewer actual employees than the standard, enter the difference in Column 11.

Information may be presented graphically each month by plotting the actual number of employees, Column 8, and the standard number of employees, Column 9, on a Manpower Control Graph (see Figure 49).

The following example is presented for purposes of illustration.

3.0	Full-time employees	$3.0 \times 173.3 = 519.9$	Column 1
.7	Borrowed personnel	$.7 \times 173.3 = 121.3$	Column 2
	Overtime hours	107.6	Column 3
	Total actual man-hours	748.8	Column 4

MANPOWER CONTROL GRAPH

○ Actual compared to standard
number of employees for _____ Plant_____
                       Period covered

NUMBER OF   ACTUAL ― ― ―
PERSONNEL   STANDARD ―――

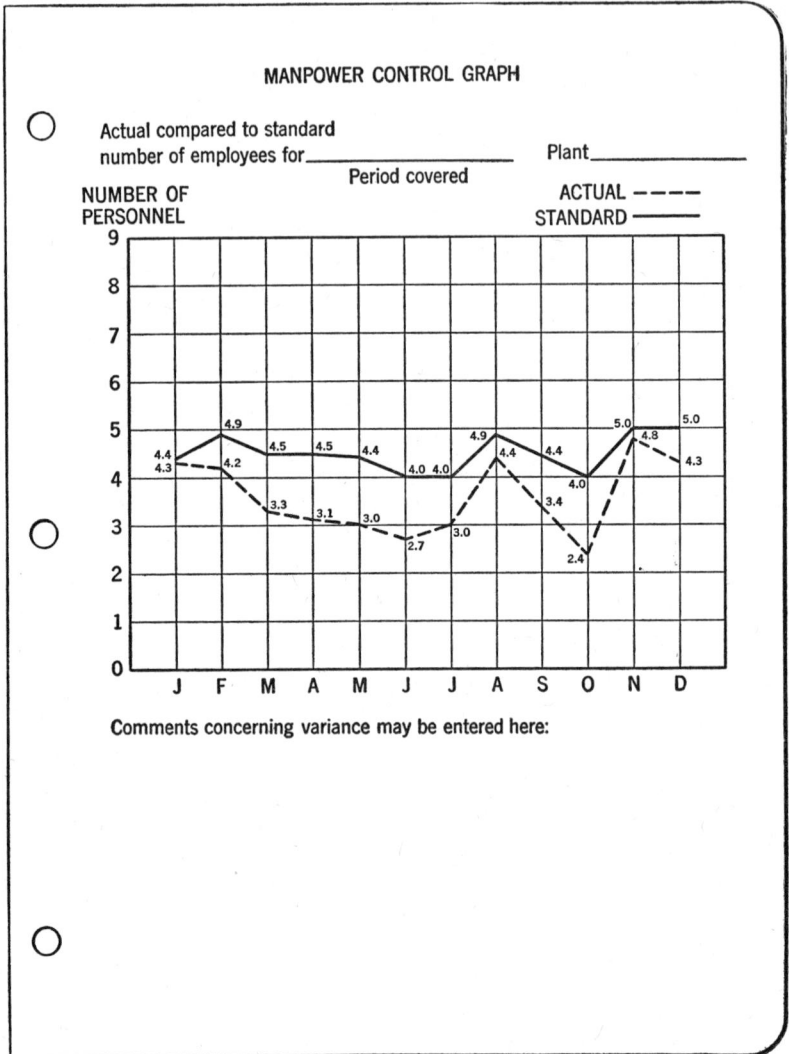

Comments concerning variance may be entered here:

Figure 49

Conversion Table for
Total Points, Man-Hours, and Employees

A	B	C
		Man-hours Converted to
Total Points	Man-hours	Employees
30–31	258–264	1.5
32–34	271–284	1.6
35–37	290–303	1.7
38–39	309–315	1.8
40–42	322–335	1.9
43–45	341–354	2.0
46–47	360–366	2.1
48–50	373–386	2.2
51–53	392–405	2.3
54–56	411–424	2.4
57–58	430–437	2.5
59–61	443–456	2.6
62–64	462–475	2.7
65–66	481–488	2.8
67–69	494–507	2.9
70–72	513–526	3.0
73–75	532–545	3.1
76–77	552–558	3.2
78–80	564–577	3.3
81–83	584–596	3.4
84–86	603–615	3.5
87–88	622–628	3.6
89–91	635–647	3.7
92–94	654–667	3.8
95–96	673–679	3.9
97–99	686–698	4.0
100–102	705–718	4.1
103–104	724–730	4.2
105–107	737–750	4.3
108–110	756–769	4.4
111–113	775–788	4.5
114–115	794–801	4.6
116–118	807–820	4.7
119–121	826–839	4.8
122–123	845–852	4.9
124–126	858–871	5.0

Formula for deriving man-hours from points
(hourly personnel activities)

Man-hours =   66.469   + (6.3836   × Location points)
          (base value)   (avg. value per point)

216   Industrial Wage and Salary Control

Manpower

Definitions and Points

Factors			A	B	C	D	E	F	G	H	I	J	K
Hourly Employees Served	D	From	0	293	585	876	1168	1460	1751	2043	2335	2626	2918
		To	292	584	875	1167	1459	1750	2042	2334	2625	2917	3209
	P		6	12	19	25	31	37	43	50	56	62	68
Accessions	D	From	0	12	24	35	47	58	70	81	93	104	116
		To	11	23	34	46	57	69	80	92	103	115	126
	P		2	5	7	10	12	14	17	19	22	24	26
Transfers	D	From	0	16	31	46	61	76	91	106	121	136	151
		To	15	30	45	60	75	90	105	120	135	150	165
	P		6	12	17	23	29	35	41	46	52	58	64
Rate Changes	D	From	0	20	39	57	76	95	114	132	151	170	189
		To	19	38	56	75	94	113	131	150	169	188	206
	P		3	6	10	13	16	19	22	26	29	32	35
Separations	D	From	0	12	24	35	47	58	70	81	93	104	116
		To	11	23	34	46	57	69	80	92	103	115	126
	P		2	5	7	10	12	14	17	19	22	24	26

* Plan should not be used for plants having less than 300 or more than 7800 hourly employees.

Find 748.8 actual man-hours in the Conversion Table for Total Points, Man-hours, and Employees to obtain the equivalent number of employees. This figure, 4.3, is entered in Column 8 of the Manpower Calculation Sheet.

Factors	Number	Points Obtained from the Manpower Evaluation Plan
Hourly Employees Served	3310	74
Accessions	8	2
Transfers	53	23
Rate Changes	29	6
Separations	16	5
	Total points	110

In the Conversion Table, find 110 total points in Column A and read the equivalent man-hours, 769, in Column B, and the equivalent employees, 4.4, in Column C. Record these figures in Columns 5 and 9, respectively, of the Manpower Calculation Sheet.

Obtain the difference between the standard and actual man-hours.

   769   Standard man-hours
−749   Actual man-hours
    20   Man-hours under standard. Enter in Column 7 of the Manpower Calculation Sheet.

Evaluation Plan*

on Degrees of Factors

L	M	N	O	P	Q	R	S	Γ	U	V	W	X	Y
3210	3501	3793	4085	4377	4668	4960	5251	5543	5835	6155	6418	6710	Over
3500	3792	4084	4376	4667	4959	5250	5542	5834	6154	6417	6709	7000	7000
74	81	87	93	99	105	111	118	124	130	136	143	149	155
127	138	150	161	173	184	196	207	219	230	242	253	264	Over
137	149	160	172	183	195	206	218	229	241	252	263	275	275
29	31	34	36	38	41	43	46	48	50	53	55	58	60
166	181	196	211	226	241	256	271	286	301	316	331	346	Over
180	195	210	225	240	255	270	285	300	315	330	345	360	360
70	75	81	87	93	99	104	110	116	122	128	133	139	145
207	226	245	264	282	301	320	339	357	376	395	414	432	Over
225	244	263	281	300	319	338	356	375	394	413	431	450	450
38	42	45	48	51	54	58	61	64	67	70	74	77	80
127	138	150	161	173	184	196	207	219	230	242	253	264	Over
137	149	160	172	183	195	206	218	229	241	252	263	275	275
29	31	34	36	38	41	43	46	48	50	53	55	58	60

Obtain the difference between standard and actual employees.

4.4   Standard employees
−4.3   Actual employees
.1   Employees under standard. Enter in Column 11 of the
Manpower Calculation Sheet.

Plot 4.4, standard number of employees, and 4.3, actual number of employees, on the Manpower Control Graph.

To assist in the interpretation of the results, unusual conditions such as strikes, shutdowns, indefinite layoffs, addition of second shifts, and other situations resulting in substantial personnel movement should be noted.

In any system of estimating manpower requirements or deriving standards, some caution should be exercised in the interpretation of the results. The amount of difference between the standard and actual manpower as well as trends in the data should be studied. If an individual location operates consistently above or below its standard, personnel should be asked to comment upon the reasons for the variance. Outer limits may be established based upon a careful study of work loads and personnel fluctuations. It would be possible, for example, to require field locations to comment upon a variance of one or more persons, provided such a condition existed for a period of four out of six months. Detailed analyses of methods, procedures, and personnel may be required at those locations where prolonged, above-standard conditions are prevalent.

The multiple correlation technique may also be used to help establish standards in individual offices where work load information is available over a period of time. The method has a tendency to reveal rather quickly any lag in adjusting to reduced work volume. There is adequate evidence in industry that many offices have experienced excessive delays in adjusting to changing conditions. The technique may also be used in forecasting personnel requirements for expanding or contracting operations.

Further research in the utilization of the multiple correlation technique as an aid in controlling manpower will undoubtedly be undertaken within the next few years. It would be interesting to combine similar data from a number of companies and use the resulting formula as a "measuring stick" to evaluate the relative efficiency of the functions studied at the companies participating in the survey. Studies might also be conducted to compare the accuracy and relative difference of standards based upon time and motion studies and standards derived with the aid of multiple correlation.

Although the manpower evaluation system is primarily concerned with the overall control of the number of persons performing a specific function, additional analyses should be made in connection with the classifications assigned to individuals at the different locations. In offices where there is a tendency to overstaff, there may also be a tendency to establish somewhat higher classifications for the employees.

One analysis conducted in a company having several branch plants producing similar products revealed considerable inconsistency in classification assignments as well as manpower assigned to perform the functions. In each instance, identical forms and procedures were in use, and variations in the work load were not significant. The functions performed by the offices being analyzed involved employment of hourly personnel, administration of rates, and maintenance of personnel records. Hourly personnel served in these eight locations ranged from 1280 to 1447 employees. In four of the eight offices, the highest classification being used was a section supervisor evaluated in salary grade 17. In the remaining four locations, the highest classification evaluated in salary grade 14. No relationship existed between the size of the eight locations and the length of service of the employees, or the salary grades being used. In the eight offices, four different clerical classifications were in use, one in salary grade

5, two in salary grade 7, and one in salary grade 9. The number of persons in the eight offices varied from two to five with the equivalent of two and a half to three and a half persons normally assigned to the work full time. In those offices having larger staffs, there was a tendency to use higher classifications for the employees.

The different classifications and number of persons being used within these offices indicate the variation which can occur in relatively small offices performing practically identical functions. Numerous cases in larger offices parallel this condition. There is a definite need in every company for top management to observe periodically the functions being performed by different groups within the organization and to evaluate the need for various operations. A searching analysis of this type frequently results in a reallocation of funds being spent for salaries, with resultant benefits to the company.

Modern industrial managers are becoming increasingly aware of the fact that accurate classification assignment is a prerequisite to effective control and forecasting of labor costs. There can be no question that improper assignment of classifications to personnel and lax rate administration result in the expenditure of thousands of dollars annually for which companies receive no tangible return. In view of the substantial portion of operating costs directly attributable to wages, it is mandatory that effective administrative controls be applied.

Effective control over salary expense requires intensive training of supervisors to assure a thorough understanding of existing policies and maximum consistency in the application of these policies to salaried employees. In the administration of hourly rates and classifications, there is less latitude for decisions, the authority for making decisions is more concentrated, and personnel having the authority are usually specialists who are familiar with company policies and rate relationships. Failure to acquaint salaried supervisors with administrative regulations and to establish other external controls, including budgetary limitations, usually lead to a gradual increase in costs.

Compilation of Statistical Reports to Aid Management Control

Another factor contributing to improved management control is an effective statistical reporting program. The basis for such a program is a sound job evaluation system, adequate job specifications, and proper classification of personnel if accurate trend or comparative analyses are to be conducted. Periodic reports may be developed which reflect information such as the following:

1. Number of persons on each classification.
2. Rates paid persons on each classification (where rate ranges are involved).
3. Average rate by classification.
4. Average rate by pay grade.
5. Distribution of employees within the quarters of each pay grade. (Statistical measures such as the standard deviation of salaries within pay grades may be studied over a period of time in order to determine the influence of management policies on payment practices.)
6. Average rate by organizational unit and for entire company.
7. Distribution of rates and personnel within a specified dollar interval.
8. Average rates of accessions and separations.
9. Number of increases per one hundred employees.
10. Average percent of increase, promotional and merit.
11. Influence of the frequency and amount of increases in different areas of the pay structure.*
12. Rate comparisons with other companies.
13. Rate relationships between foremen and the hourly workers they supervise.
14. Rate relationships between comparable jobs on the salaried and hourly rolls.

Although many of these reports are of immediate interest at the time they are prepared, trends in the data may be even more significant. Various ratios, such as the number of hourly employees to the number of foremen or supervisory personnel, may be calculated. Where similar operations or plants exist, these ratios may be compared. It is important when making comparisons of this nature to evaluate the performance or quality of the work being accomplished. Ratios which reflect relatively few supervisors compared to the number of persons supervised are not always desirable, since the work being performed may not be of the desired quality.

Reports designed for management control purposes are, at present, oftentimes incomplete. Frequently, personnel responsible for submitting reports become so engrossed in securing the figures or graphing the data that little attention is devoted to a careful analysis of the end result and making suggestions for corrective action, which are of course the real objectives of such reports. Analyses which are conducted are sometimes superficial, with the result that cause and effect relationships are not apparent. In companies having several

---

* See *Control of Salary Expense,* American Management Association Financial Series, No. 79, 1945, for a discussion of Edward N. Hay's compa-ratio system for controlling the granting of salary increases.

thousand or more employees, data which lend themselves to further analysis are practically unlimited. Under these conditions, one of the most important functions of management personnel is to decide the types of analyses which should be conducted in order to obtain the greatest tangible return for the time allocated.

10

Conclusion

The principles of job analysis and evaluation provide the most effective basis for agreement between management and unions concerning wage rate payments. The technique provides an organized approach to a mutual problem—a problem which is vital to both parties. To install a job analysis and evaluation system requires careful planning by both groups, a thorough realization by both parties of their existing problems, and a conscientious desire to develop an equitable system of payment.

As far as management is concerned, the adoption of a sound job analysis and evaluation program is fundamental to the development of an effective labor cost control system. To be of maximum value, it should function as one of an integrated group of administrative controls. Evidence is increasing that mathematical and statistical techniques help refine existing systems and provide management with new and more effective tools as a basis for reaching better decisions.

There is no single program which can be introduced in every organization to accomplish all of the desired objectives successfully. Variations will occur in the evaluation plan, the procedures used, the length of time required to introduce the program, and the policies developed for purposes of administrative control. It is essential that every company develop its own plan or thoroughly test any plan it is considering before introducing it. In recent years there have been definite indications that plans are becoming more standardized. It should not be implied, however, that further analytical work in the field is restricted. New techniques are constantly being applied to refine the systems already in use. Further research in this area will undoubtedly be stimulated by the realization on the part of industrial management that improved wage and salary controls are one of the necessary prerequisites to reduced operating expenditures.

In the process of considering a job analysis and evaluation system, both management and union representatives should know the limitations of such a system. Rates for certain jobs within the structure may not lend themselves to establishment by job evaluation. Certain extraneous factors may exert an influence on the rates paid these jobs. Rates paid by competitors for such jobs may compel adjustments not in accordance with job evaluation. In other instances, it may be desirable to exclude a job from evaluation, on the basis that it has certain unusual characteristics which cannot be adequately measured by the plan. Jobs excluded from the evaluation plan should be carefully analyzed and all facts pertaining to the job recorded. Obviously these jobs should be held to a minimum and not used for comparison purposes. It may be desirable to reach an agreement with the union whereby existing rates will be retained only in those instances where they are not contested by either management or the union.

As knowledge of the techniques of job analysis and evaluation spreads, unions will be more and more willing to take an active part in the development and administration of such programs. In the past their reluctance has been based upon skepticism—fear that they were endorsing a "pig in a poke." Point plans presented particular problems, for despite the fact that many point plans appeared to work reasonably well, there has been an area of doubt concerning the assignment of point weights to factors and degrees of factors. Moreover, there seemed to be no systematic basis for analyzing the results of the wage structure to determine whether the number of jobs which were shifting was at a minimum. The methods outlined in this book should provide management and union personnel with numerous checks which will assure them that the plan they are considering has been carefully developed.

Once a plan is installed, both management and the union will have to live with it. Oftentimes, failure of a program may be attributed to the fact that the plan was not thoroughly checked before it was introduced. It should be remembered that a certain degree of inflexibility develops whenever job evaluation is installed. This inflexibility is particularly noticeable in a tight labor market when it becomes necessary to make exceptions to policies regarding evaluated rates. Such unusual situations, if attributable to the supply of and the demand for certain types of labor, may require a training or upgrading program. As a last resort, a special rate higher than the evaluated rate may be negotiated, assuming the evaluation is correct and the job has not changed. Union negotiators advocating the granting of rates in excess of the amount resulting from evaluation should consider very carefully the influence such a policy will have upon other union personnel performing similar jobs. Both union and management representatives may find themselves in an untenable position as a result of such agreements.

Since the establishment of a wage structure presents a mutual problem of real concern to both management and labor, the development of a logical system based upon an analysis of factual information should be the objective of both groups. The field is one of vital concern to millions of wage earners and, as such, great care should be used in the constructing of wage systems. If union representatives decide that they do not want to utilize job evaluation in their negotiations, it is nonetheless vital that they be informed concerning the technique if it is being used to establish rates on jobs within their jurisdiction. Independent arbitrators as well as personnel in governmental agencies have come to realize more and more that proper application of the technique of job analysis and evaluation presents a tangible basis for equitable rate determination and the settlement of disputes involving rates.

In recent years, the federal government has taken an increasing interest in wage payments. Through the medium of minimum wage legislation, pressure has been exerted to increase rates for lower level jobs. The thought behind such a program is frequently based upon the premise that a certain minimum standard of living requires the amount specified. The eventual result of requiring a certain minimum wage without attempting to specify the type of work performed for such a wage has a leveling influence on company wage structures. In other words, rates below the minimum are raised to the minimum, but other rates within the structure do not receive a proportional increase. In lieu of minimum wage legislation, a strong argument can be made for a minimum wage structure using as benchmarks selected, well-defined jobs found throughout industry. Objections to such governmental action would come from those companies, oftentimes relatively small in size, where comparatively low rates are paid.

Whether wages are adopted on a unilateral basis, developed through negotiations with a union, or established by legislation, controversies over the amount paid for the services rendered will continue to exist between management and labor. If the parties involved are conscientiously interested in approaching the problem in a rational manner (and either one or both parties may not be interested in this approach), job analysis and evaluation provide a systematic basis for negotiations.

The techniques described in this book are not intended to imply that decisions in the field of job analysis and evaluation can be made primarily on the basis of statistical analyses. Some readers might be inclined to think that too much stress has been placed upon mathematical processes in a field which has been largely construed as based upon human judgments. Actually, the results of properly developed and interpreted statistical analyses provide an additional basis for improving the accuracy and reliability of human judgments. For personnel determining or negotiating wages, they provide numerous controls which may preclude unsound decisions. Moreover, there has been a marked tendency to neglect the treatment of mathematical techniques in a substantial portion of the job analysis literature.

Despite the additional validity given job evaluation by the more extensive use of statistical techniques, persons responsible for reaching decisions concerning introduction of the methods should realize that certain limitations exist. Insofar as there can be errors in human judgment, there can also be errors in job evaluation plans, despite extreme caution and the utilization of elaborate statistical techniques. Use of a systematic plan for determining wage payments necessarily restricts negotiations. Discussion concerning establishment of rates is channeled down definite paths, depending upon the type of plan adopted. In certain situations, particularly in large companies, decisions concerning evaluation of jobs cannot always be made by persons responsible for labor negotiations. Job evaluation specialists or technicians are usually responsible for most of the determinations which have to be made. Decisions which are reached have to be sold to management and employees on a continuing basis if the plan is to remain in effect for an extensive period. Moreover, there are always the exceptions—jobs which do not lend themselves to evaluation on the plan or jobs for which the rates must be established at levels substantially higher than the existing pattern. If the jobs treated as exceptions become too large in number, the entire job evaluation system may have to be sacrificed.

Although there are some pitfalls in the development and introduction of a job analysis and evaluation program, there are also some very definite rewards. Possibly the chief advantage is that the problem of rate determination and cost control is approached systematically. As industrial organizations have increased in size and gradually decentralized their operations, a critical need for a logical basis of establishing wage rates has developed. The number of industrial disputes emanating from disagreements over wages is ample evidence of the significance attached to the problem by both parties. There is a real need for subjecting each job to some sort of critical analysis which will establish the basis for the development of definite historical records of the work performed. With the numerous method changes and increased automation occurring within industry today, such records can be invaluable, particularly during labor negotiations.

Although it is sometimes argued that job evaluation restricts negotiations, in many instances evaluation results in negotiations in which overall wage levels, rather than rates for individual jobs or groups of jobs, are considered. A properly developed job evaluation plan should give ample assurance to all parties that the differentials between existing jobs have been properly established and that systematic methods exist for determining rates for new job classifications. It is hoped that more widespread use of the methods and controls developed in recent years will permit management and labor to take renewed confidence in job evaluation as a basis for equitable wage administration.

In an industrial society the age-old problem of payments for services performed remains very real. Wage determination and administration represent an area where additional research is certain to provide better solutions to some of today's most perplexing problems. It should be self-evident that the responsibility for a major portion of this research rests squarely on the shoulders of management. Within its jurisdiction lies not only the basic data required for the research but also the facilities for processing the data. On the other hand, union representatives must strive for an analytical approach which is both rational and objective if their constituents are to share in the beneficial results of the research conducted. Those who are responsible for controlling wages cannot take their responsibility lightly. There must be a delicate balance—a balance which for the workers leads to a constantly increasing real income and for management gives assurance that there will be an adequate return for the risks involved.

Appendix A

DICTIONARY OF STATISTICAL TERMINOLOGY APPLYING TO WAGE AND SALARY ADMINISTRATION

For the convenience of the reader, definitions of the most important statistical terms relating to wage and salary administration are presented below:

Statistical Term	Definition or Explanation
Arithmetic progression	Arithmetic progression involves the assignment of weight to degrees of a factor in such a manner that the difference between degrees varies by a constant amount. For example, the difference between the progression 5, 10, 15, 20, and 25 varies by the constant amount of 5 points.
Beta coefficients	Beta coefficients provide an accurate indication of the relative importance of the variables used in predicting the criteria.
Chi-square test	This test measures the divergences between actual and expected frequencies in order to determine whether the differences are significant. By reference to a chart such as that on page 561 of *Business Statistics*, by George R. Davies and Dale Yoder, a determination may be made concerning the degree of significance.
Coefficient of net or partial regression	A net regression coefficient indicates the relation of the criteria to one of the variables excluding the associated influences of the other variable or variables. They are, in effect, weights expressing the force to be given to the variables in combining them to predict the criteria.
Constant in the multiple regression equation	The constant in the multiple regression equation is the hypothetical value for the criteria when the other factors or variables being considered have a value of zero.

227

Correlation coefficient   The correlation coefficient involves an expression of the similarity or covariation between two or more series or variables. Correlation coefficient is a statistical term measuring the extent and direction of a particular relationship. For example, a correlation exists between total evaluation points on job classifications and rates paid on those classifications. As a statistical measure, the correlation coefficient may vary from a minus 1.00, which is perfect negative correlation, through zero, which indicates no correlation, to a plus 1.00, which indicates perfect positive correlation. The relationship between total points in an evaluation plan and present wage rates may be described by a positive correlation coefficient. The correlation coefficient assumes that the data being described are represented by a straight-line relationship.

Criteria   Criteria is a term frequently used in multiple correlation to indicate the data which are being predicted by the factors involved. For example, wage rates are considered the criteria and the factors in the evaluation plan are used in predicting these wage rates.

Curvilinearity   Curvilinearity is an expression which denotes the relationship between two or more variables. It indicates that the relationship is best expressed by a curve line rather than a straight line.

Factor analysis   Multiple factor analysis involves statistical computations to indicate those factors which can be selected from a larger number of factors and used effectively in the prediction of a certain criteria. For example, the process indicates which factors in a job evaluation plan can be used most effectively to predict wage rates. Among the several methods of multiple factor analysis, the two major alternative ones are those by L. L. Thurstone and Harold Hotelling.

Geometric progression   Geometric progression involves the assignment of weight to degrees of the factors in such a manner that the difference between degrees varies by a constantly increasing amount. For example, difference between the progression 10, 16, 29, 55, and 100 varies by an amount which is constantly increasing. When plotted on an arithmetic scale, progression is represented by a curved line which slopes upward at an increasing rate.

| Horizontal scale | Horizontal scale is sometimes referred to as X-axis or the abscissa and is used for the values of the independent variable. For example, total points are considered the independent variable and are plotted on the horizontal scale. |

Intercorrelation

Intercorrelation refers to the relationship existing between factors as reflected by coefficients of correlation. For example, in the process of computing a multiple correlation, the intercorrelations for each factor with every other factor and with rate are obtained. Study of these intercorrelations reveals the relationship which exists between factors and between factors and rate.

Interpolation

Interpolation involves the assignment of point weights between those weights already established for degrees of factors. For example, if two point weights, such as 10 and 20, were adopted on two degrees of a factor, interpolation would involve use of a numerical value, such as 15, between these two weights.

Least-squares trend line

A least-squares trend line involves precise mathematical calculations to establish the linear relationship between two series of data. It is represented by an equation: $T = a + bX$, where T represents the trend value, a is the value that defines the height of the line at the origin or starting point, and b is the measure of the slope with each variation of the independent variable. Depending upon the nature of the data to be described, a least-squares trend line may provide the best description of the relationship between total points and present wage rates.

Mean

The arithmetic mean or average is a measure of central tendency which is at the point of balance or center of gravity of a distribution. It is calculated as the sum of the items divided by the number of items.

Median

The median is a measure of central tendency occurring at the central position within an array and having an equal number of items on either side of it.

Mode

The mode is a measure of central tendency which is the most usual or typical, actual or interpolated, in a distribution.

Multiple correlation

Multiple correlation involves the prediction of a criteria by using two or more variables. For example, wage rates are predicted by using a group of factors which tend to vary with differences in job content, which in turn lead to differences in rate. Multiple linear correlation may be used when a relationship is best described by a straight line. Multiple curvilinear correlation may be used when a relationship is best described by a curved line.

Multiple correlation coefficient

The multiple correlation coefficient expresses the relationship or covariation between two or more independent variables and a dependent variable or criteria. For example the multiple correlation coefficient measures the degree of variability in wage rates which are accounted for by changes in the combined factors used in an evaluation plan.

Normal distribution

A normal distribution is described by a bell-shaped curve where the larger frequencies are clustered about its center and the distribution is symetrical around its central ordinate. The distribution represents an expression of the laws of chance or probability and as such is used as the basis for numerous statistical theories. In working with wage trend lines, it is usually assumed that a normal curve would adequately represent the population distribution around the trend line.

Second-degree curve

A second-degree curve involves precise mathematical calculations to establish the curvilinear relationship between two series of data. It is represented by an equation: $T = a + bX + cX^2$. Where T is equal to the trend value, a is the value that defines the height of the line at the origin or starting point (where the X value $= 0$), b is the measure of slope at the origin, and c is an additional increment determining the degree of curvature. The relationship between jobs plotted on the degrees of a factor such as Job Training and present rates for those jobs is usually curvilinear when arithmetic progression is used on the degrees of the factors. This relationship may usually be described by a second-degree curve.

Skewness

When a frequency distribution is not symmetrical (see definition of a normal distribution), it is said to be skewed. A curve may be skewed to the right (positive) or left (negative), depending upon the area of the distribution where the excess tail appears.

Standard deviation

The standard deviation is a measure of dispersion or scatter within a frequency distribution. If a plus or minus one standard deviation is measured from the arithmetic mean of a normal distribution, 68.27% of the data are included. Within the range of plus or minus two standard deviations, 95.45% are included, and within plus or minus three standard deviations, 99.73% or practically all the data are included. The greater the dispersion of the data, the larger the standard deviation.

Standard error of estimate

This measure may be interpreted in a manner analogous to that of a standard deviation for a frequency distribution. It provides, for example, an estimate of the range above and below the least-squares trend line within which 68.27% of the items may be expected to fall if the scatter is normal.

Variable

A variable is any numerical value which can assume different values in successive individual cases. Independent variables are usually measured on the X - axis and dependent variables on the Y - axis.

Vertical scale

The vertical scale, sometimes known as the ordinate or Y-axis, is used for the values of dependent variables. For example, wage rates are considered dependent variables and are plotted on the vertical scale.

Appendix B

CONDENSED COMPUTING FORMS

In order to simplify the computing involved in developing and analyzing wage structures, condensed computing forms are presented on the following pages. These forms reduce to a minimum the calculations necessary to secure the desired measures. Sample calculations have been included to help readers in following the steps outlined. Formulas in connection with calculation of the multiple correlation are presented for five-variable and ten-variable problems. The forms permit the calculation of:

1. Least-squares trend line, correlation coefficient, standard error of estimate, second-degree curve.

2. Factor intercorrelations, multiple regression equation, multiple correlation coefficient.

Statistical

Line	COLUMN A		COLUMN B
1 Number of employees	25 -		xxx xxxx
2 Sum of points	3 754 -	Sum of rates	4 230 -
3 Sum of squares of points	675 102 -	Sum of products of points × rate	667 680 -
4	xxx xxxx	Sum of squares of rate	125 340 -
5 A1 × A3	16 877 550 -	A1 × B3	-16 692 000 -
6 A2 × A2	14 092 516 -	A2 × B2	15 879 420 -
7 A5 - A6	2 785 034 -	B5 - B6	812 580 -
8 Check A5 + B5 = C5	33 569 550 -	Check A6 + B6 = C6	29 971 936 -
9	xxx xxxx	A1 × B4	18 133 500 -
10	xxx xxxx	B2 × B2	17 892 900 -
11	xxx xxxx	B9 - B10	240 600 -
12	xxx xxxx	Check B7 + B11 = C11	1 053 180 -
13 Square root of A7	1 668 8421	Square root of B11	490 5099
14	xxx xxxx	A13 × B13	818 583 5716
15	xxx xxxx	B7 ÷ B14	9927
16	xxx xxxx	B7 ÷ B13	1 656 6026
17	xxx xxxx	Check B16 ÷ A13 = B15	9927
18 A2 ÷ A1	150 1600	B2 ÷ A1	169 2000
19	xxx xxxx	Check A18 + B18 = C18	319 3600
20 A13 ÷ A1	66 7537	B13 ÷ A1	19 6204
21 A20 ÷ B20	3 4023	B20 ÷ A20	2959
22 A21 × B15	3 3725	B21 × B15	2918
23	xxx xxxx	B22 × A18	43 8167
24	xxx xxxx	B18 - B23	125 3833
25	xxx xxxx	B15 × B15	9855
26	xxx xxxx	1 - B25	0145
27	xxx xxxx	Square root of B26	1204
28	xxx xxxx	B27 × B20	2 3623
29 Check	B18 = B24 + (B22 × A18)		$169.2000 = 125.3833 + (43.8167)$

SUMMARY

Coefficient of correlation	B15	.9927	Average points per cent or mill	A22	3.3775
Average points per job	A18	150.1600	Average value per point (cents or mills)	B22	.2918
Average rate (cents or mills)	B18	169.2000	Constant base value (cents or mills)	B24	125.3833
Standard deviation of points (plus and minus)	A20	66.7537	Standard error of estimate for wage structure (plus and minus)	B28	2.3623
Standard deviation of rate (plus and minus)	B20	19.6204			

FORMULA: Least squares - Rate = 1.2538 + ($.02918$ × Job points)

Calculation Sheet

COLUMN C		COLUMN D (SECOND DEGREE CURVE)	
	xxx xxxx	1 Sum of points to the third power	146 249 620 –
A2 + B2	7 984 –	2 Sum of points to the fourth power	37 534 527 114 –
A3 + B3	1 342 782 –	3 Sum of products squares of points × rates	127 312 272 –
B3 + B4	1 393 020 –	4 D3A1 – B2A3	327 125 340 –
A1 × C3	33 569 550 –	5 A7	2 785 034 –
A2 × C2	29 971 936 –	6 B7	312 580 –
C5 – C6	3 597 614 –	7 D1A1 – A2A3	1 121 907 592 –
Check A7 + B7 = C7	3 597 614 –	8 D2A1 – A3A3	482 600 467 446 –
A1 × C4	34 825 500 –	9 D1A1 – A3A2 Check (D7 = D9)	1 121 907 592 –
B2 × C2	33 772 320 –	10 D4D5 – D6D7	– 584 476 945 800 –
C9 – C10	1 053 180 –	11 D8D5 – D7D7	85 382 065 265 764 700 –
	xxx xxxx	12 D10 ÷ D11 = a =	– .000068
	xxx xxxx	13 D6 – (D9D12) ÷ D5 = b =	.3192
	xxx xxxx	14 B2 – (A3D12) – (A2D13) ÷ A1 = c =	123 1052
	xxx xxxx	15 D1D12	– 9 944 9742
	xxx xxxx	16 A3D13	215 492 5584
	xxx xxxx	17 A2D14	462 136 9208
C2 ÷ A1	319 360	18 = B3	667 684 5050
	xxx xxxx		
	xxx xxxx		
Check A21 × B21 = 1	9999		

SECOND DEGREE CURVE

| (c)   (b)   (a) |

Points D14 $\underline{123.1052}$ + D13 $\underline{.3192}$ + D12 $\underline{-.000068}$ = Rate
(Base)   (× Job points)   (× Job points^2)

0	123 1052	– 0	– 0 –	= 123 1052
50	"	15 9600	– 1700	= 138 8952
100	"	31 9200	– 6800	= 154 3452
150	"	47 8800	– 1 5300	= 169 4552
200	"	63 8400	– 2 7200	= 184 2252
250	"	79 8000	– 4 2500	= 198 6552
300	"	95 7600	– 6 1200	= 212 7452
350	"	111 7200	– 8 3300	= 226 4952
400	"	127 6800	–10 8800	= 239 9052

Date

Identification

Computation of a Multiple Correlation
Five Variables, Four Factors Plus Criteria

The sample problem assumes five job classifications evaluated on four factors.

Jobs	Total Points	Effort	Skill	Responsibility	Working Conditions	Rate $
Cleaner, sweeper	44	11	11	10	12	1.38
Body bolter	79	40	11	12	16	1.58
Switchman	157	32	55	40	30	1.71
Die maker	260	47	154	48	16	2.03
First roller	355	55	170	109	21	2.33
		185	401	214	95	$9.03

Multiple Correlation — Five Variables

x = Point weights Σ = Summation $N = 5$ (Number of job classifications used in sample problem)

Line	Proof	A Effort	B Skill	C Responsibility	D Working Conditions	E Rate	F Σ (Proof)
1	Σx_o*	185	401	214	95	903	1798
51	$\Sigma x_A x_o$ (F51 = A51 + B51 + C51 + D51 + E51)	7979	18909	9886	3639	35666	76079
52	$\Sigma x_B x_o$ (F52 = B51 + B52 + C52 + D52 + E52)		55883	27594	7992	83533	193911
53	$\Sigma x_C x_o$ (F53 = C51 + C52 + C53 + D53 + E53)			15574	4489	44242	101785
54	$\Sigma x_D x_o$ (F54 = D51 + D52 + D53 + D54 + E54)				1997	17455	35572
55	$\Sigma x_E x_o$ (F55 = E51 + E52 + E53 + E54 + E55)					168747	349643
101	N(O51) − (A1)(O1)	5670	20360	9840	620	11275	47765
102	N(O52) − (B1)(O1)		118614	52156	1865	55562	248557
103	N(O53) − (C1)(O1)			32074	2115	27968	124153
104	N(O54) − (D1)(O1)				960	1490	7050
105	N(O55) − (E1)(O1)					28326	124621
150	Reciprocal of line 150 A101 B102 C103 D104 E105	.01328032	.002903568	.005553719	.03227493	.005941654	
150	Square root	75.2994	344.4038	179.0921	30.9838	168.3033	
151	O101/A150	75.29941	270.38732	130.67835	8.23380	149.73561	
152	O102/B150		344.40382	151.43849	5.41515	161.32805	
153	O103/C150			179.09220	11.80957	156.16545	
154	O104/D150				30.98393	48.08965	
155	O105/E150					168.30329	

* In Σx_o the inferior o refers to the data in the column where the calculation is being performed. For example, the figure 185 in the first line of the A factor is the summation (Σ) of the point weights (x) for the individual jobs on the Effort (A) factor. The capital O which appears first in line 101 has a similar meaning

Multiple Correlation — Five Variables — Continued

		A Effort	B Skill	C Respon-sibility	D Working Conditions	E Rate	F Σ (Proof)
201	O101/O150	75.29941	59.11664	54.94379	20.01046	66.99215	
202	O102/O150		344.40381	291.22448	60.19274	330.13018	
203	O103/O150			179.09220	68.26148	166.17618	
204	O104/O150				30.98393	8.85306	
205	O105/O150					168.30329	
251	O201/A150	1.00000	.78509	.72967	.26575	.88968	3.67019
252	O202/B150		1.00000	.84559	.17477	.95856	3.76401
253	O203/C150			1.00000	.38115	.92788	3.88429
254	O204/D150				1.00000	.28573	2.10740
255	O205/E150					1.00000	4.06185
301	O151/O150 (A301 = 1.0000)	1.00000	.78509	.72967	.26575	.88968	
302	O152/O150 (B302 = 1.0000)		1.00000	.84559	.17477	.95856	
303	O153/O150 (C303 = 1.0000)			1.00000	.38115	.92788	
304	O154/O150 (D304 = 1.0000)				1.00000	.28573	
305	O155/O150 (E305 = 1.0000)					1.00000	
350	Copy O301	1.00000	.78509	.72967	.26575	.88968	3.67019
351	O302 — (B350)(O350)		.33863	.27273	−.03387	.26008	.88258
352	O351/B351		1.00000	.71092	−.08829	.67794	2.30060
353	O303 — (C350)(O350) — (C351)(O352)			.27369	.21132	.09382	.57882
354	O353/C353			1.00000	.77211	.34280	2.11487

355 O354 − (D350)(O350) − (D351)(O352) − (D353)(O354)   .76323   −.00018   .76306
356 O355/D355   1.00000   −.00024   .99978

357 O305 − (E350)(O350) − (E351)(O352) − (E353)(O354) − (E355)(O356)   −.04047
358 O357/E357   1.00000

400 Copy E350, E352, E354, E356, E358   .88968   .67794   .34280   −.00024   1.00000

401 $\beta_{E\text{-}D}$ = D400   .34261   −.00024
402 $\beta_{E\text{-}C}$ = C400 − (D354)(D401)   .34261

403 $\beta_{E\text{-}B}$ = B400 − (C352)(C402) − (D352)(D401)   .43435
404 $\beta_{E\text{-}A}$ = A400 − (B350)(B403) − (C350)(C402) − (D350)(D401)   .29875

451 $b_{E\text{-}D}$ = (E150/D150) D401   .32197   −.00130
452 $b_{E\text{-}C}$ = (E150/C150) C402
453 $b_{E\text{-}B}$ = (E150/B150) B403   .21226
454 $b_{E\text{-}A}$ = (E150/A150) A404   .66774

500 $a = \dfrac{(E1) − (A1)(A454) − (B1)(B453) − (C1)(C452) − (D1)(D451)}{N} = \dfrac{908 − (185)(.66774) − (401)(.21226) − (214)(.32197) − (95)(−.00130)}{5}$

$= \dfrac{908 − 123.58190 − 85.11626 − 68.90158 + .12350}{5} = \dfrac{625.57876}{5} = 125.11475$

Regression Equation:

$$\underset{(E)}{\text{Rate}} = \underset{(500)}{a} + \underset{(A454)}{b_{E\text{-}A}} \left(\text{Points for Effort A} \right) + \underset{(B453)}{b_{E\text{-}B}} \left(\text{Points for Skill B} \right)$$

$$+ \underset{(C452)}{b_{E\text{-}C}} \left(\text{Points for Responsibility C} \right) + \underset{(D451)}{b_{E\text{-}D}} \left(\text{Points for Working Conditions D} \right)$$

The point values for the cleaner classification have been substituted to forecast the cleaner's rate of $1.38.

Rate = 1.25115 + (.0066774)(11) + (.0021226)(11) + (.0032197)(10) + (−.0000130)(12)

= 1.25115 + .07345 + .02335 + .03220 − .00016

= $1.37999

= $1.38

Multiple Correlation — Ten Variables

(Nine Factors plus Criteria)

Line	Σx_0	
1		
51	$\Sigma x_A x_0$	(K51 = A51 + B51 + C51 + D51 + E51 + F51 + G51 + H51 + I51 + J51)
52	$\Sigma x_B x_0$	(K52 = B51 + B52 + C52 + D52 + E52 + F52 + G52 + H52 + I52 + J52)
53	$\Sigma x_C x_0$	(K53 = C51 + C52 + C53 + D53 + E53 + F53 + G53 + H53 + I53 + J53)
54	$\Sigma x_D x_0$	(K54 = D51 + D52 + D53 + D54 + E54 + F54 + G54 + H54 + I54 + J54)
55	$\Sigma x_E x_0$	(K55 = E51 + E52 + E53 + E54 + E55 + F55 + G55 + H55 + I55 + J55)
56	$\Sigma x_F x_0$	(K56 = F51 + F52 + F53 + F54 + F55 + F56 + G56 + H56 + I56 + J56)
57	$\Sigma x_G x_0$	(K57 = G51 + G52 + G53 + G54 + G55 + G56 + G57 + H57 + I57 + J57)
58	$\Sigma x_H x_0$	(K58 = H51 + H52 + H53 + H54 + H55 + H56 + H57 + H58 + I58 + J58)
59	$\Sigma x_I x_0$	(K59 = I51 + I52 + I53 + I54 + I55 + I56 + I57 + I58 + I59 + J59)
60	$\Sigma x_J x_0$	(K60 = J51 + J52 + J53 + J54 + J55 + J56 + J57 + J58 + J59 + J60)
101	N(O51) — (A1)(O1)	
102	N(O52) — (B1)(O1)	
103	N(O53) — (C1)(O1)	
104	N(O54) — (D1)(O1)	
105	N(O55) — (E1)(O1)	
106	N(O56) — (F1)(O1)	
107	N(O57) — (G1)(O1)	
108	N(O58) — (H1)(O1)	
109	N(O59) — (I1)(O1)	
110	N(O60) — (J1)(O1)	
150	Square root	A101, B102, C103, D104, E105, F106, G107, H108, I109, J110
151	O101/A150	
152	O102/B150	

153	O103/C150
154	O104/D150
155	O105/E150
156	O106/F150
157	O107/G150
158	O108/H150
159	O109/I150
160	O110/J150
201	O101/O150
202	O102/O150
203	O103/O150
204	O104/O150
205	O105/O150
206	O106/O150
207	O107/O150
208	O108/O150
209	O109/O150
210	O110/O150
251	O201/A150
252	O202/B150
253	O203/C150
254	O204/D150
255	O205/E150
256	O206/F150
257	O207/G150
258	O208/H150
259	O209/I150
260	O210/J150

Multiple Correlation — Ten Variables — Continued

(Nine Factors plus Criteria)

Line		
301	O151/O150	(A301 = 1.00000)
302	O152/O150	(B302 = 1.00000)
303	O153/O150	(C303 = 1.00000)
304	O154/O150	(D304 = 1.00000)
305	O155/O150	(E305 = 1.00000)
306	O156/O150	(F306 = 1.00000)
307	O157/O150	(G307 = 1.00000)
308	O158/O150	(H308 = 1.00000)
309	O159/O150	(I309 = 1.00000)
310	O160/O150	(J310 = 1.00000)
350	Copy O301	
351	O302 — (B350)(O350)	
352	O351/B351	
353	O303 — (C350)(O350) — (C351)(O352)	
354	O353/C353	
355	O304 — (D350)(O350) — (D351)(O352) — (D353)(O354)	
356	O355/D355	
357	O305 — (E350)(O350) — (E351)(O352) — (E353)(O354) — (E355)(O356)	
358	O357/E357	
359	O306 — (F350)(O350) — (F351)(O352) — (F353)(O354) — (FO355)(O356) — (F357)(O358)	
360	O359/F359	

361   O307 — (G350)(O350) — (G351)(O352) — (G353)(O354) — (G355)(O356) — (G357)(O358) — (G359)(O360)
362   O361/G361

363   O308 — (H350)(O350) — (H351)(O352) — (H353)(O354) — (H355)(O356) — (H357)(O358) — (H359)(O360)
364   O363/H363 — (H361)(O362)

365   O309 — (I350)(O350) — (I351)(O352) — (I353)(O354) — (I355)(O356) — (I357)(O358) — (I359)(O360)
366   O365/I365 — (I361)(O362) — (I363)(O364)

367   O310 — (J350)(O350) — (J351)(O352) — (J353)(O354) — (J355)(O356) — (J357)(O358) — (J359)(O360)
368   O367/J367 — (J361)(O362) — (J363)(O364) — (J365)(O366)

400   Copy J350, J352, J354, J356, J358, J360, J362, J364, J366, J368.

401   $\beta_{J\cdot I}$ = I400
402   $\beta_{J\cdot H}$ = H400 — (I364)(I401)
403   $\beta_{J\cdot G}$ = G400 — (H362)(H402) — (I362)(I401)
404   $\beta_{J\cdot F}$ = F400 — (G360)(G403) — (H360)(H402) — (I360)(I401)
405   $\beta_{J\cdot E}$ = E400 — (F358)(F404) — (G358)(G403) — (H358)(H402) — (I358)(I401)
406   $\beta_{J\cdot D}$ = D400 — (E356)(E405) — (F356)(F404) — (G356)(G403) — (H356)(H402) — (I356)(I401)
407   $\beta_{J\cdot C}$ = C400 — (D354)(D406) — (E354)(E405) — (F354)(F404) — (G354)(G403) — (H354)(H402) — (I354)(I401)
408   $\beta_{J\cdot B}$ = B400 — (C352)(C407) — (D352)(D406) — (E352)(E405) — (F352)(F404) — (G352)(G403) — (H352)(H402) — (I352)(I401)
409   $\beta_{J\cdot A}$ = A400 — (B350)(B408) — (C350)(C407) — (D350)(D406) — (E350)(E405) — (F350)(F404) — (G350)(G403) — (H350)(H402) — (I350)(I401)

451   $b_{J \cdot I} = (J150/I150)I401$

452   $b_{J \cdot H} = (J150/H150)H402$

453   $b_{J \cdot G} = (J150/G150)G403$

454   $b_{J \cdot F} = (J150/F150)F404$

455   $b_{J \cdot E} = (J150/E150)E405$

456   $b_{J \cdot D} = (J150/D150)D406$

457   $b_{J \cdot C} = (J150/C150)C407$

458   $b_{J \cdot B} = (J150/B150)B408$

459   $b_{J \cdot A} = (J150/A150)A409$

500   $a =$
$$\frac{[J1 - (A1)(A459) - (B1)(B458) - (C1)(C457) - (D1)(D456) - (E1)(E455) - (F1)(F454) - (G1)(G453) - (H1)(H452) - (I1)(I451)]}{N}$$

Regression Equation:

Criteria $J = a + b_{J \cdot A}\ \overline{\text{Points for factor A}} + b_{J \cdot B}\ \overline{\text{Points for factor B}} + \cdots + b_{J \cdot I}\ \overline{\text{Points for factor I}}$

The multiple correlation coefficient may be calculated as follows:

551   $R^2_{K \cdot ABC \ldots I} = (J251)(A409) + (J252)(B408) + (J253)(C407) + (J254)(D406) + (J255)(E405) + (J256)(F404)$
$+ (J257)(G403) + (J258)(H402) + (J259)(I401)$

552   $R = \sqrt{551}$

Bibliography

Baker, Helen, and John M. True, *The Operation of Job Evaluation Plans,* Industrial Relations Section, Princeton University, p. 111, 1947.

Balderston, C. C., *Wage Setting Based on Job Analysis and Evaluation,* Industrial Relations Monograph No. 4, Industrial Relations Counselors, Inc., New York, p. 68, 1943.

Barkin, Solomon, "Wage Determination: Trick or Technique?" *Labor and Nation, 1,* 6, p. 24–26, 48, June–July 1946.

Belcher, David W., *Wage and Salary Administration,* Prentice-Hall, New York, p. 503, 1955.

Benge, E. J., *Job Evaluation and Merit Rating: A Manual of Procedures,* National Foremen's Institute, New York, p. 73, 1946.

Benge, E. J., "Statistical Study of a Job Evaluation Point System," *Modern Management,* p. 17–23, April 1947.

Benge, E. J., S. L. H. Burk, and E. N. Hay, *Manual of Job Evaluation,* Harper and Brothers, New York, p. 198, 1941.

Bloom, Gordon F., and Herbert R. Northrup, *Economics of Labor Relations,* Richard D. Irwin, Inc., Chicago, p. 292–334, 1954.

Booz, Allen & Hamilton, *Evaluating Managerial and Supervisory Jobs in the Controller's Department,* Controllership Foundation Inc., One East 42nd St., New York, p. 140, 1949.

Booz, Allen & Hamilton, *Setting Salaries in the Controller's Department,* Controllership Foundation Inc., One East 42nd St., New York, p. 59, 1950.

British Institute of Management, *Job Evaluation, A Practical Guide,* Personnel Management Series 4, Management House, 8 Hill St., London, p. 80, April 1952.

Charm, Sumner D., *Wage Policy for Management,* Funk & Wagnalls Co., New York, p. 224, 1949.

Chesler, D. J., "Abbreviated Job Evaluation Scales Developed on the Basis of 'Internal' and 'External' Criteria," *Journal of Applied Psychology, 33,* p. 151–157, 1949.

Chesler, D. J., "Reliability and Comparability of Different Job Evaluation Systems," *Journal of Applied Psychology, 32,* p. 465–475, 1948.

Chesler, D. J., "Reliability of Abbreviated Job Evaluation Scales," *Journal of Applied Psychology, 32,* p. 622–628, 1948.

Croxton, Frederick E., and Dudley J. Cowden, *Applied General Statistics,* Prentice-Hall, New York, p. 944, 1940.

245

Dartnell Corporation, *Job Evaluation Methods and Procedures*, Report No. 531, the Corporation, Chicago, p. 88, 1946.

Dartnell Corporation, *Salary Administration Plans*, the Corporation, Chicago, p. 64, 1943.

Davies, George R., and Dale Yoder, *Business Statistics*, John Wiley & Sons, New York, second edition, p. 616, 1941.

Dickinson, Z. C., *Collective Wage Determination: Problems and Principles in Bargaining, Arbitration, and Legislation*, Ronald Press, New York, p. 640, 1941.

Dickinson, Z. C., *Compensating Industrial Effort*, Chapter 11, "Job Analysis for Wage and Salary Determination," Ronald Press, New York, p. 187–218, 1937.

Dooher, Joseph M., and Vivienne Marquis, editors, *AMA Handbook of Wage and Salary Administration*, American Management Association, New York, p. 412, 1950.

Douty, H. M., *Wage Structures and Administration*, Institute of Industrial Relations, University of California, Los Angeles, p. 72, 1954.

Dwyer, P. S., *Linear Computations*, John Wiley & Sons, New York, p. 344, 1951.

Ells, R. W., *Salary and Wage Administration*, McGraw-Hill, New York, p. 120, 1945.

Ezekiel, Mordecai, *Methods of Correlation Analysis*, John Wiley & Sons, New York, second edition, p. 531, 1941.

Fryklund, Verne C., *Trade and Job Analysis*, Bruce Publishing Co., Milwaukee, p. 167, 1942.

Gitlow, Abraham L., *Wage Determination under National Boards*, Prentice-Hall, New York, p. 248, 1953.

Gray, J. S., "Adjusting Base Weights in Job Evaluation," *Journal of Applied Psychology*, 35, p. 8–10, 1951.

Gray, J. S., "Custom Made Systems of Job Evaluation," *Journal of Applied Psychology*, 34, p. 378–380, 1950.

Gray, J. S., and M. C. Jones, "Ready Made Versus Custom Made Systems of Job Evaluation," *Journal of Applied Psychology*, 35, p. 11–14, 1951.

Gray, R. D., *Systematic Wage Administration in the Southern California Aircraft Industry*, Industrial Relations Monograph No. 7, Industrial Relations Counselors, New York, p. 91, 1943.

Gomberg, William, "A Collective Bargaining Approach to Job Evaluation" and "A Rejoinder to William Gomberg" by S. Barkin, *Labor and Nation*, 2, 1, p. 51–54, November–December 1946.

Gomberg, William, "A Trade Unionist Looks at Job Evaluation," *Journal of Applied Psychology*, 35, p. 1–7, February 1951.

Hay, E. N., "The Compa-Ratio; A Means of Control of Salary Expense," *Advanced Management*, 5, p. 9–10, 42, January–March 1940.

Hay, E. N., "Technique of Securing Agreement in Job Evaluation Committees," *Personnel*, 26, p. 307–312, 1950.

Hopwood, J. O., *Salaries, Wages, and Labor Relations*, Ronald Press, New York, p. 124, 1937.

International Association of Machinists, *What's Wrong with Job Evaluation, A Trade Union Manual*, Research Dept., IA of M, Washington, D. C., p. 97, 1954.

Johnson, F. H., R. W. Boise, and D. Pratt, *Job Evaluation*, John Wiley & Sons, New York, p. 288, 1946.

Jones, Philip W., *Practical Job Evaluation*, John Wiley & Sons, New York, p. 304, 1948.

Kindall, A. F., W. Dietz, E. J. Kessler, and J. T. Hopkins, "How Job Evaluation Contributes to Cost Reduction" in "Personnel Aspects of Cost Reduction," Production Series No. 124, American Management Association, New York, 1940.

Labor Relations Institute, *How to Control Your Labor Costs Through Job Evaluation*, the Institute, New York, p. 37, 1945.

Lawshe, C. H., "Towards Simplified Job Evaluation," *Personnel*, 22, p. 153–160, November 1945.

Lawshe, C. H., and others, "Studies in Job Evaluation," *Journal of Applied Psychology:*

"Part I, Factor Analysis of Point Ratings for Hourly-Paid Jobs in Three Industrial Plants," 28, p. 189–198, June 1944.

"Part II, The Adequacy of Abbreviated Point Ratings for Hourly-Paid Jobs in Three Industrial Plants," 29, p. 177–184, June 1945.

"Part III, An Analysis of Point Ratings for Salary-Paid Jobs in an Industrial Plant," 30, p. 117–128, April 1946.

"Part IV, Analysis of Another Point-Rating Scale for Hourly-Paid Jobs and the Adequacy of an Abbreviated Scale," 30, p. 310–319, August 1946.

"Part V, An Analysis of a Factor Comparison System as It Functions in a Paper Mill," 30, p. 426–434, October 1946.

"Part VI, The Reliability of Two Point Systems," 31, p. 355–365, 1947.

"Part VII, A Factor Analysis of Two Point Rating Methods of Job Evaluation," 32, p. 118–129, 1948.

"Part VIII, The Reliability of an Abbreviated Job Evaluation System," 33, p. 158–166, 1949.

Lester, R. A., *Company Wage Policies*, Report Series No. 77, Industrial Relations Section, Princeton University, p. 45, 1948.

Lester, R. A., and R. L. Aronson, *Job Modifications under Collective Bargaining*, Princeton University Press, Princeton, p. 77, 1950.

Levitan, S. A., *Ingrade Wage-Rate Progression in War and Peace*, Clinton Press, Plattsburg, N. Y., p. 141, 1950.

Life Office Management Association, *Clerical Salary Administration*, prepared under auspices of LOMA Clerical Salary Study Committee, p. 220, 1948.

Life Office Management Association, *Job Evaluation for the Establishment of Salary Standards*, Clerical Salary Study Committee, Report No. 1, the Association, New York, p. 54 and appendices, 1938.

Livernash, E. R., "An Analysis of Job Evaluation Procedures," unpublished doctoral dissertation, Harvard University, Boston, p. 350, 1941.

Lott, M. R., *Wage Scales and Job Evaluation: Scientific Determination of Wage Rates on the Basis of Service Rendered*, Ronald Press, New York, p. 161, 1926.

Lytle, C. W., *Job Evaluation Methods*, Ronald Press, New York, second edition, p. 507, 1954.

Martucci, N. L. A., "Wage and Salary Administration, Part I, The Need for a Program, Part II, Program Planning, Part III, Job Analysis, Part IV, Job

Evaluation," *Modern Management, 5:* 3, 4, 5, 6, June, August, October, November 1945.

Metropolitan Life Insurance Co., *An Introduction to Job Evaluation,* Policy Holders Service Bureau, Metropolitan Life Insurance Co., New York, p. 40, 1947.

Michael, L. B., *Wage and Salary Fundamentals and Procedures,* McGraw-Hill, New York, p. 330, 1950.

Miles, M. C., "Validity of a Check List for Evaluating Office Jobs," *Journal of Applied Psychology, 36,* p. 97–101, 1952.

Moore, F. G., "Statistical Problems in Job Evaluation," *Personnel, 23,* p. 125–136, September 1946.

Moore, H., "Problems and Methods in Job Evaluation," *Journal of Consulting Psychology, 8,* p. 90–99, 1944.

National Industrial Conference Board, *Job Evaluation: Formal Plans for Determining Basic Pay Differentials,* Studies in Personnel Policy No. 25, the Board, New York, p. 43, 1940.

National Industrial Conference Board, *Principles and Application of Job Evaluation,* Studies in Personnel Policy No. 62, the Board, New York, p. 28, 1944.

Otis, J. L., and R. H. Leukart, *Job Evaluation, a Basis for Sound Wage Administration,* Prentice-Hall, New York, second edition, p. 532, 1954.

Paterson, D., "A Statistical Basis for Setting Wage Rates," *American Statistical Association Journal, 34,* p. 365–368, 1939.

Patton, J. A., and R. S. Smith, *Job Evaluation,* Richard D. Irwin Inc., Chicago, p. 316, 1949.

Peters, C. C., and W. R. VanVoorhis, *Statistical Procedures and Their Mathematical Bases,* McGraw-Hill, New York, p. 516, 1940.

Pipage, L. C., and J. L. Tucker, *Job Evaluation,* University of Illinois Bulletin, p. 43, 1952.

Riegel, J. W., *Salary Determination,* Bureau of Industrial Relations, University of Michigan, Ann Arbor, p. 278, 1940.

Riegel, J. W., *Wage Determination,* Bureau of Industrial Relations, University of Michigan, Ann Arbor, p. 138, 1937.

Rogers, R. C., "Analysis of Two Point-Rating Job Evaluation Plans," *Journal of Applied Psychology, 30,* p. 579–585, 1946.

Shartle, C. L., *Occupational Information, Its Development and Application,* Prentice-Hall, New York, second edition, p. 425, 1952.

Shiskin, Boris, "Job Evaluation: What It Is and How It Works," "What It Means to Unionists," and "What Should Unions Do About It?" *American Federationist,* July, p. 8–9, August, p. 20–22, September, p. 22–23, 1947.

Smyth, R. C., and M. J. Murphy, *Job Evaluation and Employee Rating,* McGraw-Hill, New York, p. 255, 1946.

Spriegel, W. R., and E. Lanham, *Job Evaluation in Automobile and Automotive Parts Industries,* Bureau of Business Research, University of Texas, Austin, p. 188, 1953.

Stanway, H. Geddes, *Applied Job Evaluation,* Ronald Press, New York, p. 81, 1947.

Stigers, M. F., and E. G. Reed, *The Theory and Practice of Job Rating,* McGraw-Hill, New York, second edition, p. 168, 1944.

United Electrical, Radio and Machine Workers of America, *U. E. Guide to Wage Payment Plans, Time Study, and Job Evaluation,* UERMWA, New York, second edition, p. 128, 1943.

Bibliography 249

U. S. Employment Service, *Industrial Job Evaluation Systems with Annotated Bibliography*, U. S. Government Printing Office, Washington, D. C., p. 69, 1947.

Western Reserve University, *Handbook of Job Evaluation for Factory Jobs, American Institute of Bolt, Nut and Rivet Manufacturers*, Personnel Research Institute, Western Reserve University, Cleveland, p. 80, 1946.

Woytinsky, W. S., and associates, *Employment and Wages in the United States*, Twentieth Century Fund, New York, p. 777, 1953.

Index

251